Historical Research

Historical Research

A Guide

W.H. McDowell

Longman

An imprint of **Pearson Education**

London · New York · Toronto · Sydney · Tokyo · Singapore · Hong Kong · Cape Town
New Delhi · Madrid · Paris · Amsterdam · Munich · Milan · Stockholm

Pearson Education Limited

Head Office:
Edinburgh Gate
Harlow CM20 2JE
Tel: +44 (0)1279 623623
Fax: +44 (0)1279 431059

London Office:
128 Long Acre
London WC2E 9AN
Tel: +44 (0)20 7447 2000
Fax: +44 (0)20 7240 5771
Website: www.history-minds.com

First published in Great Britain in 2002

© W.H. McDowell 2002

The right of W.H. McDowell to be identified as Author
of this Work has been asserted by him in accordance
with the Copyright, Designs and Patents Act 1988.

ISBN 0 582 29459 2

British Library Cataloguing in Publication Data
A CIP catalogue record for this book can be obtained from the British Library

Library of Congress Cataloging in Publication Data
A CIP catalog record for this book can be obtained from the Library of Congress

10 9 8 7 6 5 4 3 2
06 05 04 03 02

Typeset in 9.5/15pt Stone Roman by Graphicraft Limited, Hong Kong
Printed and bound in Malaysia

The Publishers' policy is to use paper manufactured from sustainable forests.

Contents

Preface

This book is intended as a guide to the study, research and writing of history. The concept for such a book emerged some time ago, and my ideas about the purpose and content of this publication have been refined as a result of my own historical research over the years, which has included the writing of projects and reports, a dissertation and a thesis, involvement in research techniques courses and the preparation of material for publication. The book provides suitable guidance on the preparation of a wide range of historical work, regardless of subject specialism. This book is subdivided into three parts: Part I focuses on the study of history; Part II provides guidance on the practical aspects of historical research, with detailed advice on research methods; and Part III includes comprehensive information and guidance on stylistic conventions appropriate to the writing of dissertations, theses, articles and books.

The book aims to be an informative and hopefully indispensable research tool for historians, yet also of considerable practical value to researchers working in other disciplines within the humanities and social sciences. For example, the book includes material on interviewing which is used in an increasing number of oral history projects. This publication highlights the qualities expected in historical researchers and is intended to assist them in planning, organising and completing better quality projects more efficiently. The book will be invaluable for history students who are engaged in writing an extended essay and simple project, or in the transition from essay writing to the research and writing of a major project, a dissertation or a thesis. The appearance of the book is perhaps timely for two important reasons: firstly, the greater attempts by Research Councils to ensure that publicly funded researchers complete their work within an acceptable timescale; and secondly, the increasing interest in recent years on the research and writing of history. No other book on research methods has been written specifically to cater for the needs of historians. There are a number of publications on historiography, but none which focus on research methods and stylistic conventions for historical researchers. Most research methods books are strongly influenced by theory, are written primarily for social scientists and sometimes give inadequate and conflicting advice on the subject of stylistic conventions. Also, study skills texts and style manuals tend not to address specifically the needs and interests of historians. This book attempts to demonstrate that the successful completion of any historical research project relies to a significant extent on a combination of the craft of writing, experience of basic research techniques and knowledge of stylistic conventions.

The book has been written with a number of readers in mind: undergraduate and postgraduate research students; practising historians, regardless of their subject specialism; and general readers who are interested in writing about history, or who are faced with the task of researching and writing a project on a historically related topic or theme. Even in secondary schools there is increased emphasis on project work and the use of primary sources, and so the book will also be of practical use for teachers of history, modern studies or related subjects. Until recently, history graduates and undergraduates were offered few formal training courses in the nature of the discipline of history, on the range of research methods, or on stylistic conventions of use in the presentation of written work. Lecturers often prepared their own research guidance notes, or expected their students to model their footnote or bibliographical references on standard history texts. Most students in the humanities traditionally learned about research techniques 'on the job' as their work progressed. But now most universities have developed research methods courses in the humanities, some of which focus specifically on the needs of historical researchers. These introductory courses for graduates complement those which have been available for several years in the social sciences. Even at undergraduate level there is evidence of a much greater emphasis on opportunities for project work using documentary sources. This book is ideally suitable for use on any course covering historical research, as well as general research methods courses within the arts and social sciences. It will be useful for students who have experience of preparing research projects, as well as those who are about to embark on such a project. For practising historians it can be used in the planning and development of research methods courses, or perhaps in the provision of useful guidance on matters such as the format for citing references in footnotes and in a bibliography. Finally, for general readers the book will serve as an introduction to history as an academic discipline, as well as providing specific advice on the writing, editing and publication of historical work.

The book covers each stage of research, from the selection of a topic for a history project and the organisation and interpretation of source material, through to the completion of a typescript for a dissertation, thesis, article or book. It is possible to dip into the book at any point if you seek advice on a specific topic, such as compiling an index for a book. The book also surveys the range of source material available to historians, and offers improved methods for the preparation of a topic outline, research notes and written drafts, as well as giving helpful advice on the citation of footnote and bibliographical references. A distinctive feature of the book is that it adopts a threefold approach by covering historiography, research methods and advice on stylistic conventions, although the primary focus is on the latter two aspects. The potential of computing for the retrieval, analysis and presentation of information is covered in several of the sections, such as in the discussion of locating and listing source material, the preparation of research notes and drafts, and in the preparation of an index. It is also covered more specifically in chapter 4 on research tools, which explores the use of computers in historical research.

Part I of this book covers the study of history and begins by focusing on a number of matters of interest to historians: the nature, value and function of history; the tasks of the historian; the development of the historical profession; and the techniques of historical scholarship. Chapters 2 and 3 contrast the discipline of history with that of the social and natural sciences. Part II covers research methods, and begins in chapter 4 by looking at research tools, particularly the potential of computers for historical research. Chapter 5 considers the range, purpose, value, location and use of various types of source material which are available to historians. It also comments on the distinction between primary and secondary sources, as well as contrasting the strengths and limitations of different types of historical evidence. This will enable readers to make a more informed decision about the selection and use of source material for their own research purposes. Chapter 6 considers a number of important factors which will contribute towards the planning and successful completion of any research project, including notes on time management and the various stages of a research project. Practical advice is provided in chapters 7 and 8 on locating, indexing and evaluating primary and secondary source material; the preparation and organisation of research notes and drafts is covered in chapters 9 and 10. Specific points to consider when incorporating different types of illustrative material in historical projects is examined in chapter 11. The final two chapters of Part II, chapters 12 and 13, offer guidance on a number of matters: the purpose, rewards and requirements of research for a higher degree; the supervision of a research degree; the procedures, aims and preparation for the examination of a dissertation or thesis, including post-examination options; and advice on the publication of history articles and books, as well as other methods for publicising research results. Part III focuses on stylistic matters and the presentation of material. Chapter 14 begins by listing abbreviations used in the research and publication of historical material, and moves on to consider the use of numbers and punctuation. Chapter 15 gives information on the sequence of material which may appear in the format of a typical typescript and offers a helpful list of items to check in a completed typescript. Chapter 16 provides a list of model examples indicating preferred formats to be used when citing footnote and bibliographical references covering different categories of source material used in historical research. The last two chapters of Part III offer some practical advice on proofreading, and detailed guidance on all aspects of preparing an index. The book includes a helpful glossary, together with an up-to-date guide to further reading, subdivided into three sections: historiography and historical research; reference sources; and research, publishing and style guides.

Finally, I would like to thank the following individuals who kindly agreed to read some sections of the first draft of the manuscript, and whose comments were greatly appreciated: on the study of history, historical sources and the location and evaluation of source material, Professor Michael Lynch (Sir William Fraser Professor of Scottish History and Palaeography at the University of Edinburgh); on the range, purpose and use of various historical source material, Dr Paul Addison (Director of the Centre for Second World War Studies, Edinburgh University); on the type of source material used by historians, Dr Henry Cowper (former Senior Counsellor and historian at the Open University in Scotland); on the nature and function of history, historical techniques and historical evidence, Owen Dudley Edwards (Reader in American and Common-wealth History at the University of Edinburgh); on the relationship between history and the social sciences, Professor David McCrone (Professor of Sociology, Edinburgh University); and on the role of computing in historical research, Professor Bob Morris (Professor of Economic and Social History at Edinburgh University, and former editor of the journal *History and Computing*). I value the advice which they have all offered and have incorporated several of their suggestions in the final draft. I have also extensively revised the original draft during the past year in order to make the contents as useful, readable and up-to-date as possible. The book does not provide rigid guidelines which must be adhered to by all researchers. Readers will gain most benefit from the book by carefully selecting the advice and suggestions which they believe will assist the completion of their own historical work and, where necessary, adapt it to suit their own circumstances. There is a distinct revival of interest in history, and this has been reflected in publications, in television and radio broadcasts and via the Internet. I hope that the appearance of this book will adequately fulfil its original aim, namely that of providing historical researchers with sensible and practical advice, together with comprehensive information on all aspects relating to the research, writing and presentation of historical material.

Bill McDowell
Edinburgh, April 2001

PART I   THE STUDY OF HISTORY

1

The nature and value of history

Everything in the social or natural world is subject to change with the passage of time. It is this process of change which humans are most conscious of, and which influences their day-to-day behaviour. Change occurs on a constant basis and so we are unable to freeze reality, except perhaps when we look at historical evidence, such as written or photographic material. We instinctively try to locate events in time and often make contrasts between past and present, perhaps hoping that knowledge of the past will help us to make informed judgements about the present. We are surrounded by traces of the past, such as buildings, the landscape, artefacts, as well as written, printed and visual records. This record of the past can help to enrich our understanding of our own society and that of other cultures, because individually we only have a fragmentary and imperfect knowledge of the past. It is the discipline of history which provides us with the opportunity to understand and appreciate the past, to distinguish myth from reality, and to see which elements of the past had an influence on future events. This image of the past is static because history can only offer snapshots of the past, albeit sometimes in profuse detail. History enables us to view ourselves and society in a proper perspective, to focus on human motives and the consequences of them for other individuals or for society, and to enhance our knowledge of the potential, as well as the limitations, of human actions.

The study of history has both a practical and educational value. It helps us develop an active enquiring mind, promotes the use of critical skills in the handling and evaluation of various types of source material and assists in the presentation of written work. Historical problems often have to be considered from different angles to arrive at a satisfactory solution; sometimes a solution is never found and instead various arguments and counter-arguments emerge, to be examined by others who look at the conflicting evidence. Some people regard history as offering a good training in how to be civilised citizens, whereas others focus on the enjoyment to be derived from reading about historical events. In an article published in the journal *History* in 1970 the value of history was summarised as follows:

> At whatever level history is studied it is highly likely to result in more active and inquiring minds, a more refined and critical judgement, a greater understanding of present-day society, nationally and internationally, an increased enjoyment of the historical artefacts left by our ancestors, even better citizens. But none of these can logically be the reason for the study, they are bonuses of a human endeavour which is legitimate in itself and not because of its utilitarian function.[1]

The discipline of history obviously has an intrinsic value, and writing about historical events can be both educative and entertaining. This provides a good starting point for looking more closely at the study of history and the task of historians. This should provide you with useful general background information and a context within which you can plan the development of your own historical research.

Historians examine the past so that we may have a better understanding of the content of past events and the context in which they took place. This can help us appreciate the similarities and differences between the circumstances and conditions which govern both past and present events. Historical research does not consist in the mere collection of 'facts', but rather in the interrelationship between factual evidence and the interpretation of this evidence by historians. We may never succeed in knowing the past exactly, but we can make progress if we use our knowledge and skills to move closer towards that ideal. The collection of facts may be appropriate in the study of the mathematical and physical sciences, but this is not the primary function of history. There is no standard text on history, nor is there any standard list of historical facts or a single interpretation of many historical events. However, there are historical events where a genuine consensus of opinion among historians does in fact exist. For example, there may be consensus about when a particular war began, including the factors which contributed to the outbreak of armed conflict. But there might not exist any consensus about which factors were more influential in triggering these events. Historical research represents a systematic enquiry into the past and an attempt to separate true from fictionalised accounts of historical events, based upon the examination of a wide range of relevant source material. This is an important task because history is the source of many of our ideas, beliefs and customs. A better understanding of the past places us in a more advantageous position to appreciate change in the present and to try and learn from past mistakes. This is not to say that the future can be predicted. A complex conjunction of circumstances may never be repeated or lead to the same outcome. We may be able to detect trends over a period of time, so there is a degree of continuity as well as change in history. The content of historical work may also vary, depending on whether we agree to view the past from the perspective of those who lived through earlier times, or from the vantage point of our present-day values and beliefs.

Each generation of historians has its own preoccupations and values and these may shape their perception of past events: what they see as significant, what they disregard, and what connections they assume between the occurrence of particular events. For example, a more pessimistic assessment of the ramifications of wars was apparent after 1918 than it was just prior to the outbreak of the First World War in 1914. We can look at previous historical research to distinguish significant from unimportant events, and to see what social, economic and political patterns emerge over a period of time. We attempt to discover what happened in the past in order to correct our interpretation of what we think may have occurred. The study of any historical topic should encourage you to develop a greater awareness and interest in the past, understand its complexity, and appreciate the forces which have brought about change in society. Herbert Butterfield once stated that 'a people that lived without any knowledge of its past – without any serious attempt to organise its memory – would hardly be calculated to make much progress in its civilisation'.[2] The study of history provides a framework which we can use to make sense of our experience and guide our actions. The future is, in any case, partly conditioned by the past: it is not entirely predictable, but equally it is not the outcome of pure chance.

The professionalisation of history and its emergence as an independent discipline can be traced to the nineteenth century in work such as that produced by Leopold von Ranke and Auguste Comte. The subject has been increasingly studied and researched since then by experts working in universities where many history departments were eventually established and where research into specialised topics proceeded. History came to be regarded as a valuable intellectual pursuit in its own right, regardless of its practical applications. Many historians emphasised the similarities between history and scientific study, which had been making significant progress during the nineteenth century. This led to greater emphasis within history on the discovery and critical examination of primary sources, combined with more training in research techniques. The study of history was regarded as the objective pursuit of knowledge and not dependent on the subjective perceptions of individual historians. Research work initially focused on political and diplomatic history, rather than on social and economic history as the Annales School of historians were later to do, because it was here that the primary sources were more readily available. These developments also coincided with the launch of several scholarly history journals aimed at professional historians, as well as the founding in 1868 of the Royal Historical Society. In January 1886 the *English Historical Review* appeared, the first journal in Britain dedicated to the study of history and targeted primarily at professional historians. In 1902 the British Academy (for the promotion of historical, philosophical and philological studies) was founded. A few years later in 1906 the Historical Association was formed by history teachers in Britain to assist in the development of history as a separate discipline and to raise professional standards. These developments were accompanied by more extensive work in archives to systematise historical knowledge, more undergraduate courses in history and the creation of national histories based on access to official papers. The subject matter of history also began to widen so that by the 1960s an increasing number of historians began to take more interest in themes developed within sociology, psychology, economics and anthropology. This represented a significant change from the former preoccupation with political and diplomatic history.

For knowledge of most historical events we rely not on our memory but on evidence, such as documents, paintings, sculpture, photographs, or sound and visual recordings. We rely partly on the work of previous generations of historians who have sifted through and analysed this evidence to present an account of what aspects they regarded as significant. Historians are expected not just to describe how things were, but why they took a particular course. This requires an appreciation of change through time, combined with a questioning attitude which seeks to discover why specific events occurred at a particular time and in a particular sequence. Historians may be unable to totally reconstruct past events but they can bring revealing insights into aspects of the past if they use their skills to accurately represent historical events. It involves not basing our assessment of the unfolding of historical events on our current prejudices and preoccupations. Herbert Butterfield believed that some historians organised their historical knowledge to fit in with a predetermined (or what was referred to as a Whig) interpretation of history. This type of interpretation equated history with evolution by identifying progress as the key theme. Butterfield argued that some historians studied the past with reference to present economic progress rather than study it for its own sake, so that the legacy of current events would be discerned by looking at the past. He called this a Whig history because the Whigs were identified as the supporters of progress. The Whig interpretation of history was regarded as one which any historian could be guilty of:

> The Whig interpretation of history is not merely the property of Whigs and it is much more subtle than mental bias; it lies in a trick of organisation, an unexamined habit of mind that any historian may fall into. It might be called the historian's 'pathetic fallacy'. It is the result of the practice of abstracting things from their historical context and judging them apart from their context – estimating them and organising the historical story by a system of direct reference to the present.[3]

It was thought to be important for historians not to ignore the meaning which past events had for contemporaries at the time they occurred because this would distort the historical record of such events. In any case, it is sometimes problematical whether progress has been the by-product of an inevitable evolutionary process, or whether it is simply the outcome of a number of unpredictable events.

To make sense of the complexity of past events we consult intentional and unintentional evidence. The past cannot be directly experienced, and those events which have been observed by other people may have been forgotten, misunderstood or misrepresented, or perhaps taken out of proper sequence. The historical evidence we have available can sometimes be selective because the occurrence of dramatic events are often recalled, whereas the passage of unremarkable events which may be of longer-term significance are less likely to have been observed and documented at the time they occurred. A proper historical perspective may enable us to see the significance of events which may not have been regarded as important to those who witnessed them at the moment they occurred. It also helps us to appreciate how and why some events became less significant with the passage of time. By developing a proper perspective on past events we may come to a different conclusion about what is historically significant.

There are two ways in which we can approach the study of the past. The cyclical view of history regards societies and civilisations as similar to living organisms which all experience a cycle of growth, maturity and decline. According to this perspective, no society or civilisation would be expected to remain static because each would experience alternating periods of growth and decline. The underlying implication seems to be that there cannot be any permanent progress or development because each new civilisation must virtually start afresh, rather than be built on the foundations of earlier ones. In contrast to this perspective, the sequential view of historical change regards history as the unfolding of a sequence of events in a linear progression. It implies that if we have some understanding of the past sequence of events we will be in a better position to predict the likely course of future events, or at least understand the nature of change in society. The outcome of events may also lead us to question either our earlier interpretation or the significance of these events so that we can provide a more accurate historical analysis. The sequential perspective appears to regard historical development as synonymous with progress, whereas the cyclical view seems to regard history as exhibiting a cyclical pattern of progress followed by decline. Adherents of the sequential view tend to see a much greater purpose to history, although this can lead to a more overtly determinist theory of historical change. The nature and subject of your own research may influence which perspective you find the most convincing. Neither theory alone provides us with a comprehensive view of historical change, yet each may be valuable for illustrating and explaining change in specific historical contexts.

Historians have an immense curiosity about the past but need to be aware of the strengths and limitations of the evidence they use. You may have formulated some questions which you hope the historical evidence will answer, but equally this evidence may persuade you to ask further questions which you had never originally thought about. A research topic must be manageable so that you can develop a good mastery of the source material. The possession of an ability to examine a subject in detail needs to be combined with the ability to see the broad picture. To make sense of the past we have to be able to see the relationship between a unique event and a general pattern of events. The search for connections between individual historical events may help us to explain the nature of a specific event. Historians are also expected to adopt a critical, but not over-critical, approach to the work of other historians. As A.F. Pollard once remarked: 'It is easy to earn a cheap reputation as a critic by pointing out details the historian has advisedly omitted. Still easier is it to earn an even cheaper reputation by using, to decry an historian's scholarship, sources which were not available when he wrote, or to stand on his shoulders and vaunt one's superior height.'[4] We cannot be seen to be selectively critical by adopting an extremely cautious attitude towards some evidence, while uncritically accepting other evidence. As G. Kitson Clark has noted:

> The blind denial of a statement can be as irrational as the blind acceptance of one, the anti-myth may supply nearly as many over-simplifications and deceptive short-cuts to truth as the myth. Moreover, scepticism may be curiously selective. Men will reject one section of a document basing their argument on facts drawn from another part of the same document. The fact that certain types of assertion have been bustled unceremoniously off the stage is often balanced by the fact that other equally unlikely assertions have been very easily accepted.[5]

We must be aware that improbable events may just be possible, the simple theory may be nearer the truth than the more complex theory and the obvious explanation may provide a more reliable guide to historical events than the less obvious.

Unless we fully appreciate the circumstances and the context in which historical events occurred, and approach them without preconceived ideas, then our speculation may lead us to the wrong conclusions. The historical record of many events is, in any case, always incomplete. Our task is to provide the best interpretation of the events which is possible and is supported by the available primary and secondary source material. The facts, as they say, do not speak for themselves. We must be aware that past generations may have viewed historical events differently from present-day historians. A degree of selection is involved in our choice of research questions, as well as in the source material we choose to examine. To write about the complexity of the past, historians are selective in what they regard were the significant events. A satisfactory balance therefore has to be reached between simplifying and oversimplifying (or sensationalising) the past. In referring to the work of the historian, it has been said that 'if he does not simplify enough, he runs the risk of being chaotic, unintelligible, unreadable, even unpublishable: if he simplifies too much, he will bore and distort.'[6] All historians inevitably differ to some degree in the extent to which they simplify the past, in what they regard as the salient issues, and in what they believe was probable given the circumstances which are known to them. Documentary evidence has to be examined without being unduly influenced by present assumptions and values or any rigid adherence to a predetermined list of questions. The historical evidence may conceal as much as it reveals. Indeed, the judgements of historians may be challenged by their successors: there is no single unanimous verdict of history, only an open and unfinished process.[7]

The aim of historical scholarship is to help your reader understand the significance of past events and not merely regard these events as an unconnected series of facts. Some historians opt for a chronological narrative whereas others prefer a thematic framework. The chronological narrative may cover several themes simultaneously and trace them over a period of time. In contrast to this, historians who choose to work with a thematic framework will deal with only one theme at a time within a specified timescale or otherwise highlight the links between different themes. Unfortunately the latter approach can fragment a chronological narrative and make the historical account appear somewhat static, since each topic is frozen in time and analysed separately. The choice between chronological and thematic approaches may be determined by the subject matter rather than the personal preferences of individual historians. In some instances it is possible to combine both approaches, particularly if a book is perhaps subdivided into parts and each part focuses on a different historical theme. There is, in effect, no single correct approach.

The techniques of historical scholarship encompass a number of activities, from selecting, evaluating and interpreting historical evidence, through to communicating these findings to your readers. Historians sometimes have to make sense of past events from the varied and often unorganised material left behind by previous generations. Much of the content of history does not consist of items of information which can be considered either true or false, but rather those which are less or more probable. Historical evidence may confirm or contradict our assumptions about past events. It is sometimes said that there are no authorities in history, only sources which must be critically examined. The goal is to produce a coherent and consistent account of historical events which will enhance our understanding of the past, whether through the discovery of new facts or the perceptive analysis of existing research data. It can be argued that the more knowledge we accumulate about the past, the greater becomes our appreciation of what we do not know. Moreover, this accumu-lation of knowledge may also increase the number of different interpreta-tions about the past, especially as historical events may appear different when viewed from various perspectives or where different sources are used. The facts in history are not necessarily value free and possess an objective reality which is the same for all historians. The selection and arrangement of historical data may lead us to draw different conclusions from the same evidence. We need to look at the range of source material used by other historians and what evidence they have used to support their assertions before we can begin to study the facts.

The implication of what has been said about historical evidence may appear to suggest that the nature of the evidence requires us to assume that there cannot be any objective interpretation of historical events, only an infinite number of subjective interpretations. With this unpalatable possibility in mind E.H. Carr noted: 'It does not follow that, because a mountain appears to take on different shapes from different angles of vision, it has objectively either no shape at all or an infinity of shapes. It does not follow that, because interpretation plays a necessary part in establishing the facts of history, and because no existing interpretation is wholly objective, one interpretation is as good as another, and the facts of history are in principle not amenable to objective interpretation.'[8] We can reach consensus about many aspects of historical events. We do not have to accept that there is either a wholly objective view of history involving the objective compilation of facts, or a wholly subjective view comprising the different interpretations of historians. According to Carr, the historical process and our knowledge of history represented the interaction between historians and their facts, so that historians may have to reconsider the facts in the light of the interpretations they make, as well as alter their interpretations according to the facts they discover. Moreover, we only have an incomplete and imperfect record of the past because past events cannot be seen in proper perspective against the much larger historical picture of which we are often unaware.

The study of contemporary history might appear to offer the best opportunity to enhance our understanding of the past. However, it can be argued that historians are too close in time to these events to examine them with a sufficient degree of historical detachment. Yet many historical judgements are interim, to the extent that there is always the potential for new evidence to appear or for new interpretations to emerge which might overturn or modify our existing knowledge of past events. Historians who study contemporary history do sometimes have the added option of being able to arrange interviews with participants of past events, although they need to be aware that individuals do vary in their powers of observation and recall. Perhaps the real difficulty with the analysis of recent historical events is that they are not fully documented, and documents can be withheld or occasionally destroyed before they can be of use to future historians. Researchers of contemporary history do undoubtedly experience the disadvantage of being unaware, so to speak, what came next.[9] Historical trends may only be evident when events are studied over long periods of time. The experience of studying history alerts us to the often unforeseen nature in which events unfold and of our imperfect knowledge of the recent or distant past. History does have a social role to play. In a presidential address delivered to the Royal Historical Society in 1976, Geoffrey Elton put forward his own views on this matter:

> What society has a right to expect from us is that we should act as mankind's intellectual conscience, helping in our sceptical way to sort the true from the untrue, the useful from the pernicious, the valid from the pretentious, and teaching others (especially our students) those proper standards of sceptical questioning which alone can protect freedom. It is our task to undermine self-appointed certainties and to break the shackles of structures, whether they dominate the mind or all of life.[10]

These are indeed admirable aims and provide ample justification for the study of history.

Historians are often reluctant to talk about the lessons of history. History does not repeat itself, but neither is any historical event totally novel when its varied characteristics are carefully examined. A sequence of historical events can never be said to be inevitable. The most we can say is that given certain antecedent conditions, a particular sequence of events is likely to follow in the manner predicted. No two events in history follow an identical path because no two events share identical characteristics. Previous generations knew as little of their future as we do of ours. But when we look to the past we inevitably look from a different perspective than those who lived in the past. As Michael Stanford noted: 'Like us, they saw their future as open, while we, looking back on that future, see it as closed. It may be that they saw choice and free will where we, with hindsight, see only necessity and faith. On the other hand, it may be that sometimes they had more choice than they thought and we are astonished at their blindness.'[11] We must be aware of this difference in perspective if we wish to avoid misinterpreting the past and the actions of individuals. They were more aware of the context within which their actions occurred, whereas we have the benefit of hindsight and can see the consequences of human actions as well as those of impersonal forces. No human actions are entirely determined, in the sense that specific events must follow on from specific causes, but many human actions may nevertheless be very predictable. Historians who are tempted to study the past with a preconceived theory are likely to produce a disjointed and distorted account of past events.

The principal task of historians is to provide an informative, accurate and balanced account of individual actions, events and historical trends.

The direction of historical scholarship does not remain static. For example, the preference for studying British political, constitutional and diplomatic history was widened to encompass an expanded field of historical study. This modified approach to the study of the past included the examination of new topics and themes, such as local, cultural, urban, business, ethnic, scientific and intellectual history. It also covered the history of other countries, such as the customs, rituals and beliefs in African and Third World countries. The greater use of social scientific methods brought new issues to the attention of historians, alerted them to the need for greater precision in historical analysis and provided new perspectives on the past. The more recent application of computers to the analysis and retrieval of information will also have a profound influence on the nature and range of historical topics which can, and will, be investigated. There also appears to be a greater willingness among many professional historians to ensure that their work appeals to a wider, and not necessarily academic, audience. This seems desirable because of the popular resurgence of interest in history, a trend which can only be advantageous in the future for historians, for historical scholarship and for the discipline of history.

Notes

1 Gareth E. Jones, 'Towards a theory of history teaching', *History*, 55 (1970), 63.
2 Herbert Butterfield, *Man on his Past* (Cambridge, 1955) p. 30.
3 H. Butterfield, *The Whig Interpretation of History* (London, 1931) pp. 30–1.
4 A.F. Pollard, 'Historical criticism', *History*, 5 (1920), 25.
5 G. Kitson Clark, *The Critical Historian* (London, 1967) p. 201.
6 John Cannon (ed.), *The Historian at Work* (London, 1980) p. 3.
7 Sankey, 'The historian and the lawyer: their aims and their methods', *History*, 21 (1936), 106.
8 E.H. Carr, *What is History?*, 2nd edn (London, 1987) pp. 26–7.
9 David Thomson, 'The writing of contemporary history', *Journal of Contemporary History*, 2:1 (January 1967), 32.
10 G.R. Elton, 'The historian's social function', *Transactions of the Royal Historical Society*, 5th series, 27 (1977), 210–11.
11 Michael Stanford, *A Companion to the Study of History* (Oxford, 1994) p. 23.

2

History and the social sciences

The study of history has traditionally been regarded as valuable because of its intrinsic interest in unique historical phenomena.[1] This has been contrasted with the social sciences where it appears greater emphasis is placed on empiricism, quantification and the use of theoretical models. Historians have tended to focus much less on social groups, social structures or patterns in human behaviour or events than those who work in the social sciences. Some historians believe that social scientists simplify reality by using trends (based on the study or observation of a number of events) to explain any specific event. The question is how different the study of history is in practice from research work in the social sciences.

A basic distinction is often made between the use of generalisations by historians and social scientists. Historians employ generalisations to assist our understanding of specific past events, whereas social scientists use them to explain mainly current events and offer reliable indicators about future events. Although historians and social scientists both use generalisations, they view the significance of general concepts from a different perspective. Chronology plays an important part in the explanation of a sequence of historical events, whereas social scientists tend to focus on patterns and trends. The contrasts which were believed to exist between historians and social scientists is clearly illustrated in the following statement, originally made by Alan Bullock in 1951, on what the proper role of the historian should be:

His whole training teaches him to break down rather than build up generalisations, to bring the general always to the touchstone of particular, concrete instances. His experience of this discipline and its results makes him cautious and sceptical about the possibility of establishing uniformities and regularities of sufficient generality to bear the weight of the conclusions then built up on them.[2]

We need to look at the distinguishing features of the social science disciplines and how they differ from the discipline of history.

During the nineteenth century, historians almost exclusively focused their attention on political history because this was where most of the documentary evidence was available. It was only towards the end of that century that some historians began to shift their focus from political and constitutional history to a consideration of social and economic history. The latter placed more emphasis on the lives of ordinary people and of mass movements, rather than that of politicians, statesmen, landowners, military leaders or entrepreneurs. This shift of focus subsequently broadened the range of historical topics under investigation to encompass local history, family history, women's history, cultural history, labour history, urban history and the history of crime and punishment. The social sciences could still be distinguished from historical research because considerably less emphasis was placed on a study of individuals and much more on social and economic structures, functional relationships and social theories. History was expected to combine narrative and analysis: narrative offered the details of actual events, whereas analysis placed those events in a broader social, economic or political context. The social science disciplines did suggest promising new areas of historical enquiry, as in psycho-history where psychology was applied to assist our understanding of the psychological motives of political and military leaders during periods of international tension or the psychological bases of popular protest.

A basic contrast has always been seen to exist between historical narrative and theoretical models in the social sciences.[3] Some social scientists believed that traditional historical narrative provided little more than a descriptive account of the past with insufficient analytical content. The greater emphasis on quantitative data in the social sciences did require the construction of abstract models; and in sociology the belief that society progresses through stages of development did favour the use of abstract concepts. The search for patterns in social development, organisations and in human behaviour naturally favoured the use of models or concepts. The latter help to explain a range of social phenomena which have certain features in common. Historians also use concepts, such as 'class', when they seek to generalise about particular features of society. But perhaps there is something fundamentally different in the language used by historians and that used by social scientists: the latter appear to use obscure language much more than would be expected by historians. More importantly, there are differences in how concepts and theories are used to explain past events. For example, sociologists think about social structures and use theories to assist their assessment of social reality. In his book entitled *Historical Sociology* Philip Abrams stated: 'Social reality stands behind social appearances not in the relation of face to veil but in the relation of process to moment. Its apprehension is more a matter of analytical structuring than of empirical seeing through.'[4] Some historians might claim that this was not the only, or even the most important, route to our understanding of the past. They could argue that abstract models may be at variance with the surviving record of the past or the memory of individuals who lived through past events.

There are differences of approach between history and the social sciences, although this may not necessarily indicate that the social sciences are closer to the natural sciences than they are to history. It is frequently stated that history is more of an art than a science, that it has a closer affinity with literary traditions and that the art of writing and the use of imagination are more important in historical research than the method of investigation. If the social sciences share similarities with the natural sciences they would need to be capable of formulating laws about society which could predict human behaviour. But there was to be no science of society. The natural sciences did not provide appropriate models for work in the humanities and social sciences. Social scientists and historians share a belief in the need to explain the significance of events, and not merely describe them. For example, a scientist may use anatomical terminology to describe human movements, whereas a social scientist would seek to explain the meaning and significance of those movements, such as that the clapping of hands is used to express approval or enjoyment. Perhaps it is in the formulation of theories and the use of quantitative techniques that the social sciences were regarded as bearing some resemblance to the natural sciences. The scope for quantitative studies and use of theory is less evident in historical studies than it is in the social sciences.

The social sciences adopted a rigorous mode of investigation and attempted to be scientific, partly in order to gain greater recognition. However, unlike the natural sciences, the social sciences do not provide us with general laws which we can use to predict events. For example, if the price of commodities increases then there is a greater likelihood that their consumption will fall, but this is not equivalent to saying that there is a general law which states that if the price increases by 20 per cent then consumption will fall by 15 per cent. Indeed, an increase in the price of a scarce or prestige commodity may serve to increase, rather than lower, demand for it. We are therefore observing the operation of probabilities, not absolute measurements, because human nature is too unpredictable to permit this. In any case, we can state that if individuals are aware that it is predicted they will act a particular way, then they may choose to act differently. The social sciences do appear to differ from history to the extent that much of the work of social scientists generates results which may be of more obvious current political, social or economic benefit. Social scientists also gain more direct access to individuals, such as through interviews and participant observation, whereas historians rely primarily on documentary evidence. The accumulation of historical and social scientific evidence does advance our knowledge of society, but not in such an obvious cumulative manner as it appears to do in the natural sciences. In science, many new studies or theories have to be built upon the foundations of earlier studies to a greater extent than they do in historical or social scientific studies. New ideas, evidence and techniques will function as useful, but not essential, building blocks for later historical studies. It has been said that this suggests that history is related more closely to literary than to scientific studies.[5]

The social sciences may claim to be closer to the natural sciences but the extent to which they are has been questioned. In arguing against the belief that the social sciences could provide a scientific explanation of social life, Alan Ryan stated: 'Many explanations look rather dubiously causal, many seem not to be backed by generalisations, much explanation seems very localised in its range, value-freedom seems extremely difficult to attain, and it seems equally hard to attain the degree of agreement on the meaning and interpretation of the data that natural scientists regularly achieve.'[6] There is perhaps another aspect which would indicate that history and the social sciences have more in common with each other than they do with the natural sciences: this is in the relationship between cause and effect. In the natural world causes always precede effects but in the social world actions do not always follow preceding thoughts because humans have the ability to envisage the possible results of certain actions and so avoid them. Social science appears to straddle the divide between history and the natural sciences because it makes use of the content of history and the methods of the natural sciences. The social sciences may be unable to offer a science of society but the work of social scientists can provide valuable material for historians.

Historians benefit from the research output of the social science disciplines, but history also plays a significant role in the content of the social sciences. Social scientists cannot always focus exclusively on contemporary social structures without considering the historical background of the subjects they investigate. A society cannot be fully understood unless it is viewed in its historical context.[7] The strength of explanations in the social sciences is bolstered through a recognition of the interplay between unique events, which are often studied by historians, and general patterns evident in the functioning of societies. As Sidney Pollard one remarked, 'history takes in all of man's social activities, including his beliefs and superstitions, his science and knowledge, his political organisation, personal eccentricities and artistic achievements. All these act and react on the material and class-oriented bases of life.'[8] The study of history does have a role to play in our understanding of contemporary events, which are the preoccupation of social scientists. Hugh Trevor-Roper stressed the importance of taking account of the historical perspective when he stated in a journal article on history and sociology that 'so much of our own contemporary history is hidden from us that we cannot hope to see it in full. It is so close to us that we cannot see it in correct proportion. It is not yet over, so that we cannot judge it by the result. Familiarity with the past can supply some of those defects. It can provide a standard of comparison'.[9]

The ability of history to provide knowledge of unique events, individuals and a chronological framework, counterbalances the emphasis within the social sciences on impersonal factors and structures, such as in the examination of economic and social trends. Alan Bullock summed this up in a lecture delivered in 1976 when he argued as follows:

> the context will be incomplete and produce a misleading picture of the past if it is confined to the description and analysis of only economic and social factors and if it excludes political history, the impact and chronological order of events frequently unpredictable in their combination and effects, the interplay of personalities, the conflicts of particular interests, the mixture of rational and irrational behaviour, the element of chance.[10]

The study of history does have a role to play in supplementing the work of social scientists, and the social sciences have in turn had an influence on the work of historians. This influence may be said to be evident in the search for precision in data through data analysis, in the range of questions based on source material, and in the need to look for general patterns in historical data. Some historians have been more willing than others to acknowledge the usefulness of the social sciences in helping us to explain the nature of historical development.

The social sciences have alerted historians to the need to move beyond an assessment of the role of individuals to consider wider social factors, such as social status, class and social mobility, which may influence human behaviour. E.H. Carr argued that proper history could not be written unless an attempt was made to study individuals in relation to their social environment. In particular contexts, class, status or nationality may exert a much greater influence on human behaviour than individual personality does. In any case, individuals act according to hidden as well as conscious motives, and their actions may be the product of unforeseen as well as planned forces or beliefs. By looking at individuals within a wider social context it is possible for historians to provide a more meaningful account of the factors which influenced the course of past events. This is particularly important when we consider that most events in history have been influenced by individuals acting within a group, occupation or class. A history which merely describes individual actions to the exclusion of the wider social context within which those actions occurred (i.e. roles, institutions and social structures) is not a complete history. E.H. Carr remarked that to write history as the product of the actions of Great Men without taking account of social forces, was to erroneously place Great

Men outside history and regard them as imposing their will on history.[11] His view was that Great Men should be regarded as both the products and agents of historical development: outstanding individuals who shaped, but were also shaped by, social forces.

The contrast between history and the social sciences involves more than simply a contrast of subject matter. The techniques used in the social sciences differ from those used in most historical research. Some historians have used social science techniques to open up new lines of enquiry, such as in the use of quantitative techniques to test the validity of qualitative evidence. This has sometimes provided a reservoir of new and fruitful source material for historians. However, there are still differences in the research techniques of historians and social scientists. Social scientists use questionnaires, sampling, interviews, participant observation, comparative methods, theoretical models, mainframe computers and statistical analysis of data. They are willing to use quantitative methods or construct mathematical models, whereas historians are more likely to rely on the critical examination of documentary evidence. This is understandable because most of the techniques used in the social sciences are not directly applicable to the study of past events. For example, oral history may be useful if we wish to fill gaps in the historical record by examining contemporary events within living memory, but it is obviously not an option for those historians whose field of study pre-dates the twentieth century. Similarly, participant observation is only an appropriate method for studies which focus on the role of individuals in the present, not human behaviour in the past. The adoption of a scientific approach by some social scientists created a division between the social sciences and the discipline of history, such as in the use of statistical analysis and theoretical models.

The precision of statistical analysis for social scientists was just as important as the reliability of documentary evidence for historians. Information presented in statistical tables gave the impression of being more precise than historical narrative, but historians argued that it was the selection and interpretation of data which were the crucial factors. Moreover, historians could argue that the presentation of statistical data might give a distorted image of reality if the data focused only on factors which regularly occurred and could be quantified, thereby omitting unexpected and accidental events. Similarly, some historians believed that the social sciences placed too much emphasis on theoretical models. It seemed that social scientists used facts to support their theories, whereas historians were more interested in only using theories if they supported specific facts. We instinctively associate theories with the social and natural sciences, and less so with the discipline of history. But can theories be developed within the discipline of history to assist us in the explanation of historical change? Is it in fact possible to provide an accurate analysis of the stages of industrial development, the class structure or the factors conducive to the emergence of dictatorships by using theory? Historians do construct a number of hypotheses when they seek to make sense of the complexity of historical events, but theories do not seem to play such an important role in historical studies because new evidence may emerge to undermine any grand theory. Indeed, a common feature of historical work in some areas is the multiplicity of competing hypotheses. Theory does not play a vital role in historical research because it de-emphasises the uniqueness of past events, as well as the role of individuals who helped to shape those events. Theory tends to portray individuals as helpless in the face of historical events beyond their comprehension or ability to modify. The use of grand theories would force historians to opt for a deterministic model of historical change. Nevertheless, if history consisted merely of a number of unique events, it would make the course of history much less comprehensible. So perhaps theory does have some role to play in helping us to understand and explain historical change.

Historians are cautious about the ability of models to provide a genuinely objective route to discovering the reality of past events. Even within the social sciences there are rival theories and models. Problems can occur when a subject is investigated from the perspective of a single theory. This is the type of criticism which has been levelled at, for example, Marxism because of its exclusive emphasis on the concept of class, to the exclusion of other divisions in society (e.g. ethnicity, nationality or religion). The existence of conflicting theories indicates that theory does not play a value-free role in explaining historical change. A more fruitful approach appeared to exist in the use of mathematical models to explain specific historical developments.

In the postwar period there has been a developing interest in the use of quantitative methods in historical research, particularly in the field of economic and social history where one social scientific method had an obvious application. The use of quantitative studies was regarded as especially useful for examining large-scale events, particularly where data existed which had been gathered over long periods of time. Examples included demographic studies using census data or perhaps an examination of price movements. It was in areas such as these that mathematical models were constructed to assist our understanding of historical change. Statements which were based on the use of quantitative data appeared more reliable and assumed a higher status than qualitative statements. Yet these techniques were unable to produce valuable results unless all the significant variables had been identified. Studies which were based only on the evidence which was available and able to be quantified were always likely to produce an incomplete and distorted account of reality. Moreover, the statistical data still had to be interpreted to make sense of it. For example, the number of products sold of specific commodities in the past may reveal little about their popularity unless analysis is extended to include other variables, such as competing commodities, prices, consumer preferences and traditions. Also, factual errors could produce a wholly inaccurate and misleading account of historical events. Historians realised that they needed to have a good grasp of the historical context before they could reach any conclusions based on quantitative data. As John Tosh indicates, 'statistics may serve to reveal or clarify a particular tendency; but how we *interpret* that tendency – the significance we attach to it and the causes we adduce for it – is a matter for seasoned historical judgement, in which the historian trained exclusively in quantitative methods would be woefully deficient.'[12]

It seems that there was only limited scope for the use of quantitative methods in history, except perhaps in areas where data were too numerous and too complex to manipulate manually.[13] But quantitative methods do force us to ask new questions, to examine new themes, to focus on old issues from a new perspective and to abandon outdated beliefs. However, if any historical research problem is not carefully defined, computers may generate so much data that its relevance may be difficult to ascertain.[14] Moreover, no proper historical account can be written unless the non-quantifiable aspects are also included in the equation. Arthur Marwick drew attention to some limitations in the scope of computers in historical research when he stated: 'Where many kinds of often fragmentary information are accumulated from a vast range of different kinds of archives there will be little possibility of the rational compilation of a database. Where issues of perception, mental attitudes, quality of life, rather than quantities, are being investigated, then the computer will remain on the sidelines.'[15] Perhaps a useful way of assessing the scope as well as the limitations of quantitative studies is to consider the work of the new economic historians.

By the beginning of the 1960s, American historians were using mathematical models to solve historical problems. The application of these models to the study of economic history formed the basis of what was to be known as the new economic history, sometimes referred to as econometric history or cliometrics. The new economic historians were so enthusiastic about quantitative methods that they used statistical data as the primary basis of their historical analysis, not merely for illustrative purposes to support existing arguments. One of the first major topics covered was the effect of slavery in constraining economic and technological development in the American South prior to the commencement of the Civil War. Quantitative studies suggested that the South was not as economically backward, nor the plantation system as unprofitable as originally envisaged, under the institution of slavery. The new economic historians therefore stated that the case for the abolition of slavery could not rest solely on the economic argument that slavery retarded economic growth, but instead had to be based on the moral argument as to whether it was humane to maintain slavery. Not all historians have accepted these results without some qualification.[16] Nevertheless, what early quantitative studies did achieve was to force scholars to reinterpret previous assumptions about specific historical events.

Another example is provided by the American historian Robert Fogel who examined the social benefits of railroads and their role in stimulating American economic growth. Fogel compared the actual level of national income with a hypothetical level which would have been reached in the absence of railroads. He wished to ascertain whether the social saving brought about by railroads was as significant as most historians believed it was. The social saving was calculated by comparing the actual cost of shipping goods by rail, with the hypothetical cost of transporting goods in the absence of railroads. The calculations were complex because of the large number of variables involved, as follows: possible economies generated by altering production and marketing sites if canals and roads alone were expected to transport commodities; costs associated with the slower transportation of goods by road and canal; inability to use canals during the winter months; an assessment of the area of land under cultivation, including changes in food prices, food consumption and land values; the proximity of farms to navigable waterways; and finally, possible damage or loss of goods if railroad transport was not available. Taking all these factors into account, Fogel argued that railroads did *not* bring about a revolutionary impact on economic growth.

In the absence of railroads, Robert Fogel argued that improvements to the canals and roads would have taken place, thereby lowering transportation costs and reducing the social savings brought about by the railroads. The controversy generated by this counterfactual model was based on the fact that it involved guessing the actions of individuals if a given sequence of events had occurred. The model tried to simplify reality so that comparisons could be made between what *did* happen in the past, with what *might* have happened if specified conditions had been different. But was there sufficient evidence available to test the reliability of the model? The real difficulty with the counterfactual model was that because the hypothetical circumstances did not occur, there was no conclusive evidence to support the validity of the assumptions made about them. Moreover, many historians disliked the use of mathematical equations and statistical sampling. In any case, the advocates of quantitative methods accepted that the discipline of history was unlikely to be transformed into a social science, even if it did make use of 'scientific' techniques.[17]

Many historians regard history as an art, not a science. Yet many historical studies appear to be closer to the social sciences, both in their subject matter and in the techniques which they use. Historians now adopt an increasingly rigorous approach in relation to their source material. For example, scientific methods may be used to date documents, to compare handwriting or to provide clear visual images of old photographs; and statistical methods are used in the analysis of demographic or electoral studies. History is also an art: the art of reconstructing the past from the documentary and other evidence available, using critical and imaginative skills. The true art of the historian's work becomes evident when the macro and micro elements, the broad picture and the historical detail, appear in proper conjunction. The study of history is the art of looking at the evidence of the past to produce an account of events which will take note of the motives of individuals, the role of wider social influences, and the interplay of chance. The purpose of historical research is to make sense of a series of events in a specified timeframe, establish their authenticity, understand the connection between them, and interpret their wider significance. Historians formulate hypotheses but do not establish general laws or models of historical development. The study of history combines elements of the foreseen and the unpredictable, individual actions and wider social forces. It appears to be more of an art than a social science.

Notes

1   Alan Bullock, 'Has history ceased to be relevant?', *The Historian*, no. 43 (Autumn 1994), 20.
2   Alan Bullock, 'The historian's purpose: history and metahistory', *History Today*, 29 (1979), 713.
3   Peter Burke, *Sociology and History* (London, 1992) ch. 1.
4   Philip Abrams, *Historical Sociology* (Shepton Mallet, 1982) p. 317.
5   Fritz Stern (ed.), *The Varieties of History* (London, 1970) p. 370.
6   Alan Ryan, 'Is the study of society a science?', in David Potter *et al.* (eds), *Society and the Social Sciences* (London, 1981) pp. 20–1.
7   C. Wright Mills, *The Sociological Imagination* (New York, 1959) pp. 149–50.
8   Sidney Pollard, 'Economic history – a science of society?', *Past and Present*, no. 30 (April 1965), 12.
9   H.R. Trevor-Roper, 'The past and the present: history and sociology', *Past and Present*, no. 42 (February 1969), 5.
10 Alan Bullock, 'Is history becoming a social science?: the case of contemporary history', *History Today*, 29 (1979), 765–6.
11 E.H. Carr, *What is History?*, 2nd edn (London, 1987) p. 54.
12 John Tosh, *The Pursuit of History*, 2nd edn (London, 1991) p. 197.
13 Daniel I. Greenstein, *A Historian's Guide to Computing* (Oxford, 1994) ch. 1.
14 Evan Mawdsley and Thomas Munck, *Computing for Historians: An Introductory Guide* (Manchester, 1993) ch. 1.
15 Arthur Marwick, *The Nature of History*, 3rd edn (Basingstoke, 1989) p. 180.
16 Lawrence Stone, *The Past and the Present Revisited* (London, 1987) pp. 32–3.
17 Robert William Fogel, 'The limits of quantitative methods in history', *American Historical Review*, 80 (1975), 329–50.

3

History and the natural sciences

With the professionalisation of history in the nineteenth century, together with the impressive results achieved by the natural sciences, the study of history was also thought to be synonymous with the scientific pursuit of knowledge. The discipline of history was increasingly expected to simulate science to the extent of developing rigorous research techniques. Historical judgements were now to be based on a careful examination of the source material. A key issue in the study and writing of history was whether the discipline could ever be regarded as a scientific endeavour which adhered to rigorous methods of logical analysis and absolute objectivity. In an inaugural address to the Royal Historical Society in 1879, the following comments were made by the chairman of Council: 'If anatomy, physiology and psychology are sciences, why not history, which is but a systematised record of man's individual and collective development? If man in his isolation as savage or prehistoric man, in anthropology and archaeology, may be treated scientifically, why not the whole of humanity in history?'[1] But the objects of study in history were clearly not necessarily identical to those studied by scientists, and neither were the concepts which were used to describe change in the external world.

History is primarily concerned with the study of human beings, their actions and the consequences of these actions for other individuals and for society. In contrast to this, the object of study in science is natural phenomena. Moreover, the techniques and instruments used in scientific enquiry are not identical to those used in historical research: historians have no microscope or telescope with which to view society. The actions of human beings simply cannot be predicted with the same degree of accuracy as events in the natural world. Moreover, the functioning of societies cannot be inferred by merely examining the actions of individuals in isolation from their relationships with one another. In the social world the whole cannot be understood merely by examining the individual parts. Historians cannot travel back in time to observe the past directly. G.R. Elton once said that 'the problem of whether the past can be known at all – since it is not now here in the presence of the observer and cannot be brought back for study – arises from the attempt to make history seem a science, comparable in purpose and method to the natural sciences.'[2] The social world is very complex and most events are never repeated. It could be said that the scientist is expected to focus on the features which individual events share in common and so produce a less complex picture, whereas the historian is more interested in relating individual events to more complex events. Scientists and historians look at individual or unique events from a different perspective: the former searches for causal laws or generalisations, the latter is more interested in connections.

The significance of those events which historians describe highlights their different approach when compared with the tasks facing scientists. Historians cannot claim to operate from a wholly objective position by merely recording historical facts: these facts have to be interpreted. Scientists are expected to establish precise facts which may give rise to the formulation of laws which have a wider application. Some historians also believe that it is possible to contrast the greater detachment between researcher and subject of those who work in the sciences from those who work in the humanities. However, the pursuit of scientific knowledge cannot always be said to be value-free, but the procedures and training adopted in scientific studies aim to achieve this objective. Perhaps this is because the greater degree of control which scientists have over events in the natural world is more obvious than the control which their counterparts in the humanities and social sciences have over events in the social world. This enables scientists to take a more detached and autonomous view of the events which they describe. As Norbert Elias has stated, 'for while one need not know, in order to understand the structure of molecules, what it feels like to be one of its atoms, in order to understand the functioning of human groups one needs to know, as it were, from inside how human beings experience their own and other groups, and one cannot know without active participation and involvement.'[3]

Historical research does not enable us to discover the past in its entirety. It can only cover those topics which historians have decided to write about, based on the evidence which they have access to. This process is clearly also governed by the time and resources at their disposal. No historian is in a position to reconstruct the past totally, but it is possible to offer a penetrating insight into snapshots of past events. A total and objective record of the past is rarely possible. The observations of historians are influenced by hindsight. If historians are aware of the outcome of past events then it is difficult to envisage how this knowledge will not somehow influence their assessment of the factors which preceded those events. John Tosh summarises the dilemma as follows: 'We can never recapture the authentic flavour of a historical moment as it was experienced by people at the time because we, unlike them, know what happened next; and the significance which we accord to a particular incident is inescapably conditioned by that knowledge.'[4] But if we wish to illuminate the causes and repercussions of a sequence of events which were unknown at the time they took place, then obviously hindsight does offer some advantages. After all, the actual repercussions may differ substantially from what was intended at the time.

The extent and reliability of historical evidence will determine to what degree past events can be reconstructed. Historians face greater difficulties than scientists in reconstructing the past because of the need to consider not simply what events did occur, but also how they believe those events were regarded by those who were present at the time they occurred. Historians are expected to move beyond the description of events: they also have to explain why they occurred. The significance of historical events may not appear obvious from the factual evidence which survives. The memory of other people has a role to play in reconstructing more recent events, but there is still the possibility that human memory will provide a distorted account of past events.[5] Moreover, it is also sometimes necessary for us to separate factors which are important in assisting our understanding of the past from those factors which appear to be important but are merely incidental.

The process of reconstructing the past is not so straightforward because we have to venture beyond the outward appearance of events to discover their hidden meaning or significance. The historian Wilhelm von Humboldt, writing over a century and a half ago, put it like this:

> The historian, like the draftsman, will produce only caricatures if he merely depicts the specific circumstances of an event by connecting them with each other as they seemingly present themselves. He must render strict account of their inner nexus, must establish for himself a picture of the active forces, must recognise their trends at a given moment, must inquire into the relationship of both forces and trends to the existing state of affairs and to the changes that have preceded it.[6]

These inner forces do not operate like scientific laws. Scientific laws can be used to assist us to reconstruct events in the natural world, but there are no laws which offer the same opportunities for historians to reconstruct events in the social world. Science can, of course, come to the assistance of historians by offering techniques to date evidence, such as that relating to material objects or handwritten documents. Statistical analysis can also be valuable in assisting our understanding of changes in population size or in price movements. Even film or audio tapes provide information which may prove to be very useful and give us a new perspective on the past. But the process of reconstructing history is clearly not identical to the process of reconstruction as it occurs in the physical sciences. Historians attempt to rediscover the past, but they can never be certain about the accuracy of this reconstruction, since there is no absolute and scientific method for comparing their reconstruction with how the past actually was.

This problem with reconstructing events forms part of a wider issue about the relative status of historical and scientific knowledge. Since the eighteenth century, science has generated a significant amount of reliable knowledge about the natural world, and there has been widespread acceptance of the results of most scientific experiments. Progress in the natural sciences has been cumulative because previous discoveries have provided the foundation for later scientific research, from which practical benefits have materialised. Scientific knowledge is normally assumed to be based on careful observation of the same phenomena over a period of time. From these observations, laws are formulated to predict the occurrence of events. Scientific knowledge advances through the assimilation of new theories and factual evidence which are found to be consistent with our observations and with our experience. But the study of human beings cannot be analysed according to the same criteria and produce predictable results. Scientific knowledge therefore appears to be based on a solid foundation in comparison with historical knowledge, but we must not forget that it is humans who perform scientific experiments, make observations and interpret the results. We cannot assume that scientists never adhere to preconceived ideas. Students of the history of science are well aware that some scientists can be as selective as some historians in what they observe and in what they are willing to accept as representing a credible hypothesis.

Historians do claim to approach their subject with a degree of impartiality, but unfortunately no scientific laws are likely to emerge from a study of human societies. We can analyse historical trends but these do not provide the basis for reliable predictions. A study of history may reveal the reasons why some societies can experience periods of progress followed by periods of stagnation or decline. Historical events are not always so unique that they cannot be classified and reveal such underlying causes and common factors, but it can also be said that neither can classifications give rise to predictions. In both science and history it is possible systematically to organise and classify knowledge but historians do not attempt to formulate laws which enable reliable predictions to be made. This perhaps helps to explain why scientific knowledge appears to enjoy a higher status than historical knowledge. Even where concepts are used in historical studies, such as democracy and dictatorship, they take on different meanings in different societies over a period of time. The beliefs, expectations and values of historians may influence, to some extent, the sources they choose to examine, their selection of facts and the interpretation which they place on the data available. Neither the historian nor the scientist can be wholly objective in their pursuit of knowledge, but equally this pursuit of knowledge cannot be entirely subjective. It may simply be that there exists a greater subjective element in historical work, and this should be viewed positively. The variety of themes and approaches to the study of history deepens and enriches our understanding of individuals and of the society in which they lived. It is this aspect, rather than any attempt to discover whether historical knowledge can be equated with scientific knowledge, which can make historical work such a worthwhile and often fascinating endeavour.

In both history and the natural sciences evidence can be used to support different, and often mutually conflicting, hypotheses. This seems more obvious in historical studies where a debate may develop over the significance of events or the techniques used. For example, historians who prefer structural history in contrast to descriptive history are more likely to be interested in the extent to which the techniques of science can be applied to the study of historical problems. The availability of evidence also highlights some differences between history and the sciences. It is a fallacy for any historian to believe that there is a finite volume of evidence available on any subject which somehow only needs to be discovered to facilitate a thorough historical examination. The evidence may be incomplete or perhaps too large to handle. Indeed, it has been argued that it is the fragmentary nature of historical source material which distinguishes history from the natural sciences.[7] Gaps in the evidence are more likely to occur in historical research and do seem to provide opportunities for historians to place their own interpretations on the evidence to a much greater extent than is possible in the natural sciences.

Some people believe that there is a greater subjective element to historical study in comparison with scientific study, but this does not make historical research less rigorous than scientific research. The writing of history is based on a mixture of factual evidence and interpretation. It is impossible for historians to step outside their own timeframe and environment to look at history objectively. E.H. Carr believed that the facts of history could not be wholly objective because they become facts of history as a result of the significance which historians attach to them.[8] However, G.R. Elton took the opposite view because he argued that the past, or facts about the past, exist independently of the historian's views about them, and so they have an objective reality. In his book *The Practice of History*, Elton argued that if history merely consisted of the interpretations of historians then history itself would be unknowable. Yet historians can never be totally objective when they analyse the actions of individuals: there must be an element of subjectivity because historians have to possess some knowledge of human nature to write about historical events.

The pursuit of total objectivity is constrained by the fact that all historians work with preconceived ideas, knowledge and values which are based on their own observations and experiences. Moreover, they invariably do not have the opportunity to come directly in contact with the facts surrounding the subjects which they investigate. As J.A. Passmore noted: 'The scientist confronts the world as it nakedly is, whereas the historian sees it, always, through the medium of someone else's testimony – a testimony he can never by the nature of the case penetrate beyond, because the events the testimony describes are gone forever.'[9] Scientists can repeat an experiment if the testimony of others is in doubt, whereas historians cannot directly observe or confirm the testimony of those no longer alive. The most they can achieve is to examine the historical evidence and look for consensus in the written or oral testimony left by previous generations. Historical events are, in any case, written from different perspectives. A social historian will focus on different themes and arguments to those an economic historian might choose, but it may be difficult to determine which of these historical analyses is the most accurate. The most we can hope for is that any reconstruction of past events corresponds as closely as possible with the known facts. It may be that scientific results are expected to be objective for all observers, whereas historical results cannot be objective from all perspectives. In most historical studies, not all factors will be regarded as of equal importance to all historians. On this basis it follows that historical judgements will essentially be subjective.

Many historians would accept that a fundamental distinction between history and the natural sciences relates to the procedure by which knowledge is generated. Experimental knowledge in the sciences accumulates in a stage-by-stage process. It is shared by most scientists until new evidence generates new hypotheses, new experiments, new facts and new laws. Historians cannot conduct experiments; they can only study what remains of the past. It seems to make the study of history more of an art than a science. But this description may not be so straightforward because it assumes that knowledge in the natural sciences only advances as a result of repeated experiments which confirm or refute scientific hypotheses. It also assumes that any scientist who repeats an experiment will obtain the same results. Scientific hypotheses must be based to some extent on inference, not merely on existing facts. Perhaps it is because historians study human beings, whose motivations and intentions are so varied and unpredictable, that leads us to make the distinction between experimental knowledge in the sciences and knowledge derived from historical analysis. A significant amount of historical analysis is involved in explaining the motives which influence individual actions, as opposed to the occurrence of historical events which were the outcome of those actions. Motives cannot be deduced from experimental procedures or from personal experience. We cannot predict actions by assuming how individuals in the past would have acted in a given situation, because human actions may the product of routine or impulsive behaviour. Historical events may perhaps have to be rewritten by succeeding generations if new evidence becomes available or more persuasive arguments are used.

Historical and scientific analysis are both based on proof and inference. Any belief that there can be proof in historical analysis would appear to require some understanding of the nature of factual evidence in historical research. Some facts may be indisputable, whereas others are subject to doubt and disagreement. The greater the extent of this disagreement, the lower the probability that certain events will be classified as facts. If the facts are in dispute then we are left with a series of inferences, some of which may appear more credible than others. Historical events may follow in succession without any evident causal connection between them, whereas in the natural sciences a causal link is normally sought. Historians aim to provide a reliable account of historical events, whereas the goal for scientists often appears to be that of absolute truth. In practice, scientists do not necessarily aim to prove which statements are true and which are false, but rather determine which statements appear more reliable and consistent, based on the degree of congruence between theoretical models and observational data.

The predictive power of science appears to distinguish it more clearly from the study of history. However, it should be noted that the power of science to predict events occurs only under specific conditions, most notably in laboratory experiments where all the variables can be measured and extraneous factors omitted. Also, in the physical sciences, predictions may sometimes be based on statistical probabilities, as they are in quantum physics. The extent to which scientific models can enhance historical knowledge depends on whether the regularities evident in the natural world can also be discerned in the social world. The interaction of specific factors which produce a given outcome seem to be more complex in social life than in the natural world. Unlike history, in science it is often possible to isolate factors, such as chemical reactions, and try to determine what the outcome of their interactions will be, based on repeated observation.[10]

Models which are developed to explain events in the physical world cannot be adopted to describe accurately a sequence of past events in human society. Human beings are not mechanical models whose behaviour can be programmed and predicted. In society it is rarely possible to identify all the relevant factors, isolate and test them, or offer precise knowledge about the likely outcome of their interactions. There are no laws or models which can predict events in history. The predictive power of science is based on the observation of uniform behaviour which leads to the formulation of general laws. The adoption of theories and the pronouncement of statements which purport to have universal validity are much less acceptable in historical studies. Indeed, the repetition of the same factors in different historical contexts may produce different outcomes. Interestingly, historians who focus exclusively on the use of theory in their research are sometimes accused of being too doctrinaire, but this is a claim which is rarely levelled at scientists.[11]

Rational explanation in history can be based on our understanding of general and unique events. For example, the invention of steam power was unique but its general diffusion throughout different societies led to the formulation of general statements about the social and economic impact of its invention. Historical models have been devised to explain the growth of industrial output, demographic trends or changes in prices. However, these models were considerably less useful in understanding the psychological factors which influenced the behaviour of statesmen, intellectual or cultural developments in society, or aspects such as religious belief. Not all avenues of research are amenable to the application of mathematical models. In any case, by the late 1970s those historians who were disillusioned with a scientific and analytical approach to history began to focus on local history and the psychology of individual behaviour, which were the domain of narrative history. The study of history at the individual or local level though did not necessarily throw light upon developments within the wider society. Quantitative methods were not rendered irrelevant but the limitations of these methods needed to be clearly defined so that they could be applied to areas where they would yield the most fruitful results. The predictive power of science could not be used to enhance historical knowledge, except in very specific areas where isolated events generated regular features which were observed or recorded in some detail. It could not be used to provide us with a complete understanding of unpredictable and unforeseen developments, such as the complex links between political structures, social and cultural change, and economic growth. As Sidney Pollard once noted, historians who focus entirely on quantitative considerations run the danger of measuring the waves and forgetting the tide.[12]

The study of history will clearly be distinguishable from the study of the natural sciences if we attempt to ascertain whether chance or determinism has a more significant role to play in historical events. The actions of individuals would suggest that chance plays a more significant role than causal laws. Historians who stress the role of contingency in history do place greater emphasis on the role of the individual in shaping historical events. But if the outcome of historical events was governed merely by chance it would represent a series of unconnected individual actions and events, which is contrary to human experience. The study of history would therefore provide no fundamental lessons for future generations. Clearly, human actions are neither totally determined nor totally free. Some historical events may be totally accidental but many others have causes which are simply not apparent to historians. Some historians believe that the facts which emerge from our study of the past could not be radically different because of the nature and arrangement of the factors involved, whether personal, social, economic or political. Nothing which occurs in history is inevitable, except in the sense that for events to have happened differently then the antecedent causes would also have had to be different.[13] In history, similar causes have a certain probability that they will produce similar effects, based on past experience. The search for historical patterns would suggest that the course of history is not purely governed by chance. Even unique events can form part of a larger and more complex pattern of historical events.

The study of history is not solely concerned with an analysis of specific, individual and unique events because it would therefore be unable to offer us general statements which could be applied with some degree of certainty to historical events. Equally, history cannot provide us with a science of society because of the unpredictability, complexity and uniqueness of events. Individuals are unique, therefore any historical study which focuses on the background, beliefs and actions of individuals will naturally develop into a history which emphasises the uniqueness of past events. Past events are unique because the combination of factors which interact to produce the characteristics of a particular event at a specific period in time cannot be repeated. Scientific experiments may be capable of being repeated, but in the study of history no such experiments can take place. This is why historians state that scientific study concentrates on similarities, patterns and common characteristics, whereas history focuses much more on differences and on the uniqueness of events.

A unique event does not necessarily have a unique cause. We may, for example, be able to specify the circumstances under which a social revolution is likely to take place but unable to predict that such an event will occur in the presence of a specified combination of circumstances. As John Tosh has remarked, the area of knowledge which can be said to be beyond dispute in history is smaller and a good deal less significant than it is in the natural sciences.[14] At a basic level historical research involves the application of common sense to a number of carefully constructed propositions based on a careful and full assessment of the supporting evidence. In dealing with complex historical phenomena the application of scientific experimental procedures would be of limited use in comparison with the indispensable skilled judgement of historians. In historical work the validity of a clear set of propositions does not always follow logically from the evidence, as it often does in science. History is closer to the arts than to science because it cannot offer us a scientific study of the past. As L.B. Namier once put it, 'the function of the historian is akin to that of the painter and not of the photographic camera: to discover and set forth, to single out and stress that which is of the nature of the thing, and not to reproduce indiscriminately all that meets the eye.'[15]

Notes

1 Gustavus George Zerffi, 'The science of history', *Transactions of the Royal Historical Society*, 9 (1881), 2.
2 G.R. Elton, *The Practice of History* (London, 1987) p. 71.
3 Norbert Elias, 'Problems of involvement and detachment', *British Journal of Sociology*, 7 (1956), 237.
4 John Tosh, *The Pursuit of History*, 2nd edn (London, 1991) p. 147.
5 W.H. Walsh, *An Introduction to Philosophy of History* (Bristol, reprint 1992) p. 85.
6 Wilhelm von Humboldt, 'On the historian's task', *History and Theory*, 6 (1967), 64.
7 Arthur Marwick, *The Nature of History*, 3rd edn (Basingstoke, 1989) p. 301.
8 E.H. Carr, *What is History?*, 2nd edn (London, 1987) p. 120.
9 J.A. Passmore, 'The objectivity of history', *Philosophy*, 33 (1958), 100.
10 G. Kitson Clark, *The Critical Historian* (London, 1967) p. 22.
11 Isaiah Berlin, 'History and theory: the concept of scientific history', *History and Theory*, 1 (1960), 9.
12 Sidney Pollard, 'Economic history – a science of society?', *Past and Present*, no. 30 (April 1965), 8.
13 Carr, *What is History?*, p. 96.
14 Tosh, *The Pursuit of History*, p. 141.
15 L.B. Namier, 'History: its subject-matter and tasks', *History Today*, 2 (1952), 161.

PART II   RESEARCH METHODS

4

Research tools

The primary purpose of Part II of this book is to provide a detailed survey of research methods and offer practical guidance on the techniques used in each stage of historical research. This advice will be helpful to you, regardless of whether your work is intended to culminate in a project, dissertation or thesis, or perhaps in the publication of a scholarly article or book. The first chapter of Part II covers research tools and begins by considering the materials which historians should have available, or have access to, before embarking on any research topic. Some of the items in the research materials list may appear obvious, others less so. You should use this as a checklist to find out whether you have all the items you require before you begin your research work. These materials range from basic items of stationery, through to specialised equipment. The section then moves on to consider in some detail the usefulness of computers as tools in historical research. Chapter 5 which follows gives advice on the various types of historical source material you may wish to use in your own research. Later chapters in Part II will consider other aspects of research methods, as follows: the qualities expected in historical researchers, and the basic elements involved in selecting and planning a research project; locating, indexing and using source material; the preparation of research notes and drafts; the special considerations which apply to the use of illustrative material; research, supervision and the examination of work for a dissertation or thesis; and finally, some helpful advice on the publication of articles and books.

Research materials

There are a number of research materials which you may require during the preparation of your project. You may need to purchase some of them before or during the course of your research work. A checklist of materials for any historical researcher may comprise the following items:

- ballpoint pens (blue, red and black; coloured pens are useful for editing drafts or marking proofs)
- pencil, sharpener, eraser, ruler, adhesive tape and glue stick; some archives permit only pencils to be used for making notes; a soft pencil, not a ballpoint pen, should be used to write on the back of photographs
- nylon-tip pens (red, green and black; these are useful for correcting written drafts; use a red or black pen to correct drafts, and a green pen to highlight the location of footnotes for easy identification)
- highlighter pens (these are normally available in a variety of colours and are very useful during the manual preparation of a book index for highlighting subjects, themes, names and titles of publications; a different coloured pen can be used to highlight each type of item)
- A4 paper (blank) and A4 refill pads
- A4 ring binders and subject dividers (numbered or colour-coded dividers can be used either to separate material on different subjects or material for use in different chapters of a book or thesis)
- clipboard (useful for holding papers when conducting interviews for an oral history project)
- self-adhesive ring reinforcements (for punched sheets of A4 paper)
- A4 typing/copier paper (minimum 80 gsm)
- writing paper, envelopes, padded envelopes and self-adhesive address labels
- typing eraser pencil or correction fluid (these will be needed if you use a typewriter which does not have a correction facility)
- A6 spiral-bound notebook (useful for jotting down ideas)
- record cards, A-Z guide cards and a card index box (the record cards can be used to prepare a subject bibliography for a book or thesis, or an index for a book)
- stapler, staples and staple extractor/remover

- paper punch, paper clips and rubber bands (it is usually better to staple sheets together than use paper clips to prevent pages going astray; important material which cannot or must not be stapled can be held together using paper clips, a rubber band or simply placed in a ring binder)
- A4 Nyrex wallet folders (useful for holding a small quantity of important letters and documents)
- A4/foolscap document wallet folders (different coloured folders can be used to file photocopied material or typescript relating to different subjects or different chapters of a book or thesis)
- storage boxes (for holding document wallet folders) or magazine files (for holding A4 literature)
- bookmarks
- calculator
- diary or personal organiser
- tape recorder or pocket/dictation memo, with spare cassettes and batteries (to record interviews or useful ideas as they come to mind)
- telephone address book
- personal computer (desktop and/or laptop, with a printer) or an electronic typewriter
- briefcase
- study desk, desk lamp and a small filing cabinet

You may also require access to a photocopier, microfilm and microfiche readers, a scanner, fax machine, online library catalogues, CD-ROM readers and databases. These should all be available in public libraries or university central, faculty or departmental libraries.

Using computers in historical research

With the expansion in the use of computers in academic study and research over the past decade, no book on historical research methods would be complete without reflecting on those areas where computers have had a significant impact on the discipline of history. Computers have multiple uses, from handling text and data, through to displaying graphics and communicating with other computer users. This expansion in the use of computers has taken place because of an increase in the power of microcomputers and the range of software available. Computers are very good at storing, accessing, handling and presenting a wide range of information. They can sometimes permit access to material which would otherwise be inaccessible in printed format, and also ensure that the information which is available is kept up-to-date more easily. CD-ROMs are also a useful research tool for historians but their major drawback is that they are a read-only research facility and so new information cannot be added. Computers can improve your efficiency because of their speed and accuracy. Keywords can be used to search databases accurately and quickly, and the results of your search can be sorted efficiently. Computers may also open up new topics of enquiry because large databases permit the exploration of subjects that would not have been contemplated without the assistance of the computer. For example, the computer can be used to view texts on screen, search for specific keywords in a text, compile statistical tables and bibliographies, or view maps, photographs and other images of locations of historical interest. Keywords may also be given on screen which will lead you to other websites of relevance to the subject you are interested in examining. Current computer hardware is capable of processing large amounts of information quickly, as well as running more sophisticated software packages which enhance the potential of computing for historians. Many history courses at undergraduate level within universities which require some research skills now include a computing element. This becomes increasingly important in the transition from undergraduate essay to dissertation and thesis, or published article or book.

Many historians were initially slow to envisage the potential of computers in historical research. Economic and social historians embraced the opportunities offered by new technology very eagerly and began to regard it as an indispensable tool. In contrast to them, other historians adopted a more cautious approach because they were suspicious that the use of computers would narrow the range of worthwhile historical topics to those which were amenable to quantification. But the increasing use of computers within and beyond the higher education sector was accelerated even faster by the user-friendliness of operating systems and the sophistication of ready-made computer programs, as well as the greatly increased filestore capability of hard disks and improved processing power. Historians no longer needed to know how to program a computer and develop their own software or rely on the advice of computer programmers who had access to large mainframe computers. Unlike the 1960s and 1970s, computers are no longer used primarily by economic historians who were interested in computing because of the ability which it gave them to perform a large number of calculations on statistical data very quickly.

The microcomputer revolution which began in the 1980s influenced both computer hardware and software. Computers became smaller, more powerful and relatively less expensive. Software became easier to use and could perform more functions, and so was more accessible to non-technical historians. Data became easier to enter and analyse, more data could be held, and information could be retrieved more quickly. The versatility, speed and mode of operation of modern computers made them more attractive to non-computer specialists. There were also notable improvements in access to data, in the exchange of data, and in the presentation of this information. E-mail was found to be useful because it permitted the fast transfer of information: it combined the advantages of the letter and telephone by ensuring that messages could be sent quickly at any time, yet able to be stored in an electronic mailbox until the recipient was ready to read them. The greater availability of computing facilities has undoubtedly assisted historians in locating historical evidence. These developments have taken place because computers are able to generate and sift through large quantities of information, such as census data, much more quickly than any historian could accomplish manually.

Recognition of the increasing importance of the computer in historical work was evident by the formation of the Association for History and Computing in March 1986 and by the publication of the specialised journal *History and Computing*. The principal uses of the computer in historical work can be summarised as follows:

- the storage and organisation of research notes
- compilation of bibliographies and indexes
- access to online catalogues of publications in libraries
- word-processing capability

- the creation of databases and spreadsheets
- graphical display of historical data
- access to remote databases via the Internet
- access to historical source material on CD-ROM
- the sending of communications by electronic mail

Universities usually encourage their students to develop a range of computing skills appropriate to their subject specialism. Similarly, many publishers also prefer work to be submitted on computer disk because it eliminates the re-keying of text, it reduces costs, and prevents new typographical errors from appearing when a book is typeset. Looking at all of this from a broader perspective, computing and research skills also have wider applications in many other areas of work in society.

Using the Internet

One of the great attractions to using a personal computer is the immense information resources which are available via the Internet. A vast number of smaller computer networks throughout the world are connected to each other to provide the communications network which is commonly referred to as the Internet. A user on any computer connected to a network is therefore able to connect to a server (a computer that stores information) via a web browser (such as Netscape Navigator or Internet Explorer) with any computer connected to any other network. Users are able to contact distant computers and transfer files and information (text and images) between computers. The Internet expanded significantly during the 1990s and continues to do so. A uniform resource locator (URL) is used to identify any document on any computer attached to the Internet. If you know the URL for a specific document it is probably much quicker to use this rather than navigate through a series of hypertext links. You can also store your most useful URLs as a set of bookmarks which can be selected for future use. However, do keep in mind that URLs change over time, hence it is better to be aware of an alternative, albeit indirect, route to your chosen websites. Search engines can be used to find information on a specific historical topic, but they can generate a large amount of irrelevant and out-of-date information. Some structured servers, such as Yahoo, which provide subject indexes are better than others.

Sometimes it is better to be directed to relevant websites via a subject gateway. The home pages of university websites provide excellent information about themselves and offer subject gateways to other useful websites. For example, you may find links to other universities, libraries, museums and galleries, historical and educational organisations, government departments and official publications, research councils and funding opportunities, data services and archives, newspapers, booksellers and publishers, and electronic journals. University websites may be very informative and include details on library and archive resources, departments, staff research interests, degrees, research opportunities, funding opportunities, press releases, lectures, a diary of events and perhaps a number of online publications, such as annual reports and prospectuses. The use of subject gateways provided by universities may be preferable to using a search engine because they will direct your search to the most relevant websites, thereby excluding irrelevant or out-of-date information which may be found on the Internet. Moreover, when you use a search engine you have to choose your keywords very carefully otherwise you will be offered information which is totally useless. In any case, the web changes so quickly that even if you do use the same keywords, these may present you with different websites if several months have elapsed between your initial and subsequent searches on the Internet. It may be difficult to ascertain whether information provided on a website is accurate because any individual with a computer and appropriate knowledge can add a web page on the Internet. However, individuals who have an expert knowledge of a particular historical subject can find it easier to share their knowledge with others on the Internet than seek to get their work published in conventional printed format by a book, journal or magazine publisher. Web pages may therefore contain very useful information for use in your research work; they may also contain incorrect information and so you should at least check the date given when the information was last updated.

There are some websites which you may find useful during the early stages of your research work. The CTICH (Computers in Teaching Initiative, Centre for History, Archaeology and Art History) website, based at the University of Glasgow, is designed to encourage the effective use of electronic resources in the teaching and research of history. This website provides general and subject-specific gateways (such as to the Institute of Historical Research or the Association for History and Computing), access to databases, electronic journals and online books, as well as relevant organisations and discussion lists. The Data Archive, located at the University of Essex, is the largest national repository of research data in the humanities and social sciences. It also incorporates the History Data Service, comprising several hundred datasets. The Data Archive holds information on several thousand datasets comprising both qualitative and quantitative data. History datasets contain information on a wide range of topics such as population data, electoral records, price data, census records, social surveys, historical revenue and expenditure, trade records, parish register information and so on. The BIRON (Bibliographic Information Retrieval Online) catalogue lists datasets and includes a bibliography of publications related to the datasets. The ESRC's database of research awards, known as REGARD, may also be worth checking. Public and university libraries should be able to supply you with further information on useful websites related to your own research interests.

Computer hardware

An increasing number of researchers have decided in recent years to purchase their own computing equipment. In any discussion of computer hardware it is possible to provide only general guidelines because new equipment with enhanced capabilities will undoubtedly emerge as technology advances. Some historians already have access to desktop computers in their place of work or study, and others purchase the equipment so that they have access to it at all times and in a familiar environment. The decision to buy a computer will depend upon several factors: the extent to which the equipment will be used; what work you will need a computer to complete; the cost; the availability of more sophisticated computing facilities in your place of work or study; and the convenience of having access to your own equipment when required. Some computer users have access to a powerful mainframe computer based within a university and may need to use the facilities which it offers. Mainframes offer the advantage of powerful processing capability which increases the speed at which tasks can be carried out. They also provide access to enhanced software and large databases, good connections to other computer networks, a more secure storage space than personal computers and access to more sophisticated printers. However, these advantages have to be weighed against the disadvantages of competition for access to the terminals, as well as a slower response from a network computer during peak periods of use. There may also be constraints on access to the terminals because of the opening times of the buildings in which the terminals are located.

Most historical researchers use desktop or laptop computers rather than mainframe computers. IBM PCs (and IBM compatibles) and the Apple Macintosh both have a graphical user interface with pull-down menus to select files and activate commands. Some may also have integral CD-ROM drives to provide users with access to text, images and sound. Purchasers of computer hardware are normally advised to choose equipment which has sufficient power and storage capacity to run the software and store data, but also some reserve power to cope with the emergence of new software packages. New and more powerful models are likely to appear and so the price of existing computers does tend to fall. All new computers will have a 12-month warranty, and it is usually possible to purchase an extended warranty. Some researchers prefer to use a laptop computer (which has a built-in flat screen and keyboard) because they are small and portable and therefore can be taken into libraries and archives. However, they are also more expensive than desktop computers, and the batteries operate for a limited period, depending on which model you choose. Some laptops have an integrated modem, whereas others have a PC card option for additional functions. With any personal computer, more powerful processors permit faster and more complex software to be run. The processor governs the amount of information that can be processed and the time it takes to process it. The amount of hard disk space required will depend upon the type and sophistication of software and data files which you wish a computer to hold. Floppy disks can be used to store both data and programs, as well as transfer work between machines. Some people find it convenient to use a separate floppy disk to store the contents of each chapter of a thesis or book because this makes it easier to locate and edit material. All work which you prepare using a computer should be dated, especially if you intend to make several copies at different times. A computer will provide you with a list of all files held, including the date they were created. To ensure the security of your data, all work must be saved regularly, perhaps every 20–30 minutes. If you intend to make extensive use of graphics facilities, then choose a good high-resolution colour monitor. There are also a wide range of printers available. Laser printers are fast, quiet and produce high resolution copies. They are more expensive to purchase than ink-jet printers but they have lower operating costs. Finally, a scanner may be of use if you intend to convert paper documents into electronic format, perhaps for editing.

Computer software

There are various specialist applications packages designed to carry out specific tasks (e.g. word processing, spreadsheets, database management) and there are also integrated packages, such as Microsoft Office, which combine a number of these functions. Single-purpose software packages provide more powerful applications which can carry out more complex tasks than integrated packages. Some applications are likely to be of more use to you than others. For example, word-processing software can improve productivity by saving time on many routine tasks, including the preparation of research notes or drafts of a book, article or thesis. A computer can be used to store your research notes under a number of headings: names, themes, topics, places and events. The notes can then be retrieved very quickly by selecting specific keywords. A more careful organisation of your research notes into relevant categories may have to be completed manually because the categories will depend on the context in which the words are used. The most useful features of word-processing packages are as follows: automated page numbering; spelling and grammar checkers; word count; numbering and arrangement of lists, pages, para-graphs or footnotes; alphabetical sorting of footnotes to produce a bib-liographical list; global editing facility to search for and replace words throughout your text; compilation of a contents page, tables, graphs and an index; selection of font (typeface and size of text); and arrangement of text layout. Print preview also allows you to see the layout of a page before a copy is printed. These are the positive benefits but you should also be aware of the limitations of computer software.

   Word-processing packages do have their limitations. For example, spell-ing checkers are unable to differentiate between words which sound the same but are spelled differently. Only the context in which a word is used will determine whether the correct spelling has been chosen. Limitations also exist if you use a computer to generate an index. If you intend to prepare a complex and therefore more useful index for a history book you will find that the computer cannot match the skill and judgement of the professional indexer. A computer will save you some time but it will only produce a basic index. The saving in time usually occurs because the index does not have to be typed from a set of manually prepared record cards after it has been compiled. The task of writing the entries on record cards is also eliminated. A computer will, however, be of use at the typesetting stage because it will save time and minimise the possibility of typographical errors occurring when your index is typeset.

Data analysis

Computers can store and manipulate a large amount of historical data. The analysis of electoral information, social data and economic statistics are areas where computing can offer you significant advantages, particularly if the information is not readily available in printed format. The data-handling properties of the computer are less beneficial for topics where the archival evidence is either fragmentary or cannot be quantified. Some historical topics may require you to compare numerical data, such as that gathered from censuses, tax rolls, business records or trade statistics. Spreadsheets are useful for analysing this type of data because text and numerical information can be entered into tables which are divided into rows and columns to form a grid of cells. Electronic spreadsheets will enable you to store, organise and calculate information, as well as produce new tables easily if information in any of the cells is altered. Computers may be used to enable you to offer a new interpretation on data which has been left unused among older historical records, either because of the bulk of material available or lack of organisation of the records. Computers have most to offer in the speed, accuracy and presentation of historical data. Graphics software may also be useful for presenting the results of your data analysis. Line graphs, pie charts, bar charts and other visual devices can assist the presentation of complex historical data, such as information on commodities, industrial growth, occupational groups, population growth, class structure, transport networks and so on. Further details on the use of illustrative material can be found in chapter 11.

Databases

Computers can also be of assistance in historical research by enabling you to search databases for information. The computer can be an excellent tool for collecting, storing and searching for information, such as financial records in old account books, property deeds or perhaps demographic data. Historians are making increasing use of the Internet as a global information resource, yet its potential is primarily dependent upon the quality and extent of material which individuals and organisations make available. In particular, it is just as easy for websites to be removed as to appear, and this can prove to be a drawback with electronically provided information. Nevertheless, the computer can save you time by linking together various items of information which would take considerably longer to find if this task was completed manually. The merit of databases is that they permit the storage of large amounts of data in a relatively small space. Information can also be kept up-to-date more easily when it is stored in electronic format, and it can be accessed more quickly than information stored in printed format.

Historical information may be available online or viewed using a CD-ROM. It is much quicker to search databases than look at printed catalogues, but the computer can really only be useful if it holds the information you require. However, computer catalogues which hold bibliographic data do possess the advantage that they can be searched under keywords or subjects, not just by author or title. Also, a printed copy can be obtained from an online search, which is obviously a quicker and more accurate method than copying details manually from a printed catalogue. Moreover, some prints may also incorporate abstracts of the items listed. The main drawback is that reading large quantities of information on a screen does produce more eye strain than looking at printed texts. Also, databases tend to cover information added in more recent years and therefore do not provide extensive coverage of older material which historians would normally be interested in examining. An increasing volume of material of historical value is being made available in electronic format, but most historical documents are simply not accessible in any database. A similar situation applies to source material other than documents which are historically of value to researchers. For example, you may be able to view recent issues of newspapers online but you will have to look at microfilm or bound printed issues if you wish to look at old newspaper articles. The searching of databases can assist you to compile a bibliography of recent secondary source material, but may be less useful in providing information on the range and content of primary sources available.

Overall, computers are useful in tackling many routine tasks which historians used to perform manually, but they are not a substitute for the intellectual tasks involved in sifting through source material to determine what is relevant and valuable and therefore worth examining in detail for any research project. It is important to be able to identify precisely those areas where computers will be beneficial, such as in the analysis and presentation of quantitative data, storing and updating information, sorting and retrieving data, or searching bibliographies and archives. The use of computers to construct models in order to answer historical questions is more problematic because by reducing the number of variables involved your model may in fact oversimplify historical reality. In any case, many historical events cannot be systematically analysed using computer models because the evidence is too uncertain or fragmentary. Nevertheless, computers do offer several distinct advantages, namely access to a vast amount of data which can be easily retrieved, simplification of data analysis, and the discovery of new topics, or new perspectives on existing subjects, for historical investigation.

5

Historical sources

The quality of your research depends to a significant extent on the availability, careful use and proper documentation of source material. The sources provide the raw material with which to reconstruct past events. There are many published guides to historical sources, and databases can also provide valuable information on the range of historical collections. It is not simply the accumulation of source material that determines the quality of a research project, but also its purpose, range and usefulness. You need to be aware of what documentary evidence is available, as well as what other historians have written on the subject of your research project, the so-called secondary evidence. This chapter will look at the range of source material which you may wish to examine for your own research project. It will consider the use of unpublished documents, letters and diaries, memoirs and autobiographies, oral evidence, official publications, business records, local history records, newspapers, paintings, prints and maps, photographs and filmed evidence. The chapter will conclude with some general comments on using historical sources.

Documentary evidence is more likely to exist where it has been compiled and retained as a matter of policy, such as in the minutes of organisations, government departments or public corporations. Private correspondence is not as widely available as it used to be because the art of writing has been increasingly replaced by other means of instant communication, such as the telephone. Moreover, you may find that documents are mislaid or destroyed, perhaps intentionally or by accident. Depending on the subject of your research, access to some private and public documents may be withheld for a specified period, or stringent conditions may be attached to access of such material. Some records might even he incomplete or stored in different locations. All these factors may place genuine constraints on the range of topics you are able to examine, as well as necessitating a greater reliance on other types of source material. This could lead you unfortunately to misrepresent past events if the documents to which you have access are not genuinely representative of those which did exist but are now no longer available. Nevertheless, it has to be said that the advent of electronic mail, the fax machine and the permanent storage of information on computer disk may provide future historians with a vast new reservoir of printed source material, although the quality of this material will have to be very carefully assessed.

Historians have traditionally made a distinction between primary and secondary source material. A written record, such as a letter, diary or report, which was compiled at the time specific events occurred will be deemed to possess a higher status than any item written at a later date. The format in which source material exists is less important than its content and the circumstances in which it was compiled. A written record which has been compiled by an eyewitness does not have to contain original thought or demonstrate literary skill to be classified as a primary source. By contrast, any historical account which is written long after an event occurred, and which is based on the use of primary sources, will contain interpretative and factual material and will therefore be regarded as a secondary source. Secondary sources are mostly written by people who were not present at the events which they describe. It is this factor, rather than simply when the material was written, which classifies this type of evidence as a secondary source.

Few historical books, articles and theses will provide a definitive account of a particular historical episode. Many historical analyses are subject to revision over time as new evidence, new techniques and new ideas and interpretations emerge. This lack of permanency about secondary sources places them in a different relationship to the original source material, which is always classed as the primary source. It is to the primary sources that you must turn to extend the boundaries of historical knowledge. The existence of the primary sources do not by themselves improve our knowledge of past events: this will only occur when historians examine the evidence and base their conclusions on an analysis of that evidence. Original documents may yield new evidence and generate new interpretations which may not have been so obvious when similar material was first examined. The discovery of new evidence may also require us to modify existing historical facts and alert us to the possibility that some primary sources could contain inaccurate data. You may need access to a wide range of source material for your own historical research project. The principal historical sources which you might consult are considered in this chapter. Information is provided here on the uses, strengths and limitations of different types of historical evidence. Information on the evaluation of primary and secondary sources for historical research purposes can be found in chapter 8.

Unpublished documents

Unpublished source material is often regarded by historians as providing a more accurate record of past events than that outlined in other printed sources, such as published reports and historical pamphlets. However, their usefulness may depend on *who* wrote them, *why* they were written, and *when* they were compiled. The minutes of a company, public corporation, government department or university may provide a more detailed and perhaps a more accurate record of events than their published annual reports, because the former are circulated to a more restricted audience and not intended to be seen by the public. Documents do not necessarily provide a complete account of past events, but it is in the unpublished minutes, memos, letters and papers that we would expect to find the reasons for decisions taken by individuals or organisations. By contrast, published material tends to record decisions already taken, rather than the reasons which lay behind those decisions. However, you should not always equate the significance of source material with whether or not it has been published. All unpublished papers need to be carefully examined to determine how useful they will be for your own research. An unpublished paper may provide an accurate record of a past event, but it could also provide little more than an impression of what the writer *believed* had taken place. Unpublished documents may be confidential but this does not prevent their contents from being misleading. If you only have access to printed documents, such as in a published volume of collected documents, their accuracy may have to be checked against the original documents to discover any printing errors. You may find that for contemporary events a sound or film recording could provide you with a more revealing record of past events, although recording tapes, like all source material, can be edited or their contents deliberately falsified.

Letters and diaries

Private letters and diaries appear to offer fruitful sources of information, but they need to be treated with some caution and carefully checked against the content of other source material. Letters may be regarded as possessing a somewhat higher status than oral testimony, but not all observations or decisions are written. You may find that information about the social and intellectual climate of a recent period in history is much more likely to be obtained from interviews than from letters and documents which may, in any case, not reveal the true feelings of the writer. A letter may have been written to exert influence on its recipient, although this can be of historical significance if it can be proved beyond reasonable doubt and is somehow relevant to your research topic. Unlike an interview, the writer of a letter cannot be cross-questioned about dubious points or asked to give information on specific matters. However, an oral account of a past event will never be described in precisely the same manner in subsequent interviews. It is also easier to detect the falsification of letters than that of tape recordings.

Some historians argue that diaries provide a more complete and truthful account of past events than would be expected in a letter. There are many well-known diaries, such as the Crossman diaries, and numerous lesser-known ones held by individuals or deposited in local, public or national libraries. All diaries have to be scrutinised very carefully, particularly in circumstances where you are aware that they were intended for publication. You may wish to find out who was expected to be given access to the contents of a diary, and whether its contents might have been deliberately changed if the intended reader had been different. You may also need to distinguish between diaries intended for publication but which may not have been published, and those which were not intended for publication but which were eventually published. Diaries often contain hearsay evidence and may have been written to justify particular actions or perhaps exaggerate the writer's involvement in the events he or she describes. Most diaries will contain a mixture of factual and subjective data: the purpose of a diary may determine the actual balance between factual and subjective information. Some writers regard a diary as a private record of past events, whereas others view it as a useful means of storing information which can subsequently be used in writing an autobiography. Any diary will be considerably less useful to you if it has not been compiled on a daily basis, because the timing and sequence of events may become distorted as a result of lapses of memory. The diaries of public officials may not necessarily be as revealing as those compiled by ordinary people. A diary may prove to be especially useful to you in circumstances where you have been denied access to sensitive documents. Such a diary will be more valuable for your research if you can prove that it contains evidence of an individual's genuine values or motives which are absent from their official correspondence. The difficulty for most historians is in detecting when this has in fact occurred.

Memoirs and autobiographies

There are many published memoirs and autobiographies which you can find by checking the *British National Bibliography* or a computer database, such as Global Books in Print. However, memoirs can be unreliable sources for a number of reasons: they give a partial account of reality because past events are viewed from a single perspective; they are normally written long after the events they describe; they are written for posterity and usually intended to impress a wider audience; they may be unrepresentative because they tend to be written by the professional classes or by important individuals in society; and they may suppress controversial information, as well as instances of confusion and indecision. Memoirs are sometimes used to justify past actions or inaction, and they can confuse facts or perhaps exaggerate insignificant historical events. Many historians believe that memoirs provide a rather selective and distorted account of historical events, although they may in fact be based on official or private papers to which historians and members of the public are denied access. This type of source material therefore cannot be ignored by historians. Memoirs are sometimes more revealing if you consider what topics they omit than what they include, because the true reasons for certain actions (or inaction) may be concealed. In these circumstances, it is perhaps much better to try and gain access to the private correspondence of individuals who have written their memoirs. At best, memoirs may illuminate the social and cultural milieu which existed at the time they were written; at worst, they may only provide an insight into the attitudes of one individual. Also, given that some people are more able and willing to write an autobiography than others, the representative nature of these accounts must be carefully considered before any extensive use is made of them. Nevertheless, as adherents of psychohistory would argue, it is important to understand an individual's private thoughts, not just their public stance.

Oral evidence

The technique of gathering evidence through interviews has been considerably developed within the social sciences, particularly in the disciplines of sociology and social anthropology. It is now being increasingly used in historical research to supplement or enhance our interpretation of written records, as well as assist our understanding of those events which have not been documented. In particular, oral evidence has been increasingly used in social history projects to gain a better insight into the lives of ordinary people which have not been documented. Very few historical topics will rely totally on oral evidence, but oral history can be useful in helping to uncover knowledge of personal experiences which might not have been obtained from any other historical source. Some professional historians do not attach the same status to recorded tapes as they do to written transcripts. However, oral historians are often able to ask questions of interviewees that may never have been considered in the past. They are also able to glean valuable information about how individuals make sense of past events and then place these experiences within a much wider social context. A basic difference between written and oral evidence is that the former exists in tangible form, whereas the latter does not exist until historians choose to create it. Oral evidence may provide us with a totally new perspective on historical events or perhaps reveal new lines of enquiry.

Nowadays the art of writing has decreased in popularity in comparison with other means of communication, such as the telephone, tape recorder, radio and television, the fax machine and the computer. Historians have to rely on an ever decreasing volume of printed material for some topics, but interviews may help to fill gaps in the available evidence. The increasing popularity of social history and local history has highlighted the importance of oral evidence. For example, although statesmen and military leaders often left diaries and a vast correspondence, this was much less common among ordinary people. In the absence of documentary evidence on working-class history and the history of the family and communities, historians were forced to consider other methods for gaining some insight into a number of factors: customs; working lives; the impact of local crafts and trades on community life; social relationships; neighbourhoods; and the leisure pursuits of ordinary people. Oral history provided an obvious method for obtaining this information. It gave ordinary people an opportunity to make sense of their own experiences. These formative experiences of the early years of their lives are likely to be the ones which older people will often remember in some detail and be more willing to speak about. Oral sources humanise and enrich history by reminding us that the study of the past should include the study of the lives of ordinary people, their attitudes, beliefs, motives, experiences and actions. But it also helps if we are aware of the limitations of human memory when eliciting information on the content or precise sequence of past events.

The extent to which the content of oral testimony diverges from written or printed sources can be significant. It may reflect deliberate distortion of either the oral testimony or the written records. It therefore helps if you have a good background knowledge about the subject you are investigating. The selection, wording, sequence and delivery of questions can influence the extent to which interviews generate meaningful results. Oral history is not simply a vehicle for obtaining facts in response to questions. Factual data may be interspersed with errors of judgement, and inconsistent replies may be influenced by opinions, values, beliefs and attitudes. The meaning of words will be conveyed by the tone, volume and rhythm of speech, and these cannot be reproduced precisely on the printed page. For example, punctuation cannot alert us to the meanings behind the rhythm of speech because slow speech may be used to indicate caution rather than emphasis. The vocabulary used in a written account may be elaborate, but the spoken word alerts us to the precise meaning which should be attached to a given statement. The principal difficulty with some oral testimony occurs where memory loss reduces the reliability of the evidence obtained, although it is possible to argue that there can also be a lapse of time between the occurrence of an event and the attempt to provide a written record of it. Historians do use primary sources which are compiled or printed some time after the events they describe, sometimes by individuals who may not have been present at the precise moment the events occurred. There are therefore limitations in the use of written accounts as well as oral testimony.

Some historians believe that oral history re-creates the past more vividly and accurately than other types of source material. They argue that it enables us to appreciate and understand more fully what it must have been like to have lived in the past because humans share a common language, emotions and experience. But it may be difficult to appreciate the experience of other individuals unless we have shared in their experience. Moreover, the recollection of any historical event may become more vivid for some individuals with the passage of time, yet less vivid for others. However, by drawing upon the experience of individuals, oral testimony offers a new perspective to help us understand the impact of historical developments. It might also persuade us to look at previously unknown documentary evidence or perhaps question existing factual evidence which had been based on written records. Written sources alone cannot provide us with a full understanding of the impact of historical events on the lives of ordinary people. Many historical events were never documented and so oral history does have something useful to contribute, particularly if we allow for the tendency of individuals to remember mainly recurrent events and situations which were especially significant or interesting for them.

Oral evidence gives us an opportunity to enhance our understanding of past events, but historians need to be aware of the weaknesses and limitations of using this type of evidence. Interviews are obviously not an option if people are inaccessible. Moreover, some people misjudge the importance of past events by confusing issues of contemporary importance with those of historical significance. Recollections are always partial because only a selection of events will ever be recalled. A degree of selectivity occurs with all oral evidence because previously forgotten facts may emerge, some may be temporarily forgotten, or a new interpretation may be placed on existing facts. An oral account of past events does not possess that permanent quality which is characteristic of written records. There is, in effect, no counterpart in oral history to the finite number of written or printed sources on a specific subject: the oral record is always an unfinished record. Also, interviewees may forget the precise sequence of events or important dates which may both be crucial in making sense of a series of past events. People also find it much easier to understand their own roles in society than to appreciate the influence of less tangible aspects, such as social structures. Excessive reliance on oral sources can therefore distort recollections of historical events by not providing information on the wider political and social context within which individuals lived their lives. Oral history can improve our knowledge of past events by providing a few missing pieces of the jigsaw, but it cannot provide the complete picture. Oral history can be a very useful additional source of material for topics where individuals have direct experience of, or involvement in, specific events, but it cannot be a substitute for the use of other types of primary and secondary source material.

Official publications

A large volume and range of publications are issued by Parliament and government departments, and these are listed in the annual catalogues of The Stationery Office. These include parliamentary debates, Bills, Acts of Parliament, Reports and departmental publications. The Government Information Service website provides links to all government departments and agencies, as well as giving information on recent UK official publications available from The Stationery Office. You should also refer to the guide to further reading at the end of this book for further information on sources to consult to locate specific official publications. For an up-to-date list of government departments and agencies, consult the current edition of the *Civil Service Yearbook*. Many libraries keep their official publications on closed access, but some university libraries keep more recent material or those up to 100 years old on open access. Departmental publications, as opposed to parliamentary publications, may be shelved in alphabetical order by the name of the department. The reports of Royal Commissions may provide a fruitful source of information for some history projects because they offer expert and informed advice on various matters which a government may wish to take into account in the framing of legislation. The reports of Royal Commissions and Select Committees are submitted to Parliament as command papers. Committees of inquiry may also be a useful source of information, particularly as these committees receive evidence from interested individuals and organisations. This evidence, together with the results of sponsored research, may be published in conjunction with a committee's main report. You may also wish to consult green papers and white papers: green papers represent tentative proposals by government, in contrast to more affirmative statements of policy (i.e. planned legislation) which are detailed in the white papers. The latter are often the subject of parliamentary debates which will provide an additional source of information.

The bound volumes of parliamentary debates contain both oral and written answers to parliamentary questions and a sessional index of subjects debated. In addition to the debates of the House of Commons and House of Lords (known as Hansard, and its predecessor which was known as Cobbett's Parliamentary History), there are also Standing Committee debates. The latter committees are appointed to consider Bills in greater detail after their second reading. To locate a debate on a Bill it is necessary to determine which Standing Committee considered the Bill; and this can be achieved by referring to The Stationery Office annual catalogues (previously known as the HMSO annual catalogues) under the heading 'Standing Committees'. The nature and scope of your historical research will determine whether public or private Bills will need to be consulted. You may wish to note that not all Bills do become Acts of Parliament, and that there may be several versions of a Bill if their contents are modified during passage through both Houses of Parliament. Public Bills *may* become Public General Acts, whereas private Bills *may* become Local or Personal Acts. Matters which are not specified in detail in Acts of Parliament are sometimes published separately as Statutory Instruments. Papers which are not presented to Parliament, such as material produced by government departments and departmental committees, are normally published by The Stationery Office as non-parliamentary publications. The records of central government departments, central and local courts, and former nationalised industries (such as gas, railways, coal, steel, electricity) are deposited in public record offices, such as the Scottish Record Office and the Public Record Office.

Business records

If you wish to research the history of a business organisation you will need to look at company records. These records may be deposited by companies in national or local archives. For example, the papers of the London and Edinburgh Shipping Company are deposited in the Scottish Record Office. You should therefore check the lists of gifts and deposits in national and local archives to find out if papers relating to a company have been deposited. In some cases, bibliographies have been published on the history of certain industries or sectors, such as the railways. You may also wish to look at published bibliographies of business histories in a library. For example, *Debrett's Bibliography of Business History* lists books which have been written on the history of different businesses, subdivided by type of business. Your local or university library will have a selection of published material on the history of companies, and these will give you advice on what other sources to consult to obtain more detailed information. There are some published guides to company information in Great Britain: check library online catalogues by subject or title of company to see what material they hold. You may also wish to refer to the annual reports of a company, review the annual publication *Who Owns Whom* or contact an organisation, such as the Scottish Business Information Service. Some university Business Studies departmental websites provide gateways to useful websites which may be of use if you intend to research the history of a specific business sector or company. Some companies may also allow you to look at some of their records. Newspaper and journal indexes should also be checked to see if any interesting articles have been published on a particular company or commercial or industrial sector. Remember to consult indexes to theses because it is always possible that a dissertation or thesis may have been written on the history of a particular organisation. The extent and accessibility of archive papers will help you decide whether to begin research on a particular company or sector. Information on useful reference sources can be found in the guide to further reading at the end of this book.

Local history records

There is a vast amount of information available for the study of local history. You may wish to begin by looking in some detail at some of the published guides to local history. Your local library may have a collection of these books, or they can be traced by checking online catalogues under the subject of local history or the name of the place you are interested in. In addition to public record offices and the national libraries, you will find that the most useful sources of information on local history are local public libraries, local record offices and local history groups. The National Register of Archives, which was set up by the Royal Commission on Historical Manuscripts, collects information about manuscript sources for the study of British history. The NRA's lists provide information on manuscripts held by local record offices, museums, national libraries and university libraries. They also hold information about the private collections of papers held by private individuals, landed estates, societies and institutions. You may wish to visit the NRA website for further and more up-to-date information. The intention of the NRA is to identify useful collections of papers, other than simply those available in public records, and give details on the nature and location of these collections. Information on record repositories in Great Britain can also be obtained from the Royal Commission on Historical Manuscripts.

You may find it worthwhile checking the Special Collections departments of university libraries because they often hold old printed books, manuscripts, maps or press cuttings collections on subjects of local interest. Their holdings may be indexed separately from the main catalogues of published material held by the university. Many local libraries, and some university libraries, also hold copies of local street directories. These directories were often published on an annual basis from the nineteenth century onwards, and provide useful information on residences, businesses, societies and public bodies, as well as street names. You may wish to supplement this with photographs, prints and ordnance survey maps which will help you to visualise change over time in streets or buildings of local interest. Other types of local records which may be of interest include architectural drawings, property records, valuation rolls, family papers and estate papers and plans. For example, estate records will give information on farmhouses, mills, cottages and schools. Estate plans may give details of the old runrig system of farming and the modern field system, as well as offer information on villages, place names, crops and so on. Similarly, town plans, building plans and transport plans will be useful for looking at the growth of towns and cities and communication links, such as roads, railways, canals, bridges and tramways. Depending on the nature of your research interests, you may also wish to look at the minutes of local councils, community newspapers, local society newsletters or the annual reports of local organisations. Parish registers and Census records will also yield useful information, some of which may be available on microfilm. The Census information will provide details on household size, occupations and so on dating back to the nineteenth century, whereas Parish registers give information on even earlier periods. You will also find that local public libraries keep press cuttings collections which may be indexed by subject, although these would need to be supplemented by looking at newspaper indexes.

Newspapers

Many libraries keep microfilm copies of old newspapers and some permit access to paper copies. Some newspapers are also available on CD-ROM, although these tend to cover more recent years and are therefore less likely to be of use for most history projects. All libraries keep lists of the newspapers they hold, and there is also a multivolume catalogue for the British Library's Newspaper Library in London. Newspapers can be a very fruitful source of information if you are aware of their limitations, which includes inaccuracies and distortion. Errors may occur because of the premium placed on speed in delivering reports for publication, and distortion may be present in eyewitness accounts of past events. Newspapers can give us an insight into the social and cultural milieu of a given period, and because they are published regularly they will offer a helpful chronology of events. Even advertisements provide us with some guidance on fashion, products, prices and entertainments. News reports and editorials alert us to changes in public attitudes. Sometimes newspapers reflect public opinion, yet at other times they help to mould it. Letters pages can reveal much about the views, values, preoccupations and prejudices of contributors (and editors) on economic, moral or political issues. Each newspaper has its own target audience and, for local newspapers, its own geographical distribution. These factors undoubtedly influence the perspective from which external events are viewed. The degree of importance which newspapers place on particular topics can normally be gauged by examining where these items appear in the newspaper, what size of typeface is used and how many columns are allocated to covering them. Photographs which accompany news reports may also be of interest. A number of positive and negative considerations have to be taken into account if you intend to use newspapers as source material.

Paintings, prints, cartoons and maps

Paintings and prints provide historians with trace evidence of past cultures which do prompt questions about the social circumstances which gave rise to the production of works of art. The messages which this type of source material reveals may not be so obvious, and may simply provide caricatures of individuals, situations or events. Visual sources tend not to be used extensively by historians: these sources range from paintings and sculpture, through to illustrated pamphlets, cartoons, advertisements and maps. Some visual sources may be symbolic rather than reflect a particular culture or period of history. The important question to consider if you use visual evidence is what they reveal about the preoccupations, values, customs and cultures of the past. Artefacts may not necessarily reflect the social context of a past age. Indeed, they might assume different meanings for different audiences if there is no single agreed social context. For example, the meaning of a work of art is not conveyed solely by the artist because it must also take account of the reaction of its public audience. Works of art clearly cannot provide us with a straightforward window on to the past. Furthermore, paintings are only sources for the period in which they were created, hence they cannot reveal anything about any other period if this differs from that in which these works of art were created. Visual sources do, in some instances, reinforce messages which have already been transmitted to subsequent generations through publications. Access to works of art is gained through national and local galleries, as well as private collections.

The key questions you need to consider when using visual sources are, firstly the audience which this material was aimed at, and secondly whether they were expected to serve any wider purpose. This can perhaps be illustrated by considering the value of political prints and cartoons as historical evidence. Political prints can be a useful source if you are interested in researching political ideology, but you cannot be certain whether prints mirrored or moulded public opinion. Historical evidence appears to indicate that eighteenth-century political prints reflected the attitudes of middle-class Londoners, rather than influenced the views of a much wider public, socially or geographically. If so, these prints probably had less influence than the content of newspapers or political pamphlets which had a wider circulation. So you have to exercise caution in the interpretations you base on the use of visual sources.

It is always important to penetrate beneath images to discover their hidden meanings; this is particularly evident if you consider the potential value of cartoons. A cartoon is a caricature of an individual and so you must infer from it what the cartoonist was implying about the characters portrayed. You also need to consider how representative the work of certain cartoonists was, what audience their work was aimed at, and whether some cartoons were perhaps toned down to avoid offending readers. Most cartoons appear in national and local newspapers, pamphlets or in other forms of advertising media. Many people look at cartoons in newspapers without reading the editorials, so to this extent cartoons may have some influence on public opinion or reinforce existing beliefs and prejudices. What cartoons cannot do is provide detailed commentary on historical events. They undoubtedly appeal more to the emotions than to the intellect. This is because cartoonists simplify reality and exaggerate beliefs and values for emotional effect. Historians therefore have to decide which features within these static images were exaggerated, and why these particular features were chosen to be high-lighted in this manner. Nevertheless, cartoons can provide you with clues about how contemporaries viewed past events, and they offer us some guidance on matters such as social dress or language. What cartoons do depend on for their effect is some shared sense of what was amusing and of topical importance, although both undoubtedly vary from one generation to the next. In other words, it is always necessary to have some general idea of the historical context to appreciate fully the ideas or concepts implied in a cartoon. You need to remember that if you use cartoons as historical evidence that it is much easier to caricature an individual or a group of people than an event, a process or a set of values. If you take these factors into account then you will provide a proper perspective about the instances when cartoons should be used as a historical source.

Architectural evidence can be very useful for social history projects. For example, visits to buildings, such as public housing schemes, will provide you with some insight into the level of amenities and the extent of social deprivation or relative affluence which existed in a particular neighbourhood. Some buildings may have been converted over the years to be used for a different purpose, but building plans which survive will indicate the original functions of buildings and may also provide a guide to lifestyle and culture. Architectural drawings or photographs may help you to date buildings and indicate what type of person was likely to have lived or worked in them. The style of a building may also help you to date when it was built. Urban maps and street directories are useful for giving information on street layouts, place names, the locations of public buildings and the names and types of local businesses. Maps can also be used to identify geographical or political boundaries. Moreover, the comparison of maps of the same area, town, city or region over a specified timescale may provide you with valuable clues about the nature of urban or rural development and patterns of human settlement. The date of compilation, the source and the general reliability of maps do, however, have to be considered to enable you to assess their usefulness in any historical research project. Archaeological evidence and artefacts may also need to be examined if you are interested in researching material for a project on ancient history.

Photographs

Historians now have access to a much richer and more diverse range of source material on the recent past than their contemporaries did a century or more ago. Photographs or sound and film recordings of past events provide new additions to the written and printed records. The advent of photography can be traced back to the mid-nineteenth century, although the arrival of the 'snapshot' did not take place until 1888 when the exposure times of photographic film were significantly reduced. Some historians believe that photographs provide us with a window to the past and a more visually realistic means of emphasising how the past differs from the present. Photographs can provide an immense amount of information and may be particularly useful if your research requires information which is not available in written or printed sources. Photographic evidence of past events and people can yield valuable evidence if it is examined and interpreted carefully. You have to consider the purpose, date and intended audience of your photographic evidence. The camera can freeze a moment in time and provide a permanent snapshot record of the past and so we no longer have to rely solely on the description of other people. This visual evidence may confirm what we already know from printed sources, it may supplement our existing knowledge, or it may cast some doubts on the accepted testimony of other individuals. Photographic evidence of undisturbed physical settings, such as the interior or exterior of buildings, may be very valuable. The genuine difficulty which you may encounter is in determining whether a photograph provides a typical image of the event it portrays. It is possible that the presence of the photographer has unintentionally distorted the scene which is captured on a photographic print. For example, a group of people may alter their pose if they are aware that they are being photographed. A truer image of reality is more likely to be obtained when you know that a particular photograph has been taken without the awareness of the participants.

There are technical considerations to keep in mind when using old photographs. For example, the long exposure periods required by early cameras hindered the identification of movement. This situation was only rectified in the last hundred years when cameras were developed which had much shorter exposure times and were therefore able to provide the typical snapshot. The introduction of smaller portable cameras was also advantageous because it increased the number and range of topics captured in photographs. Similarly, the introduction of better lighting helped to produce more reliable interior images. Notwithstanding these limitations, old photographs may provide our only record of some events in the past because many interesting historical events have never been documented. Yet many typical scenes, such as family or working life, have also never been photographed precisely because they were typical. It is the untypical events, such as weddings, holidays or reunions, which are the principal events captured in family photograph albums, but there are very few historians who are interested in the display of ritual and cere-mony at events such as weddings. In these untypical situations, people dress specially for the occasion rather than appear in normal daily attire. But for most social historians it is clearly the typical day-to-day events, rather than the exceptional ones, which are of most interest. These are the scenes which enhance our understanding of social and cultural life, as well as the physical environment. However, these are the events which are rarely captured on film. Perhaps photographic evidence of the recent past may be even more valuable to future historians given the rapid social and physical changes of modern society.

Films

In addition to photographs, you may find that newsreel, documentary or feature films can also be used as a source of historical evidence. This includes both silent and sound films, each of which has a different impact because accents and tone of delivery are absent from silent films. The historical value of film is often underrated because it can only be viewed by gaining access to the proper equipment and, unlike written records, the material cannot be rapidly scanned. The moving image does, however, have several advantages over the static image, particularly in the extent to which it can illustrate how events unfold. Its greatest use may be in documenting social conditions, cultural and leisure pursuits, or military conflicts. Amateur movies may give us an insight into historical and geographical change, but in the pre-camcorder age the quantity and quality of film may pose problems. Up until the early 1950s the film which was used is liable to spontaneous combustion and therefore may not be available. Feature films can be important sources for historians because of the myths which they propagate about, for example, the British Empire or the American Wild West. Like photography, techno-logical advances in cameras and in the processing of film has improved over time, thereby lessening the limitations imposed by the early films where cumbersome equipment limited when and where film could be used. If you choose to use film footage in your research, it must be dated and properly documented. You may also need to be aware whether or not the film you use has been edited: newsreels were, for example, often edited or censored. A further problem arises because the medium of film does not provide a permanent record of past events. All films have a limited storage life, depending upon which material was used in their manufacture. The physical condition in which films were stored, such as temperature and humidity, are also important factors which determine their quality. The digitising of old newsreel is a helpful development because film stored on nitrate media is highly flammable. Other factors you may wish to take into account are the content, size and length of film, and whether it has been fully catalogued. The proper cataloguing of film material may in fact not have occurred with original film footage which was not included in a completed film.

Historians who utilise film evidence in their research often need to be acquainted with the precise date, location and circumstances under which a film was made. Information on films which were not properly cata-logued and documented can often be ascertained from the subject mat-ter of the events covered in the film or the type and size of film used. The location of the cameraman must be considered, as well as the amount of detail recorded, the clarity of the images and some confirmation that it provides an accurate account of what it purports to describe. This evidence may be gleaned by careful examination of buildings, transport, style of clothing, or the appearance of specific individuals known to be alive at the time the film was made. In common with photographs, you must also be aware that the angle from which a scene is shot, or the use of telephoto lenses, can distort what otherwise appears to represent a straightforward visual record of events. This type of information may be obtained from scripts or camera logs, or alternatively the content of the film could be checked against the sound commentary. If used carefully, film can provide you with a valuable additional window to the past by revealing important information which may not have been recorded in written records. However, it is also important to note that most early amateur filmmakers came from the upper and middle classes rather than the working classes, hence the subject matter is not necessarily representative of events in the past.

Film evidence may be used to confirm or disprove what you already know from written or printed sources. But the interpretation of this evidence is an area where film may not be so advantageous. Film can provide a record of human behaviour and capture changes in emotions in response to external events in a variety of social settings, but what it cannot do is interpret and explain the reasons for this behaviour. The process of interpretation falls to the historian to complete. Film evidence may be used to fill gaps in our knowledge of the past and enable us to visualise a sequence of historical events or the operation of equipment. It can also help us to achieve other objectives, such as evaluating the impact of propaganda on public opinion, looking at types of local customs, examining the terrain over which wars were fought, or considering elements of change and continuity in the rural and urban environment. We should also be aware that it can open up new fields of enquiry which may not be settled except through careful examination of the written records. Film evidence may provide only a selective representation of past events. Even technical limitations restrict the use of cameras to periods when climatic and lighting conditions, or distance from an event, were favourable. These factors can introduce an element of bias into what has been captured on film. Overall, you need to remember that the photographic and film evidence to which you have access, or which you are aware exists, may not necessarily be representative of the visual sources which might or should be available.

Using historical sources

The development of an awareness of the purpose of different types of source material and the value which can be placed on them is a skill which needs to be acquired. You may wish to distinguish between witting and unwitting testimony in the sources you use. Many primary sources contain evidence which the writer intended others to see, the so-called witting testimony; others contain material which was merely unintentional, and therefore can be classified as unwitting testimony. You may choose to begin your research by examining the secondary sources because these will provide background knowledge about your subject, as well as giving you some indication of how other historians have approached the same topic. The latter may include what questions they asked, what topics they decided to omit, what themes they pursued, and what sources they used. An alternative approach is to start with the primary source material because this may encourage you to examine evidence which could have been overlooked if only secondary sources were used as a guide to which primary sources to consult. However, many historians find it difficult to begin their research by reviewing the primary sources, unless they have a satisfactory knowledge of the contours of their subject through an examination of the secondary sources. In any case, the primary sources may be too vast for you to fully appreciate the value of their contents. A solution to these conflicting approaches is therefore required.

The most obvious solution to this dilemma is to develop a more flexible approach which combines an examination of the secondary sources without finalising which primary sources should be examined. This could involve the preparation of a broad list of research questions which are capable of being modified and progressively focused as your research develops. By not specifying your research questions too precisely you will not limit your choice of source material. The most promising research projects are those where the topic is narrowly defined and the sources are not too extensive. In any case, few historians are ever likely to master all the relevant primary and secondary sources. But it is important to be aware of the possibility of distortion if any source is not fully examined and its content is taken out of context. Moreover, excessive reliance on secondary sources may not be advisable because it encourages delay in examination of the primary sources. If you are preparing work for a research degree it may not be advisable to spend more than the first term or semester looking exclusively at the secondary sources. A variety of sources will usually have to be examined and compared with one another to achieve a satisfactory assessment of any historical event.

Your choice of research topic may present you with either the prospect of an abundance of source material or the task of compensating for fragmentary evidence. The volume of evidence which is available is not, of course, a guide to its reliability or usefulness. Source material has to be selected to ensure that it is representative of the much larger amount of evidence which is available. Clearly the problem of working with unrepresentative material can be avoided if you do not select your source material with the aim of supporting a very narrow hypothesis rather than revealing the wider complexity of a subject. The abundance of source material may be regarded as a positive aspect if it assists you in formulating a wide range of research questions. You may find that it is necessary to limit your field of research and define your chosen topic much more carefully if it appears that the volume of source material is far too cumbersome to be examined thoroughly.

You may face the alternative scenario where there is a much more limited range of source material available. You will now have to take practical steps to compensate for the existence of fragmentary evidence. It may be very difficult to write convincingly on a subject if there are gaps in the evidence. In these circumstances you may be tempted to emphasise less significant events at the expense of more crucial ones and so your research may lack a coherent structure. With a limited range or amount of source material you have to be careful not to make unjustifiable assumptions based on this evidence. The implication of the limited extent of source material for your own research is that you have to ensure that the evidence which does exist is representative of the subject and themes which it covers. Careful judgement must guide any inferences which are based on limited historical evidence, particularly where this information cannot be easily corroborated. The concerns of people in the past and their perspective on events may differ appreciably from historians today, hence much of what was deemed important or taken for granted in the past may never have been recorded in any tangible form. Yet this is the type of evidence which would be of greatest value in any historical research project.

It is perhaps wise to resist the tendency to rely more heavily on the secondary sources when the primary sources are scarce. The secondary sources may place undue emphasis on the wrong aspects of past events, or regard all events in a similar manner without attempting to place them in a sensible hierarchy of importance. They may also fail to identify the proper causes of events or confuse long-term causes with more immediate precipitating factors. Alternatively, secondary sources may erroneously place undue emphasis on the consequences of the actions of individuals in circumstances where wider social, economic or political forces were more important in determining historical change. Your field of interest will have to be chosen with great care if a preliminary review of source material reveals the existence of only fragmentary evidence. Equally, it would not be sensible for you to choose a subject where the sources were abundant if there was little prospect that this subject would sustain your genuine interest or make a valuable contribution to historical scholarship. By considering the range of source material which has been referred to in this section, you should be in a position to make a more informed decision about what type of historical evidence you intend to use in your own research.

6

Planning a research project

Historical research can add immensely to our knowledge about people, cultures and past events. The quality of that research will depend to a significant extent on the methods used to plan a research project. A distinction can be made between historiography, which deals with the nature and writing of history, and historical methods, which includes the discovery of evidence and a critical examination of past records. Part II of this book covers research methods, and this particular chapter focuses on various aspects of planning a research project. It begins by looking at the qualities expected in historians and the elements of a researchable topic, then moves on to consider the preparation of a research topic outline. Useful advice is also provided on time management, and the chapter concludes by considering the various stages of a research project.

A primary aim of historical research is to look for connections between events so that a meaningful pattern or structure can be discerned. Historians normally have some general idea of the likely contribution and significance of their own research project. Exactly what that contribution is, and how significant it will turn out to be, is sometimes not evident until after the research has commenced. The careful preparation of a research project will improve the quality of the material which you produce, as well as helping you to make much more effective use of your time. The following notes begin by offering practical advice about the ideal qualities expected in historical researchers. You may wish to examine this list and identify any qualities which you could develop which are appropriate to the subject of your own research interests.

Qualities expected in a historian

There are several qualities which might be expected to be found in a competent historical researcher. You will already possess some of these qualities and may be willing to develop others. The qualities can be summarised as follows:

1 Curiosity; initiative; motivation and commitment; imagination and insight; and creativity and original thought. Historians need to have the ability to formulate clear research questions, be willing to use critical thinking skills to test accepted wisdom and adopt a methodical approach in searching for relevant source material. Basically, you need to know how, and where, to look for evidence which will assist you to answer the questions of who, what, where, why and how.

2 The ability to familiarise yourself with the concepts, language and technical terms which are appropriate to your chosen field of enquiry. Historians need to have the ability to master complex ideas and present these in a readable and concise manner.

3 The ability to analyse a topic or theme from different perspectives to provide a genuine and original contribution to knowledge.

4 A high level of enthusiasm for the research, combined with willpower and diligence to help cope with unexpected setbacks. A research plan and timetable is always useful in helping you to monitor the various stages of your project.

5 The ability to manage time and resources. You should be able to prioritise work and set realistic targets, and this must be based on a clear set of objectives or goals. The ability to cope with several simultaneous tasks depends on good time management.

6 A willingness to learn new techniques, accept constructive advice from other researchers and gain specialist knowledge. You may need to master information gathering and management skills in order to bring order to a large volume of disparate source material.

7 The confidence and ability to engage in independent research, be aware of the value of researching a particular topic and maintain high professional standards. You would be expected to acknowledge the work of others, not plagiarise material or misrepresent the views of other historians, adhere to confidentiality where this is justified and preserve

and maintain access to sources for other researchers. You would be expected to avoid bias in selectively reporting research results, or in making false claims to expertise on matters beyond the scope of your specialist field.

8 The ability to make an effective and significant contribution to knowledge by communicating ideas effectively and extending the boundaries of existing knowledge. Your historical conclusions therefore have to be adequately supported by your research data. If you are uncertain of the reliability of your data you need to make it clear that your interpretation must be qualified to some degree. It is important not to overstate, nor understate, the validity of your evidence or the results which are derived from such evidence.

9 The ability to produce a competent piece of historical work in a reasonable period of time. This includes the accurate and logical presentation of evidence in a manner which is readily understandable by your readers.

10 Possession of typing or word-processing skills; familiarity with computer software packages covering the use of spreadsheets and databases; library search skills, and knowledge of how to search for, and retrieve, relevant information from the Internet. Other specialised skills and knowledge, such as palaeography, statistical analysis, interviewing skills and knowledge of intellectual property rights, if relevant to the subject of your enquiry.

It is sensible to begin work on a topic which is sufficiently interesting to hold your attention over a lengthy period of time. You may wish to explore a topic where details are either unknown or have been misinterpreted by other researchers. There may be unanswered questions which have been ignored by other historians, but this will only be evident after you have reviewed the available published literature. A subject which has not been extensively researched might be regarded as particularly attractive, but it will probably involve a more extensive survey of the source material. If your topic is too specialised then it may be of interest only to a relatively small and select audience. It is certainly worthwhile for you to make early contact with other professionals who are working in the same field of study because they may supply you with information on work in progress. Finally, look at the annual publication *Current Research in Britain* for a general guide on the range of research projects currently in different stages of development in universities, other institutions and government departments.

Choosing a topic

One of the most difficult problems which historians encounter is that of actually choosing a suitable research topic for investigation. Your first task will be to consider in what period of history your interests and knowledge fall. The preparatory work which you will have to carry out to identify a suitable topic depends, to a significant extent, upon the scale of your intended research. Obviously a more detailed investigation of possible topics, including the implications of carrying out research in a specific subject area, is required for an extended piece of research work, such as a thesis or book, in comparison with the more limited objective of writing an article for inclusion in a book or journal. At an early stage you will have to decide whether you intend to embark on the research of a completely new topic or merely offer an alternative and interesting perspective on a topic which has already been covered by other historians. Whatever you decide, you will probably have to begin with a broad outline of the subject which interests you and then progressively narrow this subject area to a smaller number of potential topics which appear to offer promising avenues for original research. It is important to try to identify the objectives of your research, but try to allow for some degree of flexibility in defining those objectives. Your aim at this stage should be to outline the contours of a subject, not necessarily define its precise structure or choose a specific title for a research project. The choice of a suitable research topic is an important task because it will have to sustain your interest and enable you to locate relevant primary and secondary source material. If you begin work with a clearly-defined subject or theme, you are much more likely to be able to direct your efforts to locate useful and relevant source material.

The first task in choosing an appropriate topic is to consider which historical subjects have interested you the most. The most common mistake which many historical researchers experience at this stage is in choosing a topic that is too large in scope. It is obviously unwise to commence work on any research topic, no matter how important that research may appear, which is too ambitious and cannot be completed within your projected timescale. For example, a topic which will require up to three years of detailed research will not be suitable for a master's dissertation which is expected to be completed within one or two years. Even if you have a clear idea about which topic you wish to research, you will still have to do some preliminary work to discover what other historians have written on your chosen subject. The most useful way of achieving this is to examine some of the reference sources located in section 2 of the guide to further reading at the end of this book. The published volumes of *History Theses* are subdivided by subject and period, thereby enabling you to scan the titles of theses in broad subject areas and periods. If you have a clear idea of the topics which might interest you then you can also refer to the index within these volumes. The latter are also supplemented by lists of theses in progress, as well as those which have been recently completed. It is also worthwhile supplementing this by looking at Aslib's *Index to Theses* because this lists theses which are not purely on historical subjects. Moreover, recent copies of the Aslib lists also incorporate abstracts which will enable you to get a better impression of the content and treatment of the subject of each thesis. This may help to sharpen your own judgement about which topics are, or are not, worth researching. You may also wish to look at the broader picture of what historically-related research is being pursued in universities by examining the humanities and social sciences volumes of the annual publication *Current Research in Britain*. However, you should note that the latter does not necessarily provide a comprehensive or up-to-date account of all research, historical and non-historical, in universities. The content of this publication is dependent upon up-to-date information being supplied by individual history departments. Nevertheless, it will be of some use in your search for a worthwhile topic, and can be supplemented by looking at *Dissertation Abstracts*, which is also listed in the guide to further reading.

In addition to looking at lists of theses and current research in the universities, there are two other important sources which you should examine: published books and published journal articles. The *Annual Bibliography of British and Irish History* and the *British National Bibliography* are worth consulting to find out what books have been published on different subjects. You can then look at a small selection of books on subjects which are of particular interest to you and which may help to clarify your thoughts about which topic you would like to research. It is also important to look at articles which have been published in history journals. You can begin this task by selecting those history journals which publish articles on periods and subjects of interest to you, and then systematically review their contents. Most libraries normally file their current journal issues in a different location from the bound volumes of back issues. You may also wish to supplement your review of history journals by looking at *British Humanities Index*, particularly if your research is of an interdisciplinary nature. There are, of course, other possible sources of information about published and ongoing historical research which can be consulted, such as book reviews, the lecture and seminar lists of learned societies (such as the Royal Historical Society), your own lecture or tutorial notes, abstracts, computer databases and the Internet. Try to look at as many of these sources as possible because this will help you to make a more informed choice of topic. You may also wish to supplement this preparatory work by seeking the advice of tutors on the suitability of specific topics. They may be able to suggest subjects which are of suffici-ent scope and interest, or at least put you in touch with other historians who may be able to offer friendly, critical advice on your research plans. They might not be able to suggest an actual research topic but may indicate subject areas which look promising, in the sense that they offer an opportunity to make an effective and original contribution to histori-cal knowledge.

Your choice of topic may have to be limited by practical considera-tions, such as the availability of relevant source material, background knowledge or the possession of certain skills. You will have to consider how much source material is available, where it is located, and whether you can negotiate access to it. If there are no difficulties in this area then it may be possible to compensate for other problems by, for example, enhancing your background knowledge and gaining specific skills, such as in palaeography or knowledge of a foreign language. It is therefore important when choosing a topic to consider whether any specialist knowledge or skills are required. Try to assess whether you will have to acquire knowledge of, for example, statistical analysis, social psychology, historical demography, social anthropology, or perhaps economic and social theory. You should be aware of these possible constraints at the outset rather than encounter them at a later stage and perhaps have to abandon or radically change the direction of your research interests. Similar considerations apply to historical topics which are partly based on the use of oral testimony or visual material, such as maps, film, illustrations or photographs. In general, when deciding on a suitable topic you should attempt as far as possible to identify what sources you will use and what knowledge and skills you will require to complete the work successfully. If your preliminary investigations reveal any shortcomings here then it is wiser to choose a different topic. Try to consult as widely as possible when you are in the process of deciding on a topic. If you are, for example, considering the possibility of researching a particular industry, company or profession, it is always advisable to contact appropriate individuals who should be able to advise you on the feasibility of your research plans. At this stage you are not seeking to finalise all the issues you wish to examine, because many of these may subsequently turn out to be more marginal than you at first realised. Your primary aim is therefore to identify a topic which, from your preliminary enquiries, appears to be interesting and worthwhile examining, and which you are confident you have the ability to complete the research for in the time available. It is clearly important to choose a subject which will give you the opportunity to ask interesting and useful questions and which may provide the focus for continuing research work. Your ability to select a suitable topic may depend upon the extent to which you have completed preliminary enquiries on the range of research possibilities.

Elements of a researchable topic

The progress you can expect to make with a project will depend not only on your own qualities as a researcher: it will also be determined by the quality of your topic. You may therefore wish to assess how your chosen topic compares with the elements outlined in the following list. The definition of a worthwhile research topic can perhaps be summarised according to the following criteria:

1 Your topic should be sufficiently interesting, challenging and important to justify allocating research time to it. There will be clear aims and objectives and your topic should be expected to produce valuable results which significantly extend the boundaries of current historical knowledge.

2 Your topic should be amenable to the use of research methods; it should be of a suitable length and appropriate to its purpose, whether intended as an article, book or thesis; and the data should be easily accessible in public or private archives. A subject which has not been extensively researched may provide more opportunities for producing original work, but an original contribution can also be made from unoriginal sources, depending on the analysis and interpretation of the source material.

3 You should possess sufficient background knowledge to be capable of working effectively on the project. The topic should ideally be one which will sustain your energy, motivation and enthusiasm because these are key factors in the successful completion of any research project. Also, network with other researchers who may be interested in aspects of your project.

4 The research on your topic should be capable of being completed in a specified period of time. This will require a careful examination of the nature and scope of your work, as well as your other commitments. Your topic should ideally be one in which you will be able to monitor progress and cater for unforeseen difficulties and delays.

5 There should be adequate funding to see your project through to completion. Be clear about your aims and objectives when applying for research funding. Be positive and demonstrate that these can be achieved within a stated timescale. The ability to attract funding will depend upon the quality of your research proposal and evidence of the extent of preparatory work.

6 The results of your research should be capable of being disseminated through publications and should, if possible, provide opportunities for the further development of your subject.

You may find it helpful during the course of your research to use a small A6 notebook to list useful ideas that come to mind. These notes can be transferred periodically to a separate research ideas file so that you have a single and accessible list of useful ideas. Your notebook and file might also be used to outline and develop both short-term and long-term goals. Your goals are likely to alter over time as your research progresses, and so they should be kept as flexible as possible.

Research topic outline

After you have chosen a suitable research topic you should prepare a detailed outline of the various themes and issues you wish to examine. Your outline will include subjects which you hope to cover in your chapters, sections, subsections or even paragraphs. A broad outline consists of a list of chapter headings for each of the major topics which are to be covered in your project. In contrast to this, the most detailed outline will consist of a list of topics, themes or issues which link with each paragraph. The advantage of preparing a detailed outline is that it allows you to visualise the overall structure of your project. It will also enable you to decide which source material will be relevant, as well as indicating where this material will be used in your project. The preparation of a detailed outline also ensures that your narrative flows smoothly, particularly because a number of topics or themes can be arranged in a logical sequence prior to the preparation of any drafts. Your detailed research topic outline will therefore give an indication of the broad structure of your research plan, as well as its individual components. You can prepare an outline by listing individual topics on blank record cards or typing them into a computer. The titles chosen for individual chapters should not be too long, and neither should some be excessively longer or shorter than others. All the titles which you choose should accurately reflect the content of each chapter or section. If your chapters are subdivided into sections they should ideally be of approximately equal length. The chapters would therefore be written one section at a time.

You may wish to keep separate folders or ring binders for filing your notes on the various themes which emerge during the course of your research. The themes could always be developed at some stage into potential chapter headings. It is advisable to maintain a balance in the amount of notes which you keep on each topic or theme so that you do not accumulate excessive detail on some topics and a shortage of detail on others. Your topic outline should, in any case, be sufficiently flexible so that it can be modified as your work progresses. The outline is likely to be modified if new themes emerge or existing ones assume lesser or greater importance. Even if you do not intend to subdivide chapters into sections, a topic outline which is subdivided to this level of detail will assist you in producing a much more satisfactory structure for your project. Your chapters can then be built up from a number of minor topics which are arranged in a logical sequence. All major topics can normally be subdivided into a number of smaller ones which will link with subsections or individual paragraphs. The latter may be numbered temporarily if you think this will assist in arranging them prior to the preparation of your drafts: so 4.1.2 will, for example, represent the second paragraph or subsection 2 of section 1 within chapter 4. These numbers would not appear in your final work, since only the chapters are likely to be numbered in a history thesis or book.

The basic hierarchical structure for any research project will therefore consist of the following elements, not all of which may appear in any individual project:

- Chapters: the principal subdivision of the work, although in some books and theses the chapters may be grouped together into parts.
- Sections: each chapter may consist of a number of sections which are identified in the contents page.
- Subsections: these can be linked with a list of research questions and so provide the building blocks for each chapter. A number of related topics can be represented by each subsection, but your work is unlikely to be subdivided into numbered subsections which are identified in the contents page.
- Paragraphs: one paragraph should be used for each minor topic or theme. They provide the basic building blocks for all chapters, sections and subsections.

You may wish to consider using flow charts or mind maps to illustrate the links between various ideas, topics or themes and so assist in the preparation of a topic outline for your project. If mind maps are used, the principal ideas, topics or themes should be placed near the centre of your map, with less important ones near the edge. The open-ended nature of mind maps enables you to make new connections more easily than by using other visual aids. Mind maps are useful because all the mental associations generated by a single keyword can be utilised. This contrasts with a simple list of keywords because the words are often forgotten shortly after they are written, usually because you are preoccupied in searching for a new word to add to your list. The structure of mind maps permits new words to be easily added to the existing keywords to help in the formation of appropriate subheadings. Overall, there can be distinct advantages in using these visual aids in the early stages of a research project when the structure and interconnections between topics are being considered.

Time management

Before becoming fully immersed in your research work you may find it helpful to consider methods for managing your time more effectively. The development of effective time-management techniques will increase the amount of work you can complete within a given timescale, give you more control over the tasks you need to complete, and enable you to cope with unexpected delays. Creating lists can help you to identify main objectives which can then be prioritised. You will, of course, need to be realistic in deciding how much work you can complete in a given period of time. It is perhaps useful to be able to identify the locations and time of day when you work at your most, and least, productive levels. Try also to distinguish between urgent and important tasks: a task may be urgent, but not necessarily important. Priority should be given to tasks which are both urgent and important, with important tasks which are not urgent being allocated a lower priority. But note that important tasks which are postponed for a lengthy period are likely to develop into urgent tasks. You will never have complete control over your work because different aspects of your work will be at various stages of completion. For example, you may be searching for source material, reading through papers and preparing some research notes. However, you can use time management to make better use of the time available.

The best solution for coping with multiple tasks is to prioritise your work by allocating separate files for different types of paperwork: letters you need to write, those you wish to respond to urgently, or those you wish to retain for reference purposes. Reviewing your paperwork on a regular basis will give you a clearer idea of the work you really need to complete. Moreover, some information might be obtained much quicker by using alternative means of communication: telephone, fax or e-mail instead of a letter. You may also wish to consider the relative merits of storing basic information on a computer rather than on paper. It will take longer to enter, find and scan information on a computer, but the latter does permit more flexibility in sorting, cross-referencing, updating and re-formatting information. You can also seek to improve your ability to scan printed sources to determine their usefulness: look at the contents pages, indexes, summaries, conclusions or opening and closing paragraphs. The maintenance of a tidy and organised study desk will obviously save time in locating any papers and books which you need. Ideally, your desk should only be used for storing material you are currently working with, so all other material should be labelled and filed. Your research work should be regarded as a positive challenge, but if you fail to organise your work properly that challenge will become excessive and will reduce your efficiency. If you set modest targets and maintain a sense of direction and purpose you will be able to overcome perceived problems, weaknesses and limitations and therefore be able to complete your work within the time available. There are a number of time-management techniques which you may wish to adapt to your own circumstances, and these are briefly outlined in the following list:

- Set clear objectives which can be measured in terms of time and effort required.
- Prioritise tasks as urgent and important, important, urgent, and not urgent or important.
- Allocate an uninterrupted period of time for completing urgent or difficult tasks.
- Identify tasks which waste time, and identify methods to overcome these difficulties.
- Vary the tasks you complete each day in order to overcome inertia.

- Identify locations and periods of time when you are more productive at completing specific tasks.
- Take occasional breaks from your work to refresh yourself.
- Prepare 'to do' lists of work to be completed on a daily, weekly or monthly basis.
- Keep your study desk tidy and organised, and maintain an efficient filing system to enable papers to be retrieved easily.
- Place on your desk only those materials (e.g. books, papers, stationery) you need to complete a specific task.
- Subdivide large tasks into a number of smaller ones, and start with the easiest in order to gain momentum.
- Reduce the volume of unwanted paperwork, and avoid reading material more than once, unless necessary to improve your understanding of its contents.
- Develop the ability to scan and absorb the contents of printed material quickly.
- Keep a notebook to list useful ideas as they come to mind, review these lists periodically, then transfer some items to your 'To Do' lists.
- Avoid re-writing your notes because this is an inefficient use of time.
- Document all your source material carefully and accurately so you do not have to return to it to re-check bibliographical information.
- Use computer searches, where possible, to reduce the time taken to locate relevant source material.
- Make notes as you read or underline important passages in photocopied extracts to ensure that you focus on the important ideas rather than read passively.
- If you need advice on any aspect of your research, then do not delay in seeking it.
- If it is possible to delegate less urgent or important tasks, then try to do so.
- Monitor your progress to ensure that work is being completed on target.
- Plan meetings, interviews and visits to archives so that those within the same geographical area can be covered at the same time.
- Consider alternatives to writing, such as the telephone, fax or e-mail.
- Build flexibility into your work plans to compensate for delays.

The stages of a research project

There are a number of well-defined stages through which a research project will progress, from commencement to completion. Not all stages will apply to every history project. To estimate the time required for completing any project it is best to subdivide the various activities into a number of small tasks and then combine the individual estimates for each task. The principal stages in project work can be noted as follows:

1 Select a general subject area for research.

2 Define your subject more precisely to select a viable research topic. Identify key themes, issues and objectives through preliminary reading of existing secondary sources and discussions with individuals who are knowledgeable about the subject area. Define the title of your research proposal as precisely as possible, and try to prepare a flexible timetable for completion of the various stages of the work. Assess whether your research can be completed in the timescale available.

3 Index relevant source material to produce a working bibliography, and assess whether these sources are sufficient and available to enable you to complete your research. List relevant keywords and check printed sources and computer databases to assist in compiling a bibliography.

4 Review the research methods you are likely to use in your research. Assess whether your work will be primarily based on extensive literature searches, or perhaps involve interviews for an oral history project. Check that you have access to all primary and secondary source material.

5 Commence background reading and, where necessary, refine your original research proposal. Review your methodology, monitor progress and define the scope of your project and the topics to be investigated much more precisely. Use relevant, up-to-date and reliable data sources. This stage in a project may lead to the generation of several important hypotheses which you may wish to make a note of.

6 Prepare a draft outline of the structure of your project and carefully evaluate the topics you intend to cover.

7 Scan and read through source material to prepare research notes. Underline any important points in source material you have photocopied.

8 Begin an organisational review of your research notes (written or typed) and research materials (such as photocopies of documents or articles)

to produce a list of subjects or issues. Your project will be subdivided into these subjects or issues. A computer may assist in the reorganisation of notes and source material into subject groups.

9 Prepare draft chapter outlines, together with a list of research questions associated with each topic. The research questions should be chosen so that they link in with each section, subsection or paragraph within each chapter. Even if your project is to be divided only into a number of chapters and does not include sections or subsections, these sub-divisions are very useful at the planning stage because they allow individual research questions to be arranged in a logical order within each chapter. By ensuring that the topics which you cover in each chapter follow a logical sequence, this will give coherence to the development of your project as the research progresses.

10 Prepare a detailed research proposal which incorporates chapter titles and chapter outlines (i.e. summaries of the contents of each chapter).

11 Subdivide your work into manageable units, such as sections or para-graphs, and begin writing them. This first draft should be based on your chapter outlines. There is no need to wait until all your source material has been reviewed before composing a first draft: the collec-tion of additional data can take place in parallel with the writing of drafts. It is only by preparing drafts at an early stage that you may detect gaps in information which would then lead to further research in the primary or secondary sources.

12 Complete your survey of source material.

13 Edit the first draft. The draft may be written, or entered into a com-puter and edited on screen. Additional drafts may be needed before an acceptable final version is produced; the number of drafts required will depend upon the quality of your original draft.

14 Prepare a final draft.

15 Type the final draft. If a word processor has been used to type earlier drafts, this stage will be simplified and merely involve the incorpora-tion of amendments to these drafts.

16 Proof-read your typescript carefully before submitting it to a publisher, journal editor or university.

17 If your typescript is submitted to a publisher then it will be sent to be copy-edited and then returned to you for checking. You will then be

asked to return the copy-edited typescript to the publisher. If your typescript is submitted for a research degree, read through it in preparation for your oral examination.

18 For published books, check the page proofs sent to you by your publisher. Mark up the proofs using British Standard proof correction marks and return all the material to the publisher.

19 Use one copy of the page proofs to prepare an index for your book. Type and submit the index to your publisher, who will arrange for page proofs of the index to be made and checked in-house.

20 Await the publication of your book or article, or, for a dissertation or thesis, the outcome of your oral examination. This is a good time to look back at how your work has progressed and plan any future project.

7

Locating and indexing source material

The task of locating and indexing source material can begin after preliminary enquiries have been completed about the viability of researching a particular subject. Your research will be based on a selection of primary and secondary sources. Primary source material includes original material and eyewitness testimony which has not been subject to interpretation by other historians. Examples of primary source material include official papers, diaries, letters, minutes, memoranda and taped interviews. You will also wish to make use of secondary sources which consist of the interpretations of other researchers on the content of the primary sources. The secondary sources provide mainly background knowledge and are normally published as books, pamphlets or articles. This section looks at how to locate and index primary and secondary sources for use in history research projects.

The quality of a research project may depend to a significant extent on the type and range of primary sources which you use. Work on primary sources permits the creation of original material which can be used by other historians. Some historical work may require to be revised over a period of time if later historical research generates new ideas based upon access to new primary sources. Even a careful review of secondary sources may give you an opportunity to offer a new perspective on existing ideas. Your own research is likely to make use of a variety of primary and secondary sources. By examining the secondary sources you will be able to ascertain what primary sources other researchers have consulted in the course of their own work. Some historians prefer to start their work by examining the primary sources, but in practice most probably work on primary and secondary sources simultaneously. You will find it useful to make a careful assessment of what sources you actually need because it is simply unproductive to examine a large quantity of material far in excess of what is required. A comprehensive bibliography of promising source material could be prepared at the outset, but you may find that not all of this material is useful. A balance must be sought between the need to prepare a detailed bibliography of source material, yet avoid the prospect of working from an excessively unwieldy list of sources.

Locating source material

A variety of options are available for identifying and locating relevant source material: library catalogues; reference lists in books; published subject bibliographies, such as *British National Bibliography*; directories, encyclopaedias and annuals; abstracts and indexes; book reviews; handbooks; and computer databases. Library or university websites can provide a gateway to useful electronic resources and the websites of relevant organisations, other libraries, historical societies and historical journals. Electronic bibliographic databases are helpful because they permit you to search large amounts of data very quickly and store references for future use. The various reference sources listed in the guide to further reading at the end of this book will also help to point you in the right direction. A thesaurus can be used to enable you to prepare a list of keywords which will be needed to search for information on your chosen subject in the various printed bibliographies and indexes, microfiche catalogues or computer databases. Library shelves should also be scanned under specific shelf marks to gain an insight into the range of published literature on a particular subject.

Some libraries use the Library of Congress classification to catalogue their stock, whereas others use the Dewey Decimal classification. For libraries which use the Library of Congress system, history publications are listed under the main classifications C, D, E and F: for example, D represents history (general), DA represents Great Britain, DC represents France, and so on. Other classifications may also be relevant to your research: AE refers to general encyclopaedias, HN covers social history, and JA deals with political science. Your own library will have a full outline of the Library of Congress classification if it uses this system. The system basically consists of three parts, as follows:

1 Letters, such as HN for social history, which are filed in alphabetical order.
2 A classification number, such as 1572, which is filed in numerical order. The classification may comprise both numbers and letters, such as 1572 .B42, which are filed in decimal and alphabetical order. Letters are filed before numbers, so HN 1572 .B42 is filed before HN 1572 .42.
3 The first three letters of an author's name or title (e.g. SMI for Smith), which is filed in alphabetical order.

The following gives an example of the filing sequence of shelf marks:

HN 1500 BRO
HN 1500 SMI
HN 1525 SMI
HN 1525 .B3 SMI
HN 1525 .C2 SMI
HN 1525 .3 SMI
HN 1525 .3 WHI
HV 220 EVA
HV 475 MAC
HV 475 .621 TAY
HV 475 .63 TAY
HV 1352 .2 ABE

For libraries which use the Dewey Decimal Classification system, refer to the latest edition of the Dewey Decimal Index (i.e. the twentieth edition, available in four volumes) and prepare a list of library classification numbers which relate to your chosen subject. History publications are shelved under 900, but other classifications may also be relevant, particularly if your subject is interdisciplinary. The filing sequence of shelf marks under the Dewey system will be as follows:

zero 0

files before brackets ( )

files before colon :

files before hyphen -

files before numbers 1–9 (or 0–9 within brackets)

The following gives an example of the filing sequence of shelf marks:

900

902

9021

909

9(41)

9(41)01

9(41):.2

9(41):.42

9(41–42)

9(701)

9(701)01

9(701):.2

9 (701–04)

9(71)

9:.4

9:.8

9–.91

91

914

92

94

Do keep in mind that if you scan library shelves this is not a foolproof method for determining what material is available on your chosen subject. Some books may have been borrowed, in current use, ordered but not yet catalogued, perhaps transferred to a short loan collection, being bound (especially in the case of past issues of journals), or shelved incorrectly. Larger publications may be shelved separately to the main sequence of items on the same subject. Similarly, pamphlets may be shelved in boxes located close to books on the same subject. Also, some rare and older books may be held in a special collections area or department, which may also keep copies of manuscript material and university theses. If a book cannot be traced under its author, then search under its title or subject. You may find that recent acquisitions are not yet listed in a library's computer catalogue. Almost all libraries now have computerised catalogues, although you may find that older material can only be searched using card or large printed catalogues. Flipping through record cards in a manually prepared catalogue is, however, much easier on the eye than turning pages in a printed bibliography or continually shifting your eye level to scan a list of entries in a computerised catalogue. Some specialist libraries hold details of their catalogue holdings in a variety of formats: record cards, microform and computerised retrieval systems, as well as large printed catalogues. Most libraries have shifted to full computerisation of their catalogues, thus most of their material can be searched by author, title, subject and keyword, as well as by language or date of publication. The ability to search a catalogue by subject and keyword is the major advantage which computerised catalogues offer in comparison with printed catalogues. Also, some computerised catalogues will indicate how many copies there are of a particular publication and whether any of them are out on loan or are recent acquisitions. They also provide the option of giving you full or partial bibliographic information on a publication. Some university libraries allow users to borrow and renew items online, as well as offering the option of checking the items they have borrowed.

Books which are unavailable in a library may be recalled or available via inter-library loan. Journals are often an untapped source of up-to-date ideas and information, particularly in the field of history where a wide variety of scholarly journals and magazines are published. Back issues of journals are normally bound and filed separately from current unbound issues. The most recent issues of journals may also be available in electronic format and accessible via full-text databases. The *British Humanities Index* and the *Arts and Humanities Citation Index* list or cite articles from a wide range of journals. If you choose to index material from these sources you will need to prepare a list of keywords which are sufficiently comprehensive to encompass the varieties in language and terminology used by the various published indexes. You will need to pay more careful attention to your selection of keywords if your historical topic spans a long period of time. For example, in the history of British broadcasting, articles which are listed under the heading 'wireless' in earlier volumes of printed indexes might in later volumes be listed under the heading 'radio'. Citation indexes will enable you to see which authors and publications have cited the book or article you are interested in. By listing other works which refer to your chosen book or article, these indexes will enable you to obtain a more comprehensive picture of what has been published on a specific subject.

Databases are being increasingly used by many historians to gather material for their research projects. Databases can store vast amounts of information, they can be updated on a regular basis, and they permit complex searches to be made. If you decide to search a database the first requirement is to list keywords which are relevant to your subject of enquiry. You can use a dictionary, encyclopaedia or thesaurus to help identify synonyms and variations of your keywords. Broad or very narrow terms can be used when conducting a search: the choice depends upon how specialised your topic is or how many items you expect to find. Using a narrower search term will yield fewer entries, and combining two keywords can also be used to make your search more specific. For example, if you search for information on 'radio drama' you will produce fewer results than if you use either 'radio' or 'drama' as your search terms. It is also possible with computer searches to truncate your keywords to cover various alternatives. For example, if you are researching the history of broadcasting you may use the truncation 'broadcast*' instead of choosing and entering individual terms, such as 'broadcasting', 'broadcasters', and so on. A word can therefore be truncated to provide various possible alternatives which all begin with the same letters. However, you do have to be careful not to truncate a word to such an extent that it generates irrelevant references. Boolean searching which combines keywords enables you to control the breadth or depth of your search by using keywords in conjunction with the logical operators AND/OR/NOT.

The basic principles of the Boolean operators are noted as follows:

• using AND, as in radio AND drama, will only provide references containing both keywords, so your search will be more specific because fewer references will emerge.

- using OR, as in radio OR drama, will provide references relating to either keyword, hence your search will be broader because more references will emerge.
- using NOT, as in radio NOT drama, will provide references on only one of the keywords, but this option must be used carefully otherwise you will exclude potentially useful references.

You may be able to refine your search further by limiting it by name of author, title, type of document, publication date and so on. You can also achieve the same objective by selecting more specific keywords. This will depend upon how many references have been generated by your initial search. If there are insufficient references, use synonyms in conjunction with the logical operator OR; alternatively, truncate your keyword(s) if you cannot think of all suitable synonyms (e.g. broadcast* OR radio drama, *or* broadcast* OR film*). But you may find that you generate too many false hits, in which case you should use more specific keywords, combine keywords with AND or NOT, or limit your search by author(AU), title(TI), or year of publication(PY), as follows:

broadcast* AND radio drama
broadcast* NOT radio in TI
radio drama AND PY=1995

You can also combine previous short searches using AND to refine your search still further, rather than construct a long and complex search term, as in the following examples:

(broadcast* OR radio drama) AND (broadcast* NOT radio in TI)
(broadcast* OR radio drama) AND (radio drama AND PY=1995)

Some databases enable you to trace cited references to publications (i.e. sources which have cited books or articles on subjects you are interested in). This should enable you to identify which items have been cited the most frequently. Boolean searching can therefore be a useful technique for locating relevant source material on a particular subject.

Access to electronic information will be either through the Internet or stored locally on CD-ROMs. An increasing amount of information is being made available by libraries via the Internet rather than on CD-ROMs. The Internet may be a useful resource for finding information on a specific topic, but it can be slow at times to gain access to a wehsite and, more importantly, the use of a search engine to identify useful websites can lead to a lot of useless, inaccurate and irrelevant information, particularly if your keywords are not very specific. The information available via websites is often very transient and so it is perhaps understandable why many historians are not so eager to use the Internet as a resource for finding information. Moreover, not all subjects are adequately covered on the Internet. Nevertheless, if you do decide to use the Internet to locate information it is best to use subject gateways which provide links to other websites covering similar topics. In the multimedia age, historical information can be provided with sound and images, not just in traditional textual format. Moreover, this information can be updated more easily and quickly than material in printed format. Some organisations provide more detailed and informative websites than others, but the situation is continually changing and so you will have to discover which are the most useful by trial and error. However, there are a number of websites which you may wish to explore to gain some insight into how the Internet might be of use for your own research project. You may wish to visit some or all of the websites provided by the following organisations: British Library; public and university libraries; British Academy; British Standards Institution; BBC; UK research councils; national and local museums; Government Information Service, for access to the websites of all government departments; and local and national newspapers. The Centre for History, Archaeology and Art History, based at the University of Glasgow, provides links to websites of interest to historians. Other useful subject gateways include The Arts and Humanities Data Service and NISS (National Information Services and Systems). You should refer to the guide to further reading at the end of this book for details of reference sources available in electronic format. These include, for example, the *British National Bibliography*, *British Humanities Index* and UKOP (catalogue of UK official publications). The ESRC's Data Archive and Qualicat electronic catalogues may also be worth checking to see if they hold any quantitative and qualitative datasets respectively relevant to your own research interests.

Although an increasing range of information is available to historians in electronic format most will still be accessible in printed format. Local archives may publish lists of the material they hold, and this can be supplemented by looking at published bibliographies on specific subjects, although the latter can sometimes be out-of-date by the time the material is published. You will also find that many libraries hold bound or micro-film copies of old newspapers, but printed subject indexes do not exist for all microfilmed newspapers. Some libraries also keep ordnance survey topographic maps of the British Isles, which may be useful if your topic involves detailed analysis of land use in a specific area over a period of time. It may also be worthwhile keeping in touch with historians working in the same field of study because they may be able to inform you about the existence of lesser-known archive collections. You may also wish to look at the most recent edition of *Current Research in Britain*, but keep in mind that these lists of research projects are not necessarily comprehensive or always up-to-date. It can take time to track down relevant source material and so it is always worthwhile identifying the limits of your field of study at the outset. This will enable you to make constructive decisions about the relevance of specific items of source material. It is almost impossible to read or review everything which has been previously written and published on a particular subject. By setting clear limits on the extent of your research interests you will achieve a more productive outcome.

Indexing source material

One of the key tasks which you have to accomplish is to construct a working bibliography of source material. This can be done manually or by using a computer. If prepared manually, bibliographical data on each item of source material consulted should be written on separate 8″ × 5″ record cards. It is best to use the same size of card because smaller cards will be difficult to retrieve if those of different sizes are filed together. You should try to use white ruled record cards because you will find it more difficult to scan information quickly from coloured or unruled cards. It is very important that full bibliographical details are recorded for each item of source material that you consult, so that valuable time is not lost at a later stage in having to re-check data from these sources. All your references must therefore be recorded accurately and consistently. To assist in this task, a model record card can be prepared for each type, not item, of source material. These types will range from manuscripts and books, through to journal and newspaper articles. Your model cards should list the bibliographical data which must be extracted from each item of source material so that it can be entered on one side of a separate series of blank record cards. The data should ideally be recorded on the blank record cards in the same sequence as indicated in the model cards. Examples of ten types of model cards are given later in this chapter.

The blank record cards which you use to record bibliographical data on each item of source material consulted can be filed in a storage box in alphabetical or chronological order, depending on the type of source material. For example, record cards which contain bibliographical data on books or journal articles which you have consulted can be placed in alphabetical order by author (or title where there is no author), whereas it is more sensible to place those relating to official publications in chronological order, according to date of publication. If two or more record cards refer to the same author, these can be arranged in chronological order by date of publication. A–Z guide cards can be used in conjunction with your record cards to facilitate the location of cards which have been placed in alphabetical order; blank guide cards with dates entered on the tabs can be used to facilitate the location of individual record cards which have been arranged in chronological order. The identification of different *types* of source material can be assisted by using different coloured guide cards for each type. When you wish to prepare a bibliography of source material you will be able to type this directly from the information on your record cards, after a check has been made to ensure that all cards are in the correct order. Most books and theses contain a select bibliography which includes all items listed in footnotes or endnotes, plus other items which the author has found to be useful. It is not a comprehensive list of all source material consulted and so it therefore follows that those record cards which refer to items which you wish to include in your bibliography should either be marked or filed separately from all your other record cards.

The preparation of model cards for each type of source material is a very useful method for recording bibliographical data. In the following list ten different types of source material which you are most likely to use in a history project are identified. The bibliographical information which you should note for each of the ten types of source material has been identified. A model card can be prepared for each of these ten types of material: each card would therefore contain the same information as in the following lists. The advantage of this method is that the cards are portable and can be taken to any library or archive and referred to in order to know what bibliographical data should be extracted from each item of source material you consult. This data should then be entered on blank record cards or in a computer. Note that this information should be extracted from the source material itself and not copied from a library catalogue or a published bibliography as these may list incomplete or inaccurate bibliographical information. Basic bibliographical data will be needed when you prepare a list of footnotes/endnotes and bibliography or guide to further reading. Advice on the format for citing source material in a footnote or bibliography can be found in Part III of this book. The information listed under each type of source material which follows is very comprehensive. It covers all possible information for each item of source material which you consult. You may not need, or require, to include all of this information in a footnote or bibliographical entry in a book, article or thesis.

Types of source material

 1 Manuscripts and archive material
 2 Official publications
 3 Theses and dissertations
 4 Broadcasts and filmed material
 5 Interviews
 6 Books
 7 Book articles
 8 Pamphlets
 9 Journal articles
10 Newspaper articles

1 Manuscripts and archive material

- author(s)
- title of document (within single quotation marks, except for descriptive titles, such as minutes, papers, reports, memos)

- date of document
- page, folio, paragraph number(s)
- title of archive collection
- title of file
- archive or repository; shelf mark or file number

2 Official publications

(a) Parliamentary debates:
  - Commons or Lords (prior to 1909, Commons and Lords debates were bound in the same series of volumes)
  - volume number and session
  - series (optional, if year is given)
  - column number(s)
  - date of debate

(b) Parliamentary papers:
  - Commons or Lords papers
  - title (underlined)
  - volume number and session
  - serial number
  - date of publication
  - page number(s)

(c) Command papers:
  - title (underlined)
  - volume number and session
  - Command number
  - date of publication
  - page or paragraph number(s)

(d) Journals:
  - Commons or Lords
  - volume number
  - page number(s)
  - date

(e) Bills:
  - title (not underlined)
  - Commons or Lords
  - session

- serial number
- clause(s)

(f) Acts (Public General, or Local):
  - title (not underlined)
  - Regnal year (pre-1963) or calendar year (1963–)
  - chapter number (of parliamentary session)
  - part/section/subsection/paragraph/sub-paragraph
  - schedules (give part and/or paragraph number)

(g) Statutory Instruments:
  - title (not underlined)
  - year
  - number
  - page number(s) (or article, rule, or regulation)

Make a note of the library and shelf marks for all official publications you consult. For non-parliamentary papers, give the originating department, the title of the publication, date of publication, and page or paragraph numbers.

3 Theses and dissertations

- author
- title (within single quotation marks)
- degree
- university
- date
- chapter/page number(s)
- library; shelf mark

4 Broadcasts and filmed material

- title of programme (series title) (underlined)
- title of programme within a series (give number and title of episode) (underlined)
- title of film (underlined)
- broadcasting network or film company
- director or producer (for films)
- type of programme or film (optional)

- date of broadcast/year of film release
- location of material; shelf mark

5 *Interviews*

- interviewee
- occupation and designation of interviewee
- contact address
- place of interview (town or city)
- date of interview

6 *Books*

- author(s)
- title (and subtitle) of book (underlined)
- editor(s)
- compiler, reviser, translator
- title and number of series (title of series is not underlined if the title of the book is underlined)
- author of preface, foreword or introduction (optional)
- edition (if other than the first edition)
- number of volumes (for multivolume works)
- place of publication
- publisher
- date of publication
- reprint edition (give place of publication, publisher and date of publication if these differ from the original edition)
- volume number (give title and date of publication if different from other volumes; the title should be underlined)
- chapter/page number(s)
- library; shelf mark

7 *Book articles*

- author(s)
- title of article (within single quotation marks)
- editor(s)
- title of book (underlined)

- title and number of series (title not underlined if title of book is underlined)
- edition (if other than the first edition)
- number of volumes (for multivolume works)
- place of publication
- publisher
- date of publication
- volume number (with title and date of publication if different from other volumes; the title should be underlined)
- page number(s)
- library; shelf mark

8 Pamphlets

- author(s)
- title of pamphlet (underlined)
- place of publication
- publisher
- date of publication
- chapter/page number(s)
- library; shelf mark

9 Journal articles

- author(s)
- title of article (within single quotation marks)
- title of journal (underlined)
- volume number; issue number
- date of publication
- page number(s)
- library; shelf mark

10 Newspaper articles

- author(s)
- title of article (within single quotation marks)
- title of newspaper (underlined)
- place of publication (optional)

- date of publication
- page number(s)
- library; shelf mark

After locating and indexing your source material, the following chapter gives advice on the various considerations you may wish to take into account in the process of evaluating your source material.

8

Evaluating source material

The task of locating and indexing source material will be followed by the equally important task of evaluating the merits of this material. All historians need to adopt a flexible method for assessing the quality and reliability of source material. The value of any source may depend upon a number of factors, such as the elapse of time between an event and its recollection, its purpose and intended audience, physical proximity to the events observed, as well as the perspective and powers of observation of the observer. A variety of sources may have to be examined and compared to obtain a satisfactory assessment of historical events. There may be gaps in the evidence and you may be unable to confirm all the relevant facts. Although some historians are insufficiently critical of sources they trust, many tend to be too critical. Outright deception and falsification of documents may not be as widespread as commonly supposed. A careful and critical assessment of the evidence available to you from various sources should assist in providing a more coherent, accurate and comprehensive account of past events.

The authenticity and credibility of historical evidence can be an important consideration for many research projects. You may have to decide whether the content of a document, the author's signature or the date are accurate. It is reasonable to suppose that the contents of a document with a forged signature are also likely to be falsified. The content may not appear credible because the sequence of events is not in a proper chronological order. Information may also be at variance with factual evidence which you have been able to establish from other sources. The language, grammar, spelling, literary style, handwriting, typeface, type of ink or paper, or factual inaccuracies may all persuade you that source material may not be genuine. The location of a document, the envelope in which it was sent, or the circumstances in which it was discovered may also appear dubious. Evidence intended for a wide audience is probably more suspect than that intended for a restricted audience because unpleasant facts might have been concealed. We may also note that incorrect facts and interpretations may be mistakenly accepted because they appear to be consistent with existing knowledge, or because they are somehow inconvenient to believe. Problems can also arise if you discover that source material is missing, inconsistent or out of sequence. Moreover, particular care must be taken when examining statistical data, especially as this type of data can not only offer clarity and precision to ill-defined statements but can also mask individual errors within statistical averages. In any case, the use of statistical analysis to determine the probability of the occurrence of past events is problematical because in human affairs the chances that a sequence of events led to a given outcome is not as evenly balanced as throwing dice, where the probabilities can be calculated. When historians examine evidence they may be able to detect discrepancies between what is written and what is publicly known, but we should not be surprised if the occasional unusual, unexpected or coincidental event is in fact true. The information which follows will focus on the evaluation of primary and secondary source material, with particular emphasis on documentary and oral evidence because these form the basis of original historical research.

Primary sources: documents

One of the key categories of primary source material is documentary evidence. Few documents are important in their entirety, but they are a significant class of source material for historians. Some historical accounts are inevitably selective, since not all written records of past events are available. The reconstruction of past events needs to be based on an intelligent selection and interpretation of the best evidence which is available. An original contribution to a subject can be made by selecting relevant source material and providing a convincing analysis of the contents of this material. The quality of the data is more important than the type of source used, since even primary sources are likely to contain inaccurate or irrelevant information. Your historical work will contain both descriptive and analytical elements. You may pose new questions about old issues, or ask obvious questions about new themes and issues. What factors therefore should you bear in mind when examining documentary evidence?

Documents vary in their purpose, their reliability and in the type of recipient they were intended to be seen by. In general, the reliability of a document may be regarded as inversely proportional to the time lapse between event and recollection. The potential usefulness of documents which you know have been prepared near to the events they describe should not be overlooked. Also, some people were more inclined than others to write letters and keep diaries. This is a factor which you must keep in mind when reviewing the range of documentary evidence which is available. The principal points to observe when examining documents are as follows:

- consider whether documents were intended purely as a factual record of events
- observe whether documents were intended to be seen by the public or a much more restricted audience
- determine whether the documents were expected to remain confidential
- decide whether the author of a document was an expert in relation to the issues or topics discussed

You may also wish to look at literary style and grammatical errors, as well as checking to see whether confidential reports were written after the events which they describe in order to create a favourable impression. If your research work involves extensive use of personal letters, the main points which you may wish to ascertain are noted as follows:

- decide whether the letters are spontaneous, credible and likely to be truthful
- consider whether they were intended to exert influence and create a favourable impression

- determine the number of individuals who were expected to read the letters
- observe whether politeness was being used to cover up any disagreements

With all documentary evidence it is important to determine whether the material has been polished for style and precision, or perhaps to suppress conflict, indecision or confusion. Information obtained from pamphlets, speeches, essays, editorials, letters to editors of newspapers and so on, may be indicators of opinion (individual or collective), but their reliability does depend upon the competence of their authors as witnesses. It also depends upon the degree of sincerity which is expressed in the opinions emanating from these sources. The same criteria apply to unpublished documents. Your task is to review documentary evidence, take account of its credibility, reconcile conflicting evidence, draw conclusions and then discuss the implications of these conclusions. Several similar expressions of opinion on a subject do not necessarily establish anything as a fact; they merely make it more plausible. No two individuals are likely to view the same event in similar terms, not least because their impressions, attitudes, emotions and opinions are, by nature, individual.

Historians sometimes do have to be careful and avoid making dubious inferences from the content of documentary evidence to the beliefs and motives of the authors of these documents. You may find it difficult to read a document without consciously seeking to determine whether it was intended to manipulate its intended audience or merely used as a means of self-expression. You need to be aware not to make assumptions too readily about the perceptions and motives of individuals where these are not documented. Ideas and values do change over time, so you may have to take account of the historical and cultural climate which existed when these ideas were captured on paper. In particular, three obvious problems arise when the written record covers more recent historical events: the best sources are seldom available until long after the period they cover; impartiality can be difficult to achieve when describing and analysing more recent events; and the correct perspective might only be grasped by viewing events from a sufficient distance in time. There are unavoidable weaknesses where you investigate historical subjects of con-temporary interest, to the extent that these studies may have to rely too extensively on secondary sources. Indeed, the primary sources may be unavailable because of the desire to suppress embarrassing and confidential information.

A summary of the key factors which you should take into account when examining documentary evidence are noted as follows:

1 The type and the origin of the document which is available.
2 Who the author is, and what is known about the author.
3 The purpose of the document.
4 When the document was written.
5 Whether the document was written at some physical or temporal distance from the events it describes.
6 Whether the writer was willing, and able, to tell the truth.
7 The presence of factual errors in the source.
8 Whether the document makes sense, to the extent that information may have been omitted, distorted or appear contradictory. It may be possible for you to verify the contents from another source.
9 Consider whether there are several versions of the document and, if so, why. Evaluate how the document compares with other documents written by the same author.
10 Look for inconsistencies of style, spelling, grammar, dates, handwriting, ink, typeface or type of paper used. Check whether the material has been altered or if anything of substance is missing from the contents.
11 Consider the importance of the intended recipient of the document. You may wish to ascertain the number of people to whom the document was intended to be circulated: the content of documents intended for wider circulation may be highly polished.
12 If your documentary evidence is a diary, letter or document, it may be helpful to find out whether it was kept for personal use or intended to be seen by a wider public.
13 Consider the degree of involvement of the author with the events described in the documentary evidence.
14 Check if the author was seeking any personal advantage in preparing the document, such as an attempt to cover up mistakes.
15 Look at whether literary style was used to obscure the truth, or perhaps de-emphasise conflict or indecision.

16 Evaluate whether facts appear to run counter to the author's expectations, and if this is mentioned in the document. You may consider that it is unlikely that individuals will distort the truth in a manner which is unfavourable to themselves. Moreover, matters of common knowledge are also less likely to be distorted.

Primary sources: oral evidence

The gathering of source material for a history project need not be confined solely to that derived from documentary sources. Interviews with individuals who were closely involved in a subject of recent historical interest can provide valuable insights. The exploration of human memories and emotions may be used to gain knowledge of issues not covered in documentary evidence, or perhaps confirm matters already known through an examination of this evidence. In general, individuals are normally willing to provide information on events in which they have had some involvement. Some people enjoy taking part in interviews, whereas others may regard it as an opportunity to clarify issues and set the record straight. Interviews also offer historians the advantage of gaining access to a famous source who may add considerable value to the research work.

Oral testimony cannot provide a meaningful account of the past until you have subjected it to critical analysis. A central issue here is whether your interviewee is in fact telling the truth. Interviewees may deliberately distort their recollection of events to make them consistent with their own preconceived ideas, motives, attitudes and values. These may shift over time, hence you must correlate oral testimony with knowledge derived from other source material. Information derived from an interview may differ from that provided for public consumption: what is concealed is often more important than what is revealed. Individuals naturally wish to appear truthful, intelligent and in command of a situation, even if evidence obtained from other sources seems to cast some doubt on these qualities. You must therefore be prepared to challenge contradictory statements. Interviewees may seek to emphasise actions or attitudes which they believe you appear to support, or they may mask actions and attitudes which they believe you may disapprove of.

You will need to be acquainted with the techniques used in oral history research if you anticipate making extensive use of oral testimony. For example, care has to be taken in the selection and wording of questions, their sequence and manner of delivery, and in the use of probes to elicit more information. Each question sets a frame of reference for succeeding questions, and the answer to later questions can be influenced by points mentioned in response to earlier questions. So your questions may have to be asked from different angles to obtain a consistent and rounded response. A knowledge of the inferences which can often be made from vocal intonation and non-verbal clues, such as facial expression and bodily gestures, can be useful. Likewise, an awareness of instances when a question may have been misunderstood, or where replies appear contradictory, qualified or perhaps irrelevant, are factors which you have to consider. If the interview turns out to be successful, then your interviewee may be persuaded to provide you with additional material, such as letters, diaries and photographs. Few historians place sufficient emphasis on the need to collect and store oral history material. Perhaps the preservation of oral archives needs to be given as much priority as the preservation of written archives. Only then will historians be less inhibited in making use of recorded interviews and in citing oral sources in their footnotes.

Some history projects might be based on an examination of oral traditions. In pre-literate societies, knowledge about skills and rituals was passed in stories from one generation to the next by word of mouth. However, the examination of oral traditions may only have a limited role to play in historical research. Information which has been passed on by word of mouth is liable to be distorted to a greater or lesser degree: events may be misremembered, taken out of context or erroneously associated with unrelated episodes. An examination of oral tradition is most likely to be an integral element of studies which are restricted to covering isolated communities, particularly those where the written or printed word does not feature prominently in their cultural life. The study of oral tradition needs to be approached very cautiously by historians because it may be difficult, if not impossible, to determine the extent to which narrative has been modified to suit contemporary purposes. It is also important to recognise that oral evidence may provide information about societies whose history has never been written. In some instances this evidence may be the most important and fruitful source of information available to make sense of the life and culture of some isolated social groups. The precise chronology of events is, however, an aspect which is difficult to ascertain by relying primarily on evidence derived from oral traditions. Moreover, individual events are likely to be exaggerated at the expense of long-term developments. The positive features of the past assume a legendary quality and tend to be elevated at the expense of the negative features of the present. The past then becomes idealised and divorced from reality and really only significant to the extent that it influences the behaviour of current social groups, tribes or societies. Most history projects which make use of oral sources can be classified as oral history because they do not, as just mentioned, involve an examination of oral traditions.

If you decide to start work on a research project which will be partly or fully based on oral sources, you should begin by preparing a list of individuals you wish to contact. Send a polite and concise letter to them explaining the nature of your research and ask if they will agree to give you an interview at a time and place which is convenient to them. If possible, use a letter of accreditation on official notepaper from your place of study or employment, and do not forget to enclose a stamped addressed envelope for their reply. Your letter should also provide details of your background and interest in the topic, indicate what information is requested and state why this information is needed. The same advice applies if you contact anyone by telephone to request an interview. Your interviewees should be encouraged to participate, not put under any duress or sense of obligation to do so. Inform your interviewee how the information will be used, give an assurance that it will be properly cited, indicate that some material may be edited and state whether recorded tapes will be deposited in an archive. Try to plan your interviews so that several sources can be contacted on each visit, thereby saving valuable research time. You will also have to research the background of your interviewees in order to use perceptive questions and conduct informative and purposeful interviews. As a matter of courtesy, a letter of thanks should normally be sent to anyone who has participated in an interview. Recorded interviews are preferable and these offer some advantages, not least because they appear less intrusive than the appearance of an interviewer hastily writing notes as well as asking questions. A recorded interview will not provide information on facial expressions or other bodily gestures, which in themselves can be revealing, but it will minimise any disturbance to the flow of information and the interaction between interviewer and interviewee. There is, in any case, a limit to the amount of information which can be written during an interview, and there will be problems in remembering precisely the content and tone of what was said. These problems will not occur if your interview is recorded.

Interviews should be recorded using a portable battery-powered cassette or reel-to-reel tape recorder. The Sony Professional Walkman can be recommended because it is compact and provides all the facilities you will need to make good quality recordings. Whatever tape recorder is used, it is helpful if you choose one which incorporates the following features:

- Tape selector: to permit optimum recording with different types of tapes, such as ferric, chrome or metal.
- Tape counter: useful in conjunction with a reset button to index the content of your tapes.
- Dolby noise reduction selector: offering B-type and, if possible, C-type noise reduction. C-type reduces tape noise twice as effectively as the conventional B-type system.
- Review function: during recording this can be useful for listening to material just recorded. Pressing the rewind/review button permits instant change from recording to playback mode.
- Edit function: during playback this can be useful for correcting a previous recording. Pressing the record button permits instant change from playback to recording mode.
- Cue and review functions: during playback this can be useful for moving the tape forwards or backwards. Playback resumes automatically when the forward/cue or rewind/review buttons are released.
- Pause button: to pause the tape during playback or recording mode.
- Peak level indicator: to monitor input level during recording or the recorded level during playback.
- Battery indicator: to enable you to check battery condition.
- Microphone attenuator: to enable you to record a large input signal (perhaps in an outdoor location) without overloading the amplifier

and causing distortion. The Walkman Professional can attenuate the signal by 20dB.

- Automatic shut-off: to stop recorder functions automatically at the end of a tape in either playback or recording mode. Locked buttons should return to their original position automatically.
- Power sources: it can be helpful if your tape recorder can operate from different sources, such as batteries, mains current, rechargeable battery pack or 12-volt car battery.

Your recording tapes need to be labelled, indexed and properly stored, preferably away from any heat source. You should note details about the interviewees and the date and place of each recording. The tapes should be transcribed before being used in your research project. Oral material may be paraphrased or quoted, and notes should be made about the tone and delivery of speech if you believe this impinges on the content of an interview.

Recorded material may be deposited in an archive upon completion of your project, although you will have to obtain copyright clearance from your interviewees. Any details about restriction of use of recorded material should be made in writing and retained for reference purposes. Remember that although you own the copyright of any recording, copyright in the spoken words belongs to your interviewees. Try to ensure that you fully explain to your interviewees the purpose of your research, how information will be used and how your results will be disseminated. If any interview is not recorded then only brief details should be written during the interview. This information can be expanded immediately after the interview by recording your thoughts on tape or paper before your memory fades of precisely what was said: as the proverb states, the palest ink is better than the most retentive memory. During your interviews, try to get interviewees to talk freely and fully. You should ideally aim for an informal conversational style, rather than one where a large number of questions are asked rapidly, as might occur with someone responding to a questionnaire. You may find that some individuals are somewhat defensive during a first interview, so you should be cautious in probing for more information. Evidence gained through interviews is not infallible: individuals may not be consistent in their convictions, and events may have more than one cause. Faced with conflicting evidence, you may discover that some events may appear improbable, yet nevertheless be true.

The reliability of oral evidence is, in general, inversely proportional to the elapse of time between event and recollection. But there are other factors you will wish to take into account. Individuals tend to recall in more detail those situations which were more significant to them or in which they were actively involved. If you are assessing the validity of arguments it is important not to be guided wholly by the degree of conviction with which beliefs are held. Agreement among several interviewees may not necessarily establish an event as factually accurate, but it may provide compelling evidence that what is said has been accurately reported. You will probably use open questions to encourage your interviewees to talk freely on a subject, whereas close (or fixed) questions are more appropriate in situations where the alternative replies can be defined and are therefore known in advance.

Interviews will rarely be uniform. The questions which you ask should, where possible, be balanced and not unduly intrusive. It is obviously preferable to aim for genuine rapport with your interviewees because this will facilitate the free expression of opinion. You are, after all, dependent upon the information supplied by your interviewees. Sometimes it is easier to elicit information if there is some proximity in age, social class or interests between interviewer and interviewee, although this obviously cannot be arranged. If there are awkward, difficult or controversial questions, you may wish to postpone these until later in the interview when your interviewee may feel more relaxed and less defensive. You may be aware that some interviewees consciously seek to move the discussion away from difficult issues; if so, repeat or re-word the question. If it is obvious that any answers provided do appear doubtful or unclear, try to re-phrase the question or ask for clarification. Answers to your questions may be genuinely vague, rather than deliberately ambiguous. The perceptions of interviewees will be governed by their opinions, attitudes and values. They may, for reasons of expediency or vanity, modify past feelings or recollections in a selective manner to fit more comfortably into a current point of view; alternatively, they may find it impossible to recall previous events accurately.

The questions which you prepare for any interview should be arranged in a logical sequence so that each question sets the frame of reference for succeeding questions. A flow chart might assist you to plan the sequence of questions, particularly as the order in which questions are asked can influence their meaning for interviewees. In drawing up a list of appropriate questions, you may wish to keep the following general points in mind:

1 Arrange your sequence of questions in a logical order. They can be written on record cards and then re-arranged prior to each interview.
2 Define each question precisely and ensure all are relevant to the information you seek to obtain and give the intended meaning. Use a few simple familiar words devoid of jargon.
3 Do not ask too many questions, otherwise your interviewees may become bored and answer questions inaccurately or deliberately not tell the truth. Try not to interrupt your interviewees unless it is obvious that they have misunderstood your question.
4 Avoid bias or emotional language which may produce an unhelpful response. Note that tone of voice and body language (i.e. facial expression, posture or hand movements) may also indirectly influence the replies which you receive. Be relaxed, open and maintain good eye contact.
5 Avoid the use of implied alternatives. Try not to use leading questions or suggest a possible reply to them. Monitor when information is given voluntarily, and when only in response to a direct question.
6 Listen carefully and try not to anticipate what is going to be said. You may find it useful to pause occasionally to allow yourself time to think and to encourage your interviewees to talk, especially as most people feel uncomfortable with silence. Be prepared to use probing questions to obtain more information, but avoid showing undue surprise or disapproval in response to the replies you receive.
7 Make the wording of questions mutually exclusive, thus avoiding an overlap in the content of questions asked.
8 Allow for 'don't know' and 'no opinion' answers, but be prepared to probe further if the replies are too vague or incomplete. Equally, if an interviewee gives too much irrelevant detail, bring the conversation back to the original question.

 9 Be aware of the occurrence of inconsistent replies. Try to encourage replies about sensitive subjects by indicating some prior knowledge about these subjects.

10 Avoid double negatives and ambiguous words. Ensure that interviewees are aware of any fine distinctions in the wording of your questions.

11 Check the pronunciation of key words prior to interviews.

12 Distinguish between hypothetical answers you receive, and those based on past experience.

13 Avoid focusing too much on examples, since this may inadvertently divert attention from the key issues to a discussion of the examples.

14 Underline those words in your interview questions which you wish to emphasise. Equally, be aware that the tone of voice, or any hesitation by interviewees, may in itself be revealing.

15 Be careful with the use of punctuation when preparing your list of questions, because this can alter their intended meaning.

16 Note that during an interview you may need to alter or omit subsequent questions, depending upon the answers you receive to earlier questions.

17 Try to separate facts from beliefs in the replies you receive, but note that strongly held beliefs may be just as important as facts in guiding actions.

18 Try to ascertain how interviewees obtained knowledge of certain facts: through direct observation, inference or simply hearsay.

19 Take account of factors which may have influenced the ability of interviewees to give an accurate recollection of historical events they describe.

20 Adhere to progressive focusing during interviews, so do not close the discussion of any topic until it has been fully explored.

Secondary sources

Your working bibliography will also include secondary source material, such as books, pamphlets, journal articles and so on. There are a number of points you may wish to keep in mind when reviewing secondary sources. If you intend to look at a large number of published books it is generally better to begin with standard texts on a subject and then progress to a more detailed analysis of your chosen topic. The work of other historians, whether included in published books or articles, should be used as a source upon which you can draw inspiration and ideas. With any published work it is important to appreciate the reason it was produced, as well as what information it is likely to provide or omit. Make a note of any useful ideas which emerge while you are reading the secondary sources. As your work progresses, the focus of your enquiry will need to be narrowed. You will wish to refer to the most recent publications, but also show some evidence of selectivity in the material consulted. The opinions of any single author should be tested against the evidence supplied by other writers and, of course, also by the primary sources you have access to.

There are several points which should be taken into account when you wish to determine the potential use of published material in any historical research project. The number of pages in a book can be regarded as a very rough guide to its potential value, because longer books offer a more detailed treatment of a topic. The subject of a publication will also provide an indication of the level of detail provided. For example, a 500-page monograph on the origins of the Second World War will provide a more detailed treatment of its subject than a book of similar length on the history of warfare in the twentieth century. Nevertheless, do keep in mind that some shorter-length books may provide more valuable information than seems apparent if they are widely regarded as offering a classic exposition on a particular subject. In general, the potential value of publications for the purpose of historical research should be ascertained by examining the following items: foreword; preface; contents page; introduction; chapter sub-headings; first and last sentences of chapters or paragraphs; chapter summaries, if these are provided; footnotes or endnotes; conclusion; bibliography; and index. Time which you spend examining these items will prevent you from wasting time reading material which is of little direct benefit for your research purposes.

Your history project may necessitate the examination of a large number of books. If so, try to remember books by their authors rather than by their titles, since many titles sound alike. Decide which books you will have to read in detail, and those which need only be scanned for essential information. Consider whether the author is an authority on the subject covered in the publication. Bibliographical information about the author may often be found on the jacket of a book or in other specialised biographical dictionaries. Look at the date of publication to see if the work was recently published, and also check whether it is a first or a re-vised edition. It is usually better to refer to the most recent edition of a publication, unless earlier books are standard works. The latter may offer views which were regarded as orthodox at the time they were written, or perhaps give an indication of the manner in which events were spoken or written about in the past. You may also wish to look to see whether the work was published by a reputable publisher. A book with reasonably detailed footnotes and a bibliography will provide you with a more useful guide to other source material which relates to the subject matter covered in the book. However, do not rely entirely on these lists, since they merely represent the author's personal selection of further reading, rather than a comprehensive up-to-date list of what published and un-published material is available. The index entries in a publication will indicate whether a topic has been given an extended treatment or merely a brief mention. Book reviews should not be overlooked, but it is worth noting that not all reviewers can be relied upon to provide an accurate assessment of the books which they review, nor are all books guaranteed to be reviewed. Finally, where abstracts of books or journal articles are reviewed you may want to verify the details provided to ensure that they do not contain any transcription or printing errors. You will find that many journals are now available via the Internet and may be downloaded or printed.

Photocopying and the copyright of source material

Many historians make extensive use of the photocopier for copying essential source material which may then be studied in detail or used for reference purposes. Photocopying material will certainly permit you to retain a more accurate record for future use in comparison with copying information by hand. The photocopier is particularly useful for copying charts, statistical tables, maps, illustrations, important but obscure articles in books or journals, or vital unpublished documents. Access to photocopies of original documents is a more preferable option than referring to publications which merely reproduce parts of documents, especially as the latter may be taken out of context. If you do photocopy large amounts of source material you should staple the sheets together to prevent pages falling out of sequence or going astray. You should also make a note of the source from which the copies were originally taken. Your photocopies can then be filed in document wallet folders or ring binders. One distinct advantage with photocopied material is that important passages can be underlined in ink or identified using a coloured highlighter pen, and additional comments can also be written in the margins. The copies can be used to paraphrase material or provide quoted extracts for incorporation in your research project. If so, these sources should also appear in a footnote or endnote and in a bibliography. In summary, the points to consider when deciding whether to photocopy source material are as follows:

- the material should be easily accessible
- the source material is important and will be constantly referred to
- the amount you can copy from the source material under copyright law
- the amount of time saved by photocopying the source material

If these points are carefully considered then you will make a more realistic assessment about the appropriateness of photocopying source material.

You may wish to refer to the Copyright, Designs and Patents Act 1988 for full details on the amount which can be freely copied from different types of source material for private study or research. You are permitted to freely copy material only if it was last published (or written, in the case of unpublished documents) more than 70 years ago, or more than 70 years have elapsed since the author died, whichever is the later. If you have the written permission of the copyright owner you may also be able to copy material within this time limit. For the purposes of private research you are, however, permitted to make a single copy of a reasonable proportion from a book or periodical without having to seek permission from the copyright owner. In this context a reasonable proportion refers to a single chapter from a book, one article from one issue of a periodical, or up to 10 per cent from a published book. Somewhat different rules apply to the copying of official publications. These may be copied freely if at least six months has elapsed since their publication. Within this period, up to 5 per cent may be copied from parliamentary papers, such as reports and Command papers, and up to 30 per cent from Bills and Acts of Parliament. No time limit applies to the copying of material from Hansard, but copyright law does apply to the copying of material from non-parliamentary publications. Note also that copying from some academic theses may be restricted unless you obtain the author's permission. Otherwise, copying from theses will either be unrestricted or subject to the provisions of the Copyright Act. Research students are not employees of a university and so they own their own intellectual property rights. The copyright in the spoken words in a recording belongs to the interviewee. The latter may grant a written or verbal licence to a researcher to use a recording for research purposes (i.e. assign copyright to the researcher). It is therefore good practice to explain to your interviewees the purposes of your research and the uses to which information obtained will be put. An interviewee's words must not be distorted if used in any research project, even where copyright has been assigned. Refer to guidance notes provided by your university or publisher or look at the Copyright Act for further information on copyright in relation to research work.

After you have located, indexed and evaluated various types of source material, your next task is to prepare research notes which summarise the relevant points you have extracted through careful examination of the source material. The research notes will be invaluable when you are ready to prepare drafts. Advice on the preparation of these notes is the topic which is covered in the following chapter.

9

Research notes

A key element in the successful completion of a research project in history is the preparation and organisation of your research notes. It is important to prepare accurate and sufficiently detailed and organised notes which you can easily retrieve when preparing drafts. The preparation of research notes, in contrast to mere underlining of important points in a publication or manuscript, is a more active task because it forces you to think about your subject in greater detail. Indeed, it encourages you to put the essential arguments in your own words and therefore analyse your topic in much greater depth. The amount of notes you prepare will depend upon the content and usefulness of your source material. The purpose of preparing detailed notes is because you will find it easier to discard unwanted research notes when your drafts are being written, than subsequently discover that the original notes were inadequate and therefore require further research. You must be guided by the level of difficulty of your topic, your research questions and your subject knowledge in determining just how detailed these notes need to be. It may be possible to summarise information rather than prepare detailed notes. In any case, it is the appropriate use of evidence rather than its quantity which may be more important. There is little point in including irrelevant material which is unlikely to be used in your project, but this can be avoided by carefully examining the list of topics, themes and issues listed in your topic outline.

Preparation and storage of notes

It is useful to begin a discussion of research notes by making a few observations and practical comments about the methods available for recording these notes. Your notes can be written on A4 paper and filed in a ring binder or document wallet folder, they can be written on 8 × 5 inches record cards or a notebook, or they can be entered directly into a computer. The first two methods represent the most practical and flexible options for preparing research notes. A notebook can certainly be useful for jotting down ideas, but is not so practical for recording detailed notes, particularly as the pages cannot be re-arranged into subject or thematic groups as your research progresses. A computer is useful for preparing drafts, but less so for compiling research notes. It is not always practical to carry computing equipment everywhere, even with a laptop computer, so your notes should ideally be written on either A4 sheets or record cards. Some researchers do later enter their notes into a computer and assign keywords to assist in the re-arrangement and retrieval of their notes. But most historians find it easier to work with handwritten notes, thereby leaving the computer to assist in the task of preparing and revising drafts.

Some historians prefer to file their research notes in a number of ring binders or document wallet folders covering different topics or themes, whereas others prefer to enter their notes on record cards. Information which is entered on A4 paper can provide a less organised series of notes in comparison with those entered on record cards, although the latter approach does tend to generate a bulky set of notes. The use of record cards can appear bulky because ideally only one topic, theme or issue should be entered on each card. The cards will usually be assigned a keyword so that they can be easily re-arranged into various subject groups as the research proceeds. However, more detailed notes can be entered on sheets of A4 paper than can be written on record cards; and these notes can be transported more easily and securely between libraries and archives in a ring binder. They can also be transferred to other ring binders for permanent storage. Ring binders obviously offer a more secure environment than wallet folders for filing your research notes because even stapled pages may be unintentionally left out of sequence when being placed in or removed from wallet folders.

Notes on related topics can be stapled together or simply filed together in different ring binders. You may find it helpful to list main points or structure your notes so that the principal issues and themes can be easily identified. Full bibliographical details on each item of source material consulted will still have to be entered separately on record cards, even if your notes are entered on sheets of A4 paper. Your notes must be legible and their contents easy to understand. Doubtful information which you have gathered can be highlighted by placing a question mark in the margin of your notes. Unusual names or foreign phrases are best written in block capitals so that they will be readily understood when your notes are reviewed at a later date. If your notes are written on A4 paper they could be grouped into sections and numbered so that they will indicate that separate but interrelated topics are being covered. Alternatively, keywords or short phrases could be entered in red ink in the margin to enable specific topics to be quickly located and classified. The latter technique may be adopted to summarise the content of each paragraph of your notes, and could be used in conjunction with the underlining (in red ink) of important points. The purpose of these techniques is simply to enable you easily to identify and classify the content of your research notes so that they can be used effectively when you decide to prepare written drafts based on the material you have gathered.

The principal alternative to the use of A4 loose-leaf paper to write research notes is to use record cards. If your notes are to be written on record cards it is best to use white, ruled 8 × 5 inches cards. Smaller cards are impractical because they can only hold very brief notes. If you do use record cards your notes should be written on the same size of card. A separate card needs to be used for each item of source material consulted or for each topic or theme. The principal advantages in using record cards when preparing research notes are as follows: they are tough and resilient; they are easy to handle if all cards are the same size; they are compact and can be stored easily; and they are relatively easy to re-arrange and classify. To work effectively, each of your record cards should only contain one key idea, topic, theme or issue. Information should, if possible, be written on only one side of each card. Some researchers number their record cards sequentially to permit cross-references to be made to other cards and to the bibliographical record/source cards. The difficulty with this method is that all your bibliographical source cards then have to be re-arranged into alphabetical order to compile a bibliography.

In summary, the basic components of research notes, regardless of which material they are written on, can be noted as follows:

1 A descriptive heading which identifies the topic or theme which is covered in your notes.

2 The chapter (or section) number which the notes relate to. This should be possible to identify if you have prepared a detailed research topic outline. Your numbering system will enable notes which relate to the same chapter or section to be kept together. The chapter or section numbers should be placed in the top right-hand corner of each set of notes so that they can be easily identified when sorting the notes into a logical sequence in preparation for writing drafts.

3 Your notes, including any quoted extracts or paraphrased material, should be clearly distinguishable from one another. Quoted or paraphrased material within your notes can be identified by being placed within square brackets. This will enable you to avoid confusion between comments you make on the source material, with extracts quoted or paraphrased from that material.

4 The source material upon which your notes have been based. It is usually sufficient to provide minimal details of the source because full bibliographical details for each item of source material consulted should be written on a separate series of record cards. For example, if the source material is a book it should be sufficient to note the author's surname, title and relevant page numbers. You only need to provide enough information to enable the particular item of source material used in your research notes to be identified and cross-referred to the appropriate (and more detailed) bibliographical record/source card.

If you have been unable to prepare a detailed outline of your project before work begins, the subjects and themes should emerge as the research proceeds. You will discover some of them by looking at the descriptive headings or titles allocated to your research notes. This emphasises the importance of properly classifying your notes by topic or theme as the work proceeds. Even where a detailed project outline has been prepared, you may find that your notes provide ideas about new topics and themes which had not been thought about when the project was originally planned.

Content and use of research notes

With the completion of a small amount of work each day your project will soon begin to take shape. The interrelationship between various issues will become apparent as the work progresses. It may inevitably take some time to gain a good grasp of your subject and the associated research methodology. But even where progress appears slow it can be assisted if you give careful attention to several factors: select only relevant information from your source material; summarise ideas, but ensure that your notes are neither too concise nor too lengthy; and organise and label your notes so that it is easy to locate and retrieve information from different sources. Your notes should attempt to provide an objective account of what has been found in the source material. The relevance and relative importance of various items of information for your history project may alter over time. Sometimes significant patterns in the nature of the work will only emerge when the research is sufficiently well advanced. No general rule applies here because each research project generates its own individual characteristics, possibilities and practical difficulties.

Your research notes will need to distinguish factual information from analysis and commentary supplied by you or by the author of the source material which you consult. If this separation does not take place when your notes are prepared, it may be impossible to distinguish facts from commentary when your notes are read weeks later. Moreover, your notes should not contain emotional language, slang, clichés, jargon, colloquial expressions or too many abbreviations. Do abbreviate words where possible to save time and space, but try to ensure that your notes will still be comprehensible if reviewed some time later. Quoted extracts need to be copied verbatim, not abbreviated. Material can also be paraphrased, although some care needs to be taken not to misinterpret the meaning supplied by the author of the source material. The art of paraphrasing material is a skill that should be developed because it represents a step on the road to preparing a first draft. Indeed, it forces you to make the effort to understand fully the source material; without such an understanding, no source material can be properly paraphrased. The amount of material you choose to paraphrase in your notes will, to some extent, depend upon the importance and usefulness of the sources you consult. Finally, important ideas which emerge from your research can be easily high-lighted within your notes if they are indented, numbered, underlined and assigned a short title.

Quotations and references

This section on the preparation of research notes concludes with some useful advice on how quoted extracts and paraphrased material can be incorporated in your notes. Quotations and paraphrased material must be easily identified, and this can be achieved by adhering to the follow-ing advice. Place this type of material within square brackets to separate it from your own comments on the source material; give a precise refer-ence; and use single quotation marks where a passage has been quoted from source material. The following two examples illustrate how extracts which have been quoted and also paraphrased would appear in the research notes. The material in both examples is based on G.R. Elton's book *The Practice of History*.

Example 1: a quoted extract occurring within research notes
Historians can never succeed in knowing the past in its entirety. There are also variations in the quality of historical writing, although most historians believe that they are capable of reproducing the truth. ['There is no final end to the study of history; the true and complete past can never be described because not enough of it survives and because what survives must be interpreted by human minds. All problems except the simplest, and sometimes so simple a point as a date or place, continue to be open to argument and doubt.' (p. 123)] So perhaps it is useful to study the historian if we wish to understand the past. Yet the reality of the past still exists independently of any observer; and it is this reality that historians seek to capture and faithfully reproduce through the techniques of historical scholarship.

Example 2: a paraphrased passage occurring within research notes
The study of history covers all aspects of human behaviour. But perhaps some reservations are required here. [The past in its entirety is not recoverable, so the study of history is, in effect, confined to a study of the traces of the past which do survive into the present. (p. 20)] Historians therefore cannot ask questions

about aspects of the past for which no material evidence exists. What they do is try and reconstruct the past if, and only if, the past has left sufficient traces for such a reconstruction to take place. This will, of course, limit the range of historical enquiry.

Note that a quoted extract can be converted into a paraphrased passage by simply paraphrasing the words used in a quotation. However, it is not possible to convert a paraphrased passage into a quoted extract unless you return to the original source material, locate the relevant passage, and quote the material word for word. This is a factor worth keeping in mind when you decide to incorporate quotations and paraphrased material in written drafts. The final example which follows illustrates a method for dealing with a quotation which extends over two pages in the original source. When copying such a quotation it is very useful to indicate where the page break occurs. This can be achieved by inserting two oblique lines or also including page numbers on either side of these lines. The following example refers to a quotation taken from E.H. Carr's *What is History?* which extends from the bottom of page 29 to the top of page 30.

Example 3: a quoted extract which extends over two pages
['The historian starts with a provisional selection of facts, and a provisional interpretation in the light of which that selection has been made – by others as well as by himself. As he works, 29//30 both the interpretation and the selection and ordering of facts undergo subtle and perhaps partly unconscious changes, through the reciprocal action of one or the other.' (pp. 29–30)]

This method is particularly useful if only part of a quotation is subsequently used in a written draft. The indication of the page break saves time, since it avoids the necessity of having to re-check the original quotation to ascertain exactly where the page break occurred.

Having looked at the preparation, format and content of research notes, attention will be focused in the following chapter on how these notes can be used in the preparation of drafts. It will also consider the different options for organising your material for a history project, the use of quotations and the purpose and format of footnotes, as well as the revision of drafts.

10

The preparation of drafts

The preparation of a first draft is often regarded by many writers as a rather daunting prospect. Most of your source material will have been located, indexed and evaluated by this stage. Your research notes will also have been compiled. The crucial task of preparing a first draft now has to be tackled. The preparation of a first draft is often more difficult than the process of revising it and producing later drafts. But it is important not to delay the writing of this draft until either all your source material has been reviewed or all your research notes have been written. The main benefit of preparing a first draft at an early stage is that the interconnections between various aspects of a topic, or gaps in the subjects or themes covered, may not be apparent until your writing begins. Some historical projects require a lengthy period during which source material is reviewed and research notes are prepared, but it would be wrong to suppose that the stage of writing drafts only begins when these tasks have been completed. The original and creative element of your work can only be accomplished by the art of writing, not by thinking about writing.

The first draft

A first draft allows you an opportunity to experiment in marshalling factual data and supporting arguments. The material which you eventually include in a first draft will be selected from a much larger volume of research notes. The quality of the first draft will depend, to some extent, on the quality of these notes. A flexible timetable therefore needs to be devised for the completion of drafts of the various chapters or sections. You may find that the writing of a draft often leads to the emergence of new ideas and new lines of enquiry. It is wise to be alert to these ideas at an early stage, rather than postpone writing until all your material has been gathered and assimilated. To assist the preparation of a first draft and to help maintain momentum, you may find it useful to set completion dates for each chapter. Begin writing early in the day and aim to complete a specified number of pages or words each day. Your first draft should ideally be written quickly and on a regular basis, so that perhaps a section of each chapter is completed every day.

The initial draft may be written or entered into a computer and edited on screen. If your draft is written then it is better to write only one paragraph on each page, because this makes it much easier to revise the work and alter the sequence of paragraphs. You may also find it beneficial to break off at a point in your work where it is relatively easy to restart writing. Your draft pages should have wide margins and use double spacing, whether written or typed, so that additional material and corrections can be incorporated when the material is revised. Try to avoid interrupting the flow of words in a first draft merely to confirm a fact, spelling, quotation or reference. It is much better not to edit your material or improve the style while preparing the draft. You may discover when writing commences that new ideas and thoughts will come to mind and thereby make subsequent sentences that much easier to write. Your aim throughout the preparation of a first draft should be to develop rapid mental association, whereby links are established between different ideas and concepts. The primary objective of a first draft is to establish the descriptive element and the essential structure of the argument, because supporting evidence can be added later and then revised.

Clear stretches of time should be allocated for the uninterrupted writing of drafts. In theory, it should be possible for you to write fluently and creatively in the knowledge that this first draft can be amended at a later stage. Your first draft should not be excessively long, although all first drafts will understandably be longer than a final draft. Begin by writing the easiest sections first: your drafts need not be written in the order in which they will appear in the final version. The easiest sections may be those in which you have gathered most information. Not all of your research notes will be useful when the time comes to prepare the first draft, but these notes are not wasted because they could be used for writing articles or form the basis of another book on a related subject.

Organising the content of drafts

Your written material should be organised so that it forms natural subject groups which provide the basis for the construction of individual chapters. Two of the most important methods for organising material in a thesis, book or article can be referred to as the chronological and the thematic approaches. The chronological approach traces the development of historical events in a chronological sequence. It is based on the assumption that we can explain historical events if we understand their causes, and this in turn means focusing attention on chronology. However, the chronological approach can be arbitrary and unduly simplistic, to the extent that it combines insignificant with important events without any clear system of subordination. Also, it inevitably tends to combine events that occur only once (with direct consequences), with those which operate continually and are perhaps of more long-term significance, the so-called background causes. In history, the causes of events cannot always be determined by examining their chronological development. The chief drawback of the chronological approach is that it prevents historians from tracing the development of individual issues and topics which exhibit any degree of complexity, or from dealing adequately with events which occur simultaneously.

In contrast to the chronological approach, the thematic approach traces one event at a time, and gives precedence to the thematic structure over any chronological sequence. It is possible to divide a subject into sub-periods arranged chronologically, and then write about different themes within these sub-periods. However, the thematic approach also has its limitations, because it leads to the repetition of events over the same time span in order to cover different topics and issues which fall within the same chronology. The thematic approach gives the impression of a snapshot of a particular historical period, in effect a static account devoid of the appreciation of movement through time. It is an approach which is not really suitable for studies which extend over a long period of time. Moreover, not all historical periods can be characterised by the presence of a single dominant theme: history is not as predictable, nor can it be as neatly labelled as most historians would suppose, or would like it to be. The thematic approach can tempt historians to choose themes which may not be wholly appropriate. Whatever approach is chosen, chronological or thematic, it must be dictated by the subject matter.

Perhaps the best approach to this dilemma is to combine the chronological with the thematic arrangement. Looked at from this perspective, the chronology moves your narrative and analysis forward relatively smoothly within and between each chapter, while also embracing each topic or theme and giving an occasional backward or forward glance as required. Good historical writing should look at long-term background causes, as well as the more immediate causes of historical events, rather than focus on one to the exclusion of the other. This will enable you to see both the patterns and the detail of historical events.

If your chapters are subdivided into sections, then each section could cover a distinct topic, or at least one aspect of a topic. Transitional devices can be used to move the story forward from one chapter to the next. Your chapters should be approximately equal in length, as well as importance, in relation to the subject as a whole. The presence of too many chapters will make your work lose some coherence by introducing too many breaks; conversely, if there are too few chapters this will prevent the introduction of suitable breaks in the text. The number and length of chapters will probably be determined by the nature and treatment of your subject. Some chapters will move the chronology on much further than others, whereas other chapters will be more descriptive by consolidating existing knowledge or preparing your readers for the discussion of subsequent events. You may wish to introduce topics at the end of each chapter so that they can be related to succeeding chapters. Alternatively, a new chapter may begin the discussion of a new subject or perhaps refer back to an earlier chapter. Both methods can be used to enable you to vary the style and pace of the narrative. Any gaps in subject coverage or an overlap of topics needs to be avoided between chapters. It also makes sense to recognise the important role of your first chapter or paragraph:

its style and content may determine whether your readers are persuaded to read on and explore the rest of the chapter, thesis, book or article.

In addition to the chronological and thematic approaches discussed here, there are a few other methods for organising research material in a draft. Firstly, you may wish to note the contrast between deductive and inductive reasoning. Deductive reasoning proceeds from the general to the particular, so that particular facts or conclusions are deduced from a generalisation. In contrast to this, inductive reasoning proceeds from the particular to the general, so that generalisations are made which are based on specific historical facts. Another contrast is that between the whole-to-part and part-to-whole ordering of material. In the former, a complete subject is examined by considering its individual elements, issues or topics; in the latter, the discussion moves from the separate topics to a consideration of the whole subject. In historical work it may be more desirable to move from familiar to unfamiliar material, from simple ideas to a more complex subject. The approach which you adopt can be influenced by your own preferences and the nature of the subject which you investigate. Topics can also be arranged in increasing or decreasing order of importance. They may also be arranged spatially, a method which is particularly useful for providing a description of an organisation, or of historical events which are geographically separated.

The organisation of the content of your project has to be accompanied by the organisation of your research material or notes. Before writing a first draft, arrange your research notes in the subject order which corresponds with the sequence of topics you aim to cover in the project. Try to think of your work as an assembly of parts, composed of individual paragraphs. Begin by writing paragraphs, which should cover only one topic or a small number of closely related topics. These should link in with the sequence of topics covered in your project outline, which was discussed in chapter 6. Your paragraphs need not be as rigidly structured as chapters or parts, but it is much better if they cover only one topic because you will find it easier to edit and re-arrange them. If your work is entered directly into a computer, then page numbers can be altered if new pages are added or deleted during the preparation of a draft. But if your first draft is handwritten, new pages will have to be identified differently: for example, three pages inserted between pages 2 and 3 should be labelled 2a, 2b and 2c respectively. In practice, this re-numbering will not be necessary if you subdivide each chapter or section into a number of paragraphs which are composed separately, since no paragraph will extend over one or two pages. You only need to identify the topic covered in each paragraph and ensure that the drafts of each paragraph are arranged in a logical sequence corresponding with your project outline. If you have developed a logical and coherent structure for the project outline, this will be reflected in the arrangement of the paragraphs, and consequently in the content of each chapter.

Begin each paragraph with a short topic sentence to introduce the theme of the paragraph. Short sentences are effective in introducing a new topic, emphasising each step in an argument, or concluding a discussion; longer sentences are more useful for developing a point. Each paragraph should expand upon the principal idea outlined in your topic sentence. These sentences are important in capturing the interest and imagination of your readers. They do not always have to be placed at the start of a new paragraph and can be placed at the end to summarise the content of preceding sentences. Try to incorporate a mixture of short and long sentences and vary the length of each paragraph. Long sentences can be broken up using colons, semi-colons and dashes. Excessively long paragraphs may also have to be subdivided, otherwise your readers will lose the thread of your argument. You may also wish to avoid the frequent use of brackets within sentences and only underline words which are to be printed in italic. Unusual or technical terms can, of course, be placed within single quotation marks rather than italicised. Double spacing, not double-double spacing, should be left between paragraphs. Be prepared to support your statements and opinions with evidence, examples, quotations or illustrations: evidence needs to be discussed, not merely presented. Although you will have to provide sufficient information to give a full explanation of the historical events which you describe, it is best not to use so many words that your meaning becomes obscured. Finally, a point worth reiterating is that the amount of space you allocate to each topic should not be based solely on the volume of research notes and source material which you accumulate. If you do, you may focus greater attention on concrete items of relatively minor importance at the expense of intangible items of much greater importance.

Using quotations

All historical work will incorporate material which has been directly quoted from another source. Historians use quotations where it is important to capture the precise language used in the original source. However, a quotation will still not be effective unless sufficient information is provided to enable readers to place the quotation within its appropriate context. Quoting material is used for illustrative purposes, whereas citing this material in a footnote or endnote is used to enable others to verify the source and the context in which the original quoted extract appeared. A source footnote enables readers to assess the validity and accuracy of an assertion. You may notice that quotations will illustrate a point, but will rarely prove it. Moreover, some sources undoubtedly have greater authority than others. You may wish to use the precise words of another author if they provide supporting evidence for a particular argument. A quoted extract may also be used if you believe that a statement made by another author is of fundamental importance, or if the author's mode of expression appears significant in relation to the argument you are developing. Quotations should be used sparingly and extracts should not be longer than necessary to illustrate a given point. Equally, very short quotations need to be treated carefully to prevent those extracts from being taken out of context. Your purpose in using a quotation may differ from that of the author of the extract because you will be selecting material to emphasise or support a particular argument. A quotation must focus precisely on the point which is being made. You may decide to use merged quotations to save space and a certain amount of repetition; several quoted extracts can be merged into your own sentence.

When you are preparing drafts you should be aware that there is no requirement to substantiate every assertion with a quotation. However, when you do quote material, the wording, spelling, capitalisation and punctuation in the original source should be copied precisely. It is not worthwhile restating a quotation in your own words, since this wastes space and irritates the reader. A quoted extract by an author who has made a succinct and classic statement which could not have been put more concisely without losing accuracy will not have to be restated: its meaning should be self-evident to your readers. A quotation may consist of a few words, a phrase, a sentence or a short paragraph. If the quotation is longer than about five lines (or sixty words) of text, it should be treated as a block or displayed quotation and indented. Block quotations do not require opening or closing quotation marks. However, it is best to avoid the frequent use of long quotations because they are liable to distract the attention of the reader from the kernel of your argument. Any important long quotations could, if necessary, be included in an appendix. An additional reason for not including too many long quotations is that their inclusion may, rightly or wrongly, give the reader the impression that you are uncertain about the strength of your arguments and therefore feel obliged to rely too much on the arguments of others.

The format for quoted extracts is just as important as your reasons for quoting material. The first letter of a quotation can be lower case, even if it is capitalised in the original. The first letter can also be capitalised if it is introduced by a colon. Single quotation marks should be used for quoting smaller extracts, with double quotation marks for a quotation within a quotation. As already noted, block quotations should be used if you wish to quote longer extracts. The latter are introduced with a colon and quotation marks are omitted. An exception occurs where quotations occur within a block quotation, in which case single quotation marks are used. Short quotations can be incorporated into your own sentence without the need for any introductory punctuation (such as a colon or ellipsis points) because it is clear that the quotation represents only part of a longer sentence. Square brackets are normally used to insert your own comments within a quotation to distinguish them from parenthetical statements which appear in the original quotation. You should underline or italicise words within a quotation which you wish to emphasise. The latter quotation will therefore have to be followed by the words 'italics mine' in round brackets (if placed after a quotation) or within square brackets (if placed within a quotation). To omit irrelevant material, use ellipsis points, thus . . . or [. . .], rather than use a single line of dots. Errors which you discover within quoted extracts should be followed by [*sic*]. You may wish to note that ellipsis points can be used at the beginning or end of a quotation to adjust it to the grammar of your sentence or to omit less relevant material. Remember to use four dots, not three, if you omit material at the end of a sentence, because a sentence would close with a full stop anyway. Source material can also be paraphrased rather than quoted. A paraphrase should be used in circumstances where the content or the underlying ideas are regarded as important, but where the language or mode of expression is not so important.

Using footnotes

Material which you quote or paraphrase will have to be cited in footnotes (or endnotes, if placed at the end of a chapter, book, thesis or article). Footnotes are most often used to cite sources rather than provide additional material not included in the text. They are not needed for passing phrases or anonymous remarks, and it is better not to use them to include remarks which you can easily incorporate in the text or in an appendix. The main uses of footnotes are as follows:

- to provide bibliographical notes
- to include cross-references to other pages or chapters
- to give information on the source of quotations or paraphrased material
- to outline the views of other writers, if peripheral to main argument
- to operate as content footnotes which provide additional evidence

All your footnotes should be numbered consecutively within each chapter. However, if your first draft has been handwritten rather than word processed, footnotes would not be assigned numbers because it is impossible to predict just how many citations will be added or deleted in later drafts. You would therefore place the source within square brackets immediately after the quotation or paraphrase to which it refers, and perhaps highlight it in red ink for easy identification. At the stage when a final draft is being prepared, these footnotes can be listed on a separate sheet and numbered sequentially. Within your typescript, footnote numbers are entered in superscript (i.e. half a space above the line of text) and placed immediately after the word or sentence to which they refer. They should also be placed after punctuation marks, although not necessarily always at the end of a sentence. A short line can be used to separate the text from the footnotes: if so, two blank lines should be left above and below this line. In a book, footnotes will normally be printed in smaller type and so this line may be omitted, since the text will not be confused with the footnotes. Notes can also be placed at the end of a chapter and referred to as endnotes.

Revision of drafts

The aim of a first draft is to organise your ideas, based on a careful review of the source material and your research notes. Later drafts provide an opportunity to reflect more carefully and in a little more detail on the content of what you have written, as well as focusing on style and presentation. These drafts permit you to improve clarity of expression, the logical development of your argument, the balance between description and analysis, and the amount and accuracy of detail provided. A good first draft will require less editing, but all your work needs to be revised to eliminate repetitive expressions or to rephrase points which are unclear. You may find that it is best to leave a period of time between the completion and editing of drafts so that your work can be viewed from a better perspective. This will enable you to identify what material needs clarification, what needs to be expanded and what can be deleted. The extent of revision will also be governed, to some extent, by your estimation of the background knowledge which can be assumed among the readers of your thesis, article or book.

The chapters of a thesis or book can be written one section at a time as material becomes available, so that reading can be interspersed with writing up the results of your research. It is advisable not to wait until all source material has been gathered and reviewed before deciding to prepare, or revise, any drafts. Your drafts should be written and revised at an early stage as your topic begins to take shape. The revision of a draft which is prepared using a computer can be done on screen, or better still from a printed copy. You may find that it is useful if amendments are made in red ink. Revision should not be carried on endlessly; you must instinctively know when the task of revision must cease. Missing words or phrases may be easier to identify when the revision of your drafts has actually begun. Moreover, try to stop writing at the point where you know momentum will be regained the following day. The latter can be achieved by composing the topic sentence of the next paragraph before ceasing work on any particular day. If you do lose momentum during revision of your work, re-read previous sentences or paragraphs to help regain some continuity of thought.

The most basic elements which you need to check when revising drafts are spelling, punctuation, grammar, sense and style. Your narrative should be interesting and written in a style that conveys a variety of pace and emphasis, just as you would expect in speech. Aim for a certain degree of selectivity in your choice of factual data and evidence to support your historical analysis. Ideas and supporting evidence should ideally be presented concisely, precisely, accurately and clearly. Try not to assume too much, or indeed too little, information known by your readers. What may appear simple and obvious to you may not be so simple or so obvious to your audience. Your drafts should be carefully read and revised with a view to eliminating clichés or ambiguous words and phrases. The inclusion of double negatives, tautology, circumlocution and plagiarised material must all be guarded against. Your historical narrative should, as far as possible, avoid giving the impression of perpetual indecision. It is the task of all historians to question existing ideas and perceptions and to provide alternative explanations if these are justified by the available evidence. If sufficient care is taken during the preparation of a final draft to the general points discussed in this section, then the product of your labour will offer much which is of interest and value to your readers.

11

Illustrative material

Many historians surprisingly make little use of illustrative material, believing somehow that it is more appropriate to include this type of material in scientific and social science publications. However, illustrative material can add value to the content of some research projects by making them both more interesting and comprehensible. Illustrative material can range from photographs and artwork, through to tables, charts and graphs. This section will focus in particular on the latter types of illustrative material which you may have to prepare yourself for a history project. It will look at the advantages of using tables, charts and graphs in any history project, and will also outline the various purposes which each type of material can accomplish. This section will also draw attention to the format for presenting these three categories of illustrative material.

There are perhaps a number of reasons why it may be useful to consider the use of illustrative material in any research project. The incorporation of this type of material can be helpful in reinforcing specific points, summarising ideas or simplifying complex data. The effectiveness of illustrative material generally depends upon the nature and complexity of the subject matter of your thesis, article or book. You may find that some historical data is very relevant to your subject, yet too detailed or complex to be explained satisfactorily without unduly affecting the continuity of your narrative. Visual material has a much greater impact than words alone can achieve and so can be used to enable your readers to understand historical data much more easily. There are various uses to which illustrative material can be put: population trends can be visualised more easily by looking at a line graph; the production of commodities can be understood much better by using a pie chart or pictorial graph; transport statistics are more easily absorbed if they are incorporated in a table; the comparison of class or occupational structure can be appreciated more readily by using a bar chart; and the decision-making structure of any organisation can be grasped more fully by using a flow chart. It is therefore useful for you to consider whether any type of illustrative material would be appropriate for your own historical research project.

Illustrations are capable of conveying complex ideas more clearly and briefly. They enable the writer and reader to think through a problem logically. Various types of illustrative material may appear close to that part of the text where they are discussed, they may be gathered together at the end of a chapter, or may appear in one or more appendices. There are a large number of computer software packages available which are capable of creating various types of graphical information. You should initially decide which type of illustrative material you require and then select a package which will be capable of producing this material. An alternative approach is to use a ready-made illustration from another source, such as a government report, the annual report of a company, or material which appears in a published book or pamphlet. However, illustrations which are taken from another source will be protected by copyright and so permission will have to be sought for their use. A fee may also have to be paid if this material is intended for reproduction in a published book.

Tables

One of the three most common types of diagrammatic material to be found in history publications are tables. Tables are ideally suited for displaying a wide range of numeric data, but they are less useful for displaying trends. You will find that graphs are much better for giving an indication of trends in the data or for comparing two or more variables. Patterns and trends in historical data can, of course, be identified to some extent in a table, but only if row and column averages are provided. There is normally no need to repeat in a chapter any data which you decide to include in tables. The exception would be where a particular point has to be emphasised, such as a trend which does not appear to be evident from the figures provided. The data which you present must be accurate, so all the figures must be carefully checked. All tables which you incorporate into a history project should be numbered and provided with clear and concise headings. The caption which you allocate to each figure should be placed below the appropriate figure.

Figures can be numbered in a single sequence or separately by chapter so that, for example, figure 2.3 will refer to the third figure which appears in chapter 2. Visual material can be referred to in the text by drawing attention to figure and page numbers by stating, for example, 'see fig. 2.3, p. 125'. If you wish to include tables within the chapter of a book it is best to avoid stating 'see table below' or 'see table above' because the position where a table appears in your typescript will not always correspond with where it appears in the book. So always try to refer to a table by its number rather than by the page number. If a table has been copied from another publication, rather than constructed from raw historical data, the source of this information must be provided in a note placed below the table, preceded by the word 'source'. The source should be treated like a footnote, so that details are entered in your bibliography. These sources can also be incorporated in a list of illustrations or in a separate acknowledgements section. Note that in a list of illustrations no full stop is required after the number or at the end of each entry. Explanatory notes may accompany any table, in which case they should be placed below the source. If you have to include several of these notes, each should be numbered using arabic numerals, just like footnotes below a page of text. All tables should be separated from the text by two or three lines in order to improve the presentation of material on the page. Long tables which are not immediately relevant to the discussion in the text can be placed in an appendix. If you do have a large amount of data which you wish displayed on a page, consider preparing two or more simple tables rather than one complex table.

The design of a table should be determined by the nature of the data which is displayed, not by the spacing of the row and column labels. It is much easier to read data by scanning down a column than by reading across a row. The independent variables in your table should therefore form the row headings, whereas the dependent variables should form the column headings. Column headings, which can be ranged left or centred, are best kept as brief as possible. They can be numbered (1), (2), (3), and so on within brackets and placed beneath the heading of each column. Try to ensure that the space between column and also between row headings is equal. The columns are best kept close together so that the data can be compared more easily. It is normal practice now among publishers to use spacing rather than vertical rules to separate columns, unless this procedure begins to hinder the presentation of data. In any case, try not to leave excessive space between the columns because this will make it more difficult to scan your table horizontally; vertical rules also make horizontal scanning more difficult.

A table may contain two levels of column headings, in which the first level is normally centred above the secondary headings. Column headings may also be typed vertically (usually at an angle of 45 degrees to the column) to save space if it appears that they will be too long to be included across the column. Where the latter situation occurs, column headings should be positioned so that they can be read easily from the bottom of the page. In wide tables, row headings can be provided at both ends of the row, not just down the left of the table. Where the row headings are long, these can be split into two or more lines: the runover lines should be indented about three spaces to improve clarity. In tables where runover lines appear, the data in the columns must be aligned with the second or last line in the row. If necessary, you may decide to include leaders (i.e. spaced dots) between row headings and the columns so that your readers will be able to see more easily that row headings are aligned with related items in the columns. It is also helpful for readers to include a rule above the totals at the foot of each column. This rule should extend across the columns but not across the stub (i.e. the left-hand column which contains the row headings, but which itself does not include a heading).

There are various methods which you can use to highlight individual figures within a table. They can be underlined, entered in bold print, accompanied by symbols such as asterisks, or identified by footnote letters or numbers. Footnotes will need to be used to clarify information in row or column headings or numerical data within the table. Footnote indicators within a table normally appear in superscript, as in a footnote, or in parentheses (i.e. round brackets). Letters may be used in place of numerals as footnote indicators in a table. If you decide to incorporate a table within the text, rather than place it in an appendix, the notes to that table must be placed below the table; they should not be placed at the foot of the page on which the table appears, unless the table is the last item which appears on the page. Footnotes to a table are usually used for one of the following purposes: 1 to identify the source from which the table was copied, in part or in full; 2 to provide comments on any aspect of the table; and 3 to refer to specific parts of the table.

Tables can be very useful in summarising numerical data and in providing valuable information which supplements that contained in the text. The following information summarises the main points which it would be helpful for you to observe in the construction of tables for a history project:

1 Try to fit tables across the width of a page because this prevents your readers from having to turn the page on its side to read the material. If this is impossible, the position of the table can be altered but the information it contains must face the bottom of the page and away from the spine (so that the top of the table is close to the spine). In a wide table, consider providing row headings at each end of the row. If your table extends over two facing pages, repeat the row headings (or their numbers, if the headings are numbered) on the second page. Column and row headings should be repeated if a table extends over two or more pages; the table number should also be repeated, but not the title of the table as in, for example, 'table 2 – continued'.

2 If your captions are longer than one line, shorten them or set them in two lines at most.

3 Use rules to separate tables from surrounding textual material. There should be a horizontal rule at the top of the table above column headings, as well as a single rule at the bottom of the table. Omit vertical rules at either side of any table. Use space to separate the columns within a table; space can also be used after every fifth row to assist readers to scan the rows. Space or rules can always be used within a table if it helps your readers to make better sense of the data you provide.

4 Column or row headings can be arranged in a hierarchical order using different type sizes, bold print or italic, rules or a numbering system.

5 Column headings should be ranged left or centred. If ranged left, the headings should be aligned with the longest numerical data which appears in each column. Try to leave the same amount of space above and below the subheadings and keep the column headings as brief as possible. Remember to state which units are being used, and place this information in parentheses below the headings.

6 Try to keep row headings about the same length. If this is not possible, split them into two lines; the data must then be aligned with the second line of the row heading.

7 Align all decimal points within the columns; for correlations of less than one, include a zero before the decimal point; and round up all decimals and large numbers to the nearest whole number.

8 If data is missing from a column, place a dash in the column rather than leave it blank. You can always include an explanation in a footnote to explain the omission of such data. When choosing whether to arrange data within rows or columns, remember that columns are easier to scan than rows.

9 Footnote numbers or letters within a table should appear either in superscript or in parentheses so that they cannot be confused with the numerical data in the table.

Charts

Various types of chart can be used in a project to make sense of complex historical data. The type of chart used will depend upon the nature of your data. A bar chart will, for example, convey different information from a flow chart. The type of chart you may wish to incorporate in a project is likely to be one or more of the following: bar charts, histograms, pie charts, pictorial charts, scatter diagrams, flow charts and maps. All these charts need to be identified by a title so that your readers will be able to grasp exactly what you are seeking to illustrate.

Bar charts

These charts can be used when there are no intermediate values between observations of a variable along the x-axis. Bar charts permit immediate comparisons to be made of several items, but they are not so useful in comparing a large amount of data or at indicating exact comparisons of figures. These charts work best where you wish to compare two, or at most three, separate variables. The columns in bar charts represent class intervals and the bars can be positioned vertically or horizontally. The charts are sometimes referred to as column charts when the bars are positioned vertically. The bars can also be shaded in strong contrasting tones so that comparisons between each item in the chart will be identified more easily. It is advisable to avoid placing text or figures on a shaded background because they might not be easily seen. A key is normally placed beside a bar chart so that readers will be able to identify what each shaded bar represents. If several component bar charts are being compared with one another, the shaded areas must be presented in the same order in each chart. A key should also be provided alongside such charts to indicate what the different patterns of shading within the bars represent. You should note that in bar charts it is the height, not the area of the bar that is important, so the columns must be of equal width. The columns can either be arranged in ascending or descending order to indicate their order of importance, or merely arranged in any order with greater ranked alongside lesser columns. In contrast with the component or stacked bar chart which is divided into different components, a paired bar chart can often be useful for indicating the similarities and differences between two variables. In a proportional component bar chart the components are shown as proportions: the bars must all be vertical and the same height. This type of chart can be used to indicate how the proportions of any item have changed over time. Finally, there is the three-dimensional bar chart which uses shading to suggest shadows so that the bars appear solid. In the latter chart, information is based on measurements using the x, y and z axes. It is worth noting that three-dimensional bar charts are difficult to produce unless you use a computer with a graphics software package; these charts can also be difficult for readers to comprehend.

Histograms

A variation of the bar chart can be found in the histogram. A histogram is similar to a bar chart except that the bars will touch, thus indicating the continuous nature of the variable. A histogram provides a graphical representation of a frequency distribution. Histograms are used to represent the frequency of occurrence of a variable so that a visual comparison can be made. In a histogram, the class boundaries are marked along the x-axis; these class intervals do not necessarily have to be equal and so the width of each column need not be the same. Unlike bar charts, it is the area of the bar that is important in histograms, not just the height. The area of the bar is proportional to the frequency of the class, so the columns can have an unequal width because the histogram deals with frequencies. Histograms differ from bar charts because they can take account of these variations in class intervals.

Pie charts

Another type of chart which often appears in history publications is the pie chart. Pie charts are used to indicate the importance of different items as a proportion of the whole. It therefore follows that your data must total 100 per cent. Pie charts are really only useful when comparing a limited number of items, perhaps up to a maximum of five or six variables. The individual components in the pie chart can be illustrated by shading the various segments. This type of chart can also be drawn to illustrate a segment detached (i.e. an exploded segment), should you wish to highlight information in a single segment. It is possible to use more than one pie chart if you want to indicate changes in the proportions of the various items over time, as well as use three-dimensional pie charts for greater visual impact. However, the segments in each pie chart must therefore be shown in the same sequence to facilitate comparisons. You may find that it is more difficult to compare the segments in a pie chart than the lengths of bars in a bar chart, and this may therefore influence the type of chart which is used. Also, pie charts take up more space than bar charts because the segments have to be sufficiently large to allow room for a label which identifies what each segment represents.

Pictorial charts

The pictorial chart is used less frequently in historical work. This chart uses pictorial symbols to represent data. The symbols are normally all of the same size and are arranged in groups of five or ten to assist counting. Pictorial charts do require more space than other types of chart, although the data they represent can normally be easily understood. Information must be given to enable readers to know precisely what each symbol represents. Computer programs offer clip-art facilities so that you can incorporate computer-based images into your chart. The symbols used in pictorial charts should bear some relation to the subject of the chart. For example, the figure of a bottle may be used to represent wine production. The main problem with the pictorial chart is that too many symbols make it difficult to count items, and too few mean that parts of symbols have to be used to represent specific quantities.

Scatter diagrams, flow charts and maps

Scatter diagrams are useful if you intend to illustrate the spread of data, but they cannot be used if more than one type of data is presented. Also, they cannot show trends in the data because their primary purpose is to indicate the spread of data. Scatter diagrams are, in any case, more widely used in scientific than in historical studies. Flow charts are perhaps more appropriate for some historical studies because they can indicate complex relationships, such as the sequence of events in an operation or the structure of an organisation, as in an organisation chart. The thickness of lines in these charts can be varied to indicate the relative importance of each part of a system, organisation or process. Alternatively, you may wish to include maps in your history project, many of which are often available ready-made and therefore only require the addition of page and figure numbers, together with a caption. Maps which are too detailed are less useful because they may be difficult to read when photographically reduced. If you do include several maps in your project and these have to be reproduced to permit comparisons to be made with one another, they should be of the same size and placed in the same orientation (i.e. all portrait or all landscape).

Graphs

In addition to tables and charts, graphs are the third major type of illustrative material which can be used to simplify the presentation of complex historical data. You will find that graphs are particularly useful for displaying trends in data if there is a continuous relationship between the variables. All graphs should be labelled as figures and assigned a number and a heading. Line graphs are much better than tables in high-lighting distinct and subtle trends in data and in making comparisons between data, such as the growth in population of different countries over a specified period of time. They are less useful for indicating exact quantities or in presenting a large amount of numerical data. You will probably have appreciated that it can be difficult to extract precise data quickly from a graph in comparison with a table. However, graphs are useful if you wish to indicate the relationship between two sets of data over time. If there are no intermediate values between the variables, a bar chart might be considered instead of a graph.

Computer software packages will make the production of graphs a much less daunting prospect. There are, however, a few points to keep in mind if you decide to incorporate graphs in your work. The axes lines in a graph need to be clearly identified and the labels assigned to them should be brief, informative and placed parallel to the axes. Axes lines should end at a value near the last data point. You should not extend graph lines past the last data point without providing an explanation in a footnote. Begin your scales at zero and use equal intervals along the axes. In graphs the x-axis represents the independent variables, which in tables would be represented by the rows, whereas the y-axis covers the dependent variables, which in tables would be represented by the columns. The dependent variable in graphs varies according to changes in the x-axis. The use of three-dimensional graphs which incorporate a z-axis should not normally be needed, and are probably best avoided.

You may find that you wish to compare two or more graphs in order to highlight important differences. If so, they should all be placed in the same orientation (i.e. portrait or landscape). Graphs can be very useful for interpolating and extrapolating values based on the data points given, although care must be taken to ensure that this is justified by the nature of the data so that incorrect assumptions are not made. Open or closed circles can be used to represent data points. If a data point lies on the axis line, cut the line at this point so that the data point can be seen. The scales along each axis should appear at equal intervals, but if the scales are not equal then the axes lines must be cut by two oblique lines to indicate the point where the scale alters. This latter type of graph which has uneven scales should be avoided unless absolutely essential because it can give a misleading representation of the data. To distinguish between different data lines on a graph, especially where these lines intersect, you may find it useful to use a mixture of solid and broken lines. Try not to include too many data lines, otherwise a line graph will be too complex for your readers to understand. Your data points are best joined by a curve rather than straight lines, unless the points are very far apart. The use of lines to join points on a graph may give a misleading impression about trends in the data which you provide. All graphs should be numbered by chapter so that, for example, figure 6.2 represents the second graph which appears in chapter 6. Finally, remember that if you copy a graph directly from another source, permission must be sought for its reproduction. The copyright source must also be identified in a note which is placed below the graph and possibly also included in an acknowledgements page.

There can be little doubt that the careful choice and use of illustrative material, such as tables, charts and graphs, can assist our understanding of complex historical data. This type of material has understandably been used more frequently in economic and social history publications because of the nature of the subject matter and the availability of statistical data. However, there are many other areas of historical study and research where it can also be of some benefit. You therefore need to consider whether your own project might be improved through the use of illustrative material. It may, after all, help both you and your readers to appreciate and understand more fully the wealth of information contained in a surprisingly wide variety of historical sources.

12

Research for a higher degree

Research for a historical subject may take place with the purpose of sub-mitting a dissertation or thesis for a higher degree. This provides an opportunity to consolidate existing knowledge and enlarge and deepen understanding of a particular subject. The work may be challenging but can also be very rewarding. You may have to identify the objectives of your project, how you propose to complete the work and assess what benefits will arise from its completion. It does present several challenges, and the tasks involved range from working under the guidance of aca-demic supervisors, submitting progress reports and developing research skills, through to the production, submission and examination of a thesis. The varied skills required to complete this work successfully are best tackled if you have sufficient guidance on the purpose and requirements of historical work which is submitted for a postgraduate degree. This section looks at the various stages of preparing work for a higher degree. It covers the purpose of a research degree, supervision, the preparation of progress reports and the special requirements involved in submitting a dissertation or thesis. The section concludes by examining the aim, con-duct and content of the oral examination which is an essential com-ponent of most postgraduate degrees in history.

Purpose and rewards of research

There are a number of reasons for pursuing research as a candidate for a higher degree. The subject may not have been extensively researched, the area of study could be very interesting, it represents an intellectual challenge, and it provides the opportunity to obtain a major qualification. It is generally recognised that a higher degree which is awarded on the successful completion of a dissertation or thesis will assist the cultivation of independent and original thought, as well as the development of a range of transferable skills, such as computing, communication skills and the ability to organise and prioritise work. This is particularly true where researchers plan and work on a project independently of others, and where the results of this research are the product of the systematic study of primary source material, as is the norm in historical research. The nature of this sustained work does provide historians with an opportunity to become specialists in a particular subject. It may not be too difficult to become a specialist on a topic which is very narrowly defined and then studied in some detail, but you still face the initial task of selecting a subject area where you believe an original contribution to knowledge can be made. A thesis, even in a specialised field of enquiry, will though not be expected to be original in all its features. But it must provide a significant contribution to existing knowledge in a well-defined subject area by offering new perspectives, be manageable in the time available, and possibly also offer a springboard for further research on related issues or themes. This is why it is important to be aware at the outset of the aims and justification for your research, as well as how much work will be involved. A good research topic is one which will offer plenty of scope for the display of originality, creativity and initiative. After all, unlike an undergraduate essay, a dissertation or thesis is expected to venture beyond describing what is already known about a topic, to focusing much more about what is unknown, or perhaps misinterpreted. It also requires the ability to take a more active part in organising time and resources than would be expected at undergraduate level.

The award of a higher degree confers professional status and indicates that an individual is capable of conducting extensive research independently. It also assumes that historians will develop a range of skills which can be used in other projects. A dissertation is normally submitted for a master's degree after one or two years of full-time study, whereas a thesis is normally required from candidates who submit work for a doctorate. The normal minimum length of full-time research for a doctorate is three years. A dissertation may be up to 60,000 words in length, whereas a doctoral thesis can range from 80,000 to 100,000 words. Clearly, a doctoral thesis represents not only a more extensive piece of work based on a more exhaustive search of source material, but is also expected to make a more original and significant contribution to knowledge. Candidates who wish to register for a doctorate are usually registered initially as supervised postgraduate students. This enables a university to assess the research potential of a candidate before retrospective registration for a particular degree. The submission of a dissertation or thesis demonstrates that an individual has acquired a number of skills: the ability to organise a large volume of source material; the ability to study a topic in depth through a systematic analysis of the sources; the ability to master the complexities of a subject; and the ability to present the results of the research in an extended piece of work which is satisfactory in both style and content and can be completed within a reasonable timescale. This work may lead to the questioning of existing beliefs or factual evidence, particularly with a subject which has not been extensively researched, documented and discussed in published historical literature. Researchers engaged in such work will be anxious to publish research papers or a book. The submission of a thesis may therefore be followed by the publication of work which establishes the author's academic authority. The realisation of all these objectives depends primarily on the qualities displayed by the researcher and the value of the research project, as well as the facilities and support provided by the institution.

Research supervision

An important element in the successful completion of a research degree is the quality of supervision which is offered. This is particularly important during the early stages of your work where supervisors can help in identifying a suitable focus for your study and channel your enthusiasm in a constructive direction. It also helps if a supervisor is receptive and open and that there is a good rapport between research student and supervisor. Many universities have prepared their own code of conduct on the supervision of research students. There can be some variations in supervisory practice and so the comments which follow therefore offer only general guidance on what may be considered best practice. The role of supervisors is to guide and encourage their research students to formulate a workable research programme. It goes without saying that academic supervisors should demonstrate an interest and competence in the general subject area of your chosen topic, as well as having experience in supervising research students. The best supervisors are able to communicate their knowledge and experience effectively. They would be expected to help their students to plan and organise their research and reflect on their work strategies to encourage independent study, as well as the management of time and the prioritising of tasks. In essence, supervisors provide feedback on progress and performance so that their students can derive maximum benefit from their research. They may also encourage their students to develop transferable skills, such as communication skills which will be of use in their future careers.

Supervisors need to be available in the early stages to guide you through the relevant literature, offer help to overcome study difficulties, clarify areas of misunderstanding, interpret results and offer general guidance on the organisation of research notes and source material. They need to be aware of alternative methods for achieving research objectives, and be able to communicate this knowledge so that your work can move forward without unnecessary delays. They will also monitor progress to ensure that your topic is manageable, can be completed in the time available and will meet university regulations. Supervisors may also wish to ensure that the tasks which you carry out are varied so that, for example, information searches, reading and writing can be interchanged at various stages during completion of your work. They therefore need to be prepared and willing to give time and attention to the supervision of the research project, suggest suitable ideas and sources which can be consulted, set goals and indicate how various research techniques might be adapted to the specific needs of the project. They may also advise you on the availability of relevant research training courses. Moreover, it is perhaps also important for supervisors to convey their own enthusiasm for research, as it is to encourage researchers to engage effectively with the source material, or to assist them in setting and determining priorities. Supervisors will wish to ensure that you do make proper use of research, library, computing and administrative facilities within your institution. If possible, they may also draw your attention to relevant professional historical organisations, departmental seminars and expertise available in other academic institutions. Researchers do, of course, have a responsibility to meet their supervisors on a regular basis, keep them fully informed about progress with their work and submit any material requested at agreed times.

One of the central aims of academic supervisors is to encourage you to think critically and imaginatively (i.e. to think logically, but also to stimulate independent and original thought). It is also important for you to become progressively more self-reliant and able to take increasing responsibility for the research. By helping students gain a greater insight into the research process, supervisors will have persuaded them to examine their strengths and weaknesses, whether this relates to the management of various components of the research project or the writing of drafts. Research students who intend to carry out research for a doctorate are normally expected to take more initiative in planning their work and in locating source material than students registered for masters degrees. Sometimes two supervisors are appointed to oversee a particular research student. One may be designated the principal supervisor, and the other may be referred to as the assistant supervisor. Both supervisors may be based in the same department or work in closely related departments, especially if the project is interdisciplinary in nature. The appointment of two supervisors may be beneficial because it provides some degree of continuity if one of them is temporarily absent. Meetings do, however, have to be coordinated to ensure that on most occasions both supervisors will be present.

In circumstances where there are two or more supervisors they would, in general, try to avoid offering conflicting advice. If their roles are clearly defined at the outset then this will not be a problem. Your supervisors will wish to be supportive and provide constructive criticism and consistent advice on the material they are asked to comment on, such as draft chapters of a dissertation or thesis or perhaps on your proposed methodology. If you have invested a large amount of time, effort and money in your project you will hope to receive sufficient advice of a high quality. Equally, you are expected to be open to suggestions from your supervisors, as well as being capable of demonstrating initiative. You are, after all, solely responsible for the quality of the work you produce. You may face difficulties but you should regard this as a learning experience. Your supervisors are usually expected to submit annual reports on your progress. The latter will be monitored through regular well-planned meetings, and these offer an opportunity for potential difficulties to be resolved and for the standard of work expected to be indicated to you. Meetings will tend to be more frequent in the early stages of your research, such as the first two terms or semesters. The dates, times and location of meetings, including any suggested work to be completed prior to them, are best agreed upon in advance, perhaps towards the end of the previous meeting. A realistic length of time needs to be set aside for each meeting with your supervisors to ensure that all relevant issues are covered.

Regular meetings between research students and supervisors form a vital element in the successful completion of a research thesis or dissertation. They are particularly important during the early stages of your research, as well as the later stages when you submit drafts of the material you have prepared to your supervisor. Supervisors normally try to be available for consultation at reasonable times, especially during the early and later stages of a project. To ensure that all your meetings are productive it is advisable to prepare research plans or keep a research diary which can form the basis of a research progress report. Your progress reports should ideally be forwarded to your supervisor prior to each meeting and should, if possible, contain the following items:

1 A summary of work carried out since the previous meeting.
2 Comments on selected issues and themes which are being developed, including those arising out of points discussed in previous meetings.
3 Future research plans.
4 Items for discussion, including questions and queries on which advice is sought.
5 A list of individuals or organisations contacted for advice or information, arranged in either alphabetical order or chronological order by date of contact.
6 A summary of written correspondence with anyone on any aspect of your research.
7 A bibliographical list of all source material consulted since the previous meeting.

Your progress reports should be typed, dated and submitted at least one week before each meeting. Photocopies of the reports can be filed in a document wallet folder or ring binder. A small A6 notebook may also be used for jotting down useful ideas which come to mind and may be expanded later to provide the basis for your future research plans. Any goals which are set, together with a timetable for completing specific tasks, have to be kept under review. Your supervisor may be expected to respond to the submission of these progress reports at each meeting, or alternatively provide some feedback soon afterwards. Feedback may provide further leads which can be followed up, such as individuals or organisations to contact, archive sources to consult or publications to review. The primary purpose of each meeting is to monitor the scope of your project, discuss progress and review the goals which were set at previous meetings. This will ensure that any problems are dealt with before they can cause serious disruption to the overall progress of your project. It may also assist the setting of a realistic completion date.

Some research students find it helpful to write brief notes during each meeting with their supervisors so that important points will not be forgotten. After each meeting, a fuller account can be prepared of points discussed, ideas generated and conclusions reached. These fuller notes might be labelled research discussion/meeting notes. They could be filed together with your research progress reports and be used as the basis for future research plans. The plans may be subdivided into a number of short, medium and long-term goals. This type of approach will provide a focus and guide to your work. It is sensible to list more tasks than you can accomplish because extra tasks can function as alternatives if the principal tasks cannot be completed on time. It may also be useful to keep an alphabetical index of people or organisations which you may wish to contact. These sources may not always prove to be fruitful, but it is important to keep a record of them to avoid the duplication involved in contacting the same sources on more than one occasion. A note or summary of any visits you make will provide useful information which can be used to prepare a formal written account for incorporation in research progress reports.

During the later stages of any research project, meetings with your supervisor will increasingly be devoted to discussions about the drafts of your thesis or dissertation. Supervisors normally encourage students to begin writing at an early stage rather than concentrate this activity towards the end of their research. It may, in any case, take approximately six months to write the final version of a PhD thesis. Supervisors may see your drafts in the form of individual chapters and not necessarily as a whole. They will examine the level of arguments used and the quality of expression, as well as matters such as style, presentation, spelling, grammar, punctuation and use and acknowledgement of sources. Your supervisor should be able to provide adequate guidance on the standard of work expected and on the criteria that are applied in judging a dissertation or thesis. They can offer helpful advice but are not responsible for the final version of work which you produce. Unlike the research student, the supervisor does not get so closely involved in a project and so may be able to see matters from a broader perspective. Supervisors will comment on drafts, but they will not be expected to know as much detail about the content of the research project. Moreover, any comments which they make on the quality of your work cannot be taken as a guarantee that your work will be approved by the examiners. They will, however, provide vital support, encouragement and critical advice during the crucial phase when your drafts are being completed. A principal supervisor will try to ensure that a dissertation or thesis is submitted on time. Supervisors may also perform a beneficial role by assisting research students to publish material in the form of articles or books, arrange part-time teaching or research appointments, attend conferences, take part in seminars or contact academic colleagues working in the same field of study.

Thesis and dissertation format

Academic supervisors perform a useful role, not only in motivating, encouraging and giving feedback, but also in advising their research students on the regulations for the preparation and submission of theses and dissertations. Many universities and individual history departments produce their own guidance notes for researchers and academic staff. These notes may cover a variety of different matters, as in the following list:

• layout of the typescript, such as the type of print and size of margins

- minimum thickness of paper to be used
- placement of page numbers, headings, diagrams and published papers
- content of the title page
- format and number of copies of an abstract to be submitted
- word limit, and circumstances in which it may be exceeded
- number of copies of the thesis to be submitted
- type of binding and lettering for a thesis or dissertation
- rules governing the extension of time permitted for submission
- copyright and how to temporarily restrict access to a thesis

It is your responsibility to be aware of the rules and guidelines which apply within your own institution. This can be supplemented by the advice given in Parts II and III of this book, as well as referring to the relevant British Standards which are listed in the Guide to Further Reading. Universities usually expect to be given sufficient notice (normally three months) of a candidate's intention to submit work for examination, primarily to allow time to appoint external examiners. Research students are responsible for the final quality of the work they submit and so are ultimately responsible for the success or failure of their thesis or dissertation.

Special requirements are involved in the preparation of a thesis or dissertation. The following points are generally applicable to all theses and dissertations. The title page will normally include the title of your project, name of author, degree, department or faculty, university, and month and year of presentation. A thesis will normally have to include an abstract, perhaps about 300 words in length. The abstract is, in effect, a synopsis of your work, summarising both organisation and content: it does not perform the function of a conclusion. However, in common with your introduction and conclusion, your abstract should be prepared *after* the thesis has been written. The abstract will briefly outline the scope of the work, the method of investigation, the structure of the thesis and summarise the content of your project. A thesis differs from a published book because it is expected to incorporate a signed declaration by the author stating that the work is entirely the product of his or her own work. If this work represents part of a much larger project because a student is a member of a research team, the contribution of other researchers must be identified in this signed declaration. The latter type of arrangement is more likely to occur with scientific or social science projects. In history projects researchers tend to work exclusively on their own topics. Some historians do, however, wish to acknowledge advice received during the completion of their research: this can be incorporated towards the end of a preface or in an acknowledgements page. This differs from a book where the acknowledgements page is normally used only to list copyright holders who have agreed to permit the reproduction of copyright material. The type of assistance which might be acknowledged in a thesis may include the following: special access to unpublished papers; the cooperation of individuals who agreed to provide taped interviews; and acknowledgement of specific ideas, theories or important factual material. A doctoral thesis of 100,000 words may take eight months to complete all stages, from the preparation of a first draft, through to the submission of the final work. You will need to be guided by the advice of your own institution as to whether your work should be bound prior to the oral examination.

The oral examination

Most postgraduate students who submit a thesis will have to prepare for an oral examination. This is less common with a dissertation, especially those which are submitted in partial fulfilment of the requirements for a master's degree extending over twelve months full-time study or its part-time equivalent. Although the oral examination is not mandatory for a doctorate, special reasons normally have to be given for this requirement to be waived. For example, a thesis would have to be of an outstanding quality were the examiners prepared to recommend that a degree should be awarded without the need for any oral examination. A thesis must represent an original piece of work which makes a significant contribution to knowledge and contains material worthy of publication. Its originality may be based on the ideas which it presents, in the methods which it adopts, or in a combination of the two. It must demonstrate that you possess an adequate knowledge of the field of study, can identify the key issues and are familiar with the relevant primary and secondary source material. In addition to being satisfactory in historical analysis, literary presentation and selective use and documentation of source material, a thesis is also expected to have a coherent structure which can be related to the much wider field of study within which it exists.

The purpose of the oral examination is to establish the authenticity of the thesis, provide an opportunity for you to outline which research techniques were used and clarify specific points within the thesis. The examination will test your knowledge of the much wider field of study to which the subject of your thesis relates. It will also give an opportunity for examiners to offer their criticisms of any aspect of the work. A candidate for a research degree therefore has to prepare for the oral examination by re-reading their thesis critically in order to refresh their memory of its contents and anticipate any points which the examiners are likely to make. This preparation makes it much easier to know how to defend some points, expand upon others, or perhaps explain why some sources were omitted. This will, of course, be known for certain only on the day of the examination.

You will normally be given sufficient prior notice about the date, time and location of your oral examination. You will probably also be given information on the names of all those who will be present at the examination. Academic supervisors try to ensure that theses do attain an acceptable standard before they are seen by any examiners. A copy of the thesis would usually be brought to the examination so that you can refer to specific pages in response to questions from the examiners. It is possible that the examiners may ask you to justify what you have written and envisage what developments you expect to follow on from the work. The oral defence of a thesis may be sufficient to dispel any doubts about weak points. It is worth noting that your external examiners may feel that they are examining not only your work but also that of your supervisor, because criticisms directed at the former may adversely reflect on the latter. Nevertheless, in the role of internal examiner, supervisors do preserve some distance between themselves and their research students. It is this which encourages, or should encourage, a greater degree of independence on the part of the research student. You may find that you have to defend parts of the thesis which had to be limited in scope or treatment, perhaps through lack of access to appropriate historical archive material or because of time or word constraints. You should certainly explain the contribution to knowledge which is made by your thesis, but not seek to claim more for it than is proper.

If your thesis has considerable merit there may be some advantage in being examined by an external examiner who is eminent in your chosen field of study and may add prestige to the project. In many instances the external examiner will be the individual whose work is cited most frequently in the footnotes. All examiners naturally expect their work to be cited and discussed in the thesis. In some subject areas there may only be a small number of competent examiners. All internal and external examiners are chosen because they have some knowledge and interest in the subject of your thesis. If only one external examiner is appointed, there will normally be two other internal examiners, one of whom may be your principal supervisor. The other internal examiner may be a member of staff from another department within the same institution. Some universities, however, do not permit supervisors to be chosen as internal examiners. In some instances a supervisor may, at the discretion of a Board of Examiners, be invited to attend the examination as an observer.

Sometimes a problem can arise in locating suitable examiners where the topic is interdisciplinary. If there are only two examiners, the main (i.e. external) examiner will usually cover one discipline, and the internal examiner will cover the other one. The external examiner is likely to have been chosen because of his or her competence in the major subject area of your thesis. This individual will also be a respected academic whom you have not previously contacted for advice or information on any aspect of your thesis. Candidates usually discuss with their supervisor when their work is likely to be submitted for examination and may be asked to comment on the names of potential examiners suggested by the supervisor. Some universities permit candidates to suggest the names of potential external examiners, and any comments they make may be taken into account when examiners are chosen. However, candidates have no right of veto over the final choice of examiner. Your supervisor may send the abstract of your thesis to any potential examiner to ascertain the willingness of that individual to be considered as an external examiner.

Candidates who submit work for a research degree are expected to demonstrate, through their written work and the oral examination, that they are capable of pursuing original research in their chosen field of study. They are also expected to present material which is properly documented and contains material worthy of publication. You will have to demonstrate that you can relate a specific research project to the general body of knowledge in the same subject area, as well as presenting the results in a critical and scholarly manner. The oral examination will, within reason, test whether you are capable of meeting these objectives. During the oral examination, try to give answers which are fluent, accurate and concise. The overall conduct of the examination may vary from that of a stern test of professional knowledge, through to a more relaxed conversation about your research project. Whatever the approach, questions need to be answered as fully and as clearly as possible in a confident and relaxed manner. Examiners normally try to make a candidate feel comfortable, but will also attempt to conduct the examination from the standpoint of independent objective assessors. Your oral examination may last from thirty minutes to two hours, but typically extends over one hour. You should not be afraid to ask the examiner to clarify points which seem unclear, or defend points which arise during the oral examination. Examiners are unlikely to expect candidates to offer instant solutions to problems which are insoluble. You should accept justifiable criticisms, yet also try to think about why an examiner has asked a particular question. On occasion, examiners may offer alternative interpretations of historical data which you have presented in your thesis. Note also that some examiners do check bibliographical details, footnotes and quoted extracts, so it is important to ensure that these are accurate.

To assist in your preparations for the oral examination you may find it helpful to keep the following questions in mind because these questions, or at least variations of them, may be asked by your examiners:

1 Why the topic was chosen by you.
2 What approach was adopted, and why the subject was regarded as important.
3 What research methods were used, what sources of information were consulted and what research skills you acquired during the course of your work.
4 Whether any problems emerged, such as lack of time, access to facilities and sources or the constraints imposed by the word limit.
5 Which topics you enjoyed the most, and which the least.

6 Which topics you found to be the easiest, or most difficult, to comprehend.

7 Whether information you discovered was surprising or merely confirmed your existing views.

8 Why certain issues, themes or topics were examined and others not covered, or at least not covered in the same amount of detail.

9 Whether you are able to identify the strengths and weaknesses of your work.

10 Assess how your thesis contributes to existing knowledge, what new perspectives emerged and what you perceive its most original aspects are.

11 Consider how your views about the subject have altered, if any, since your research began.

12 Identify how your work relates to other published work currently available.

13 State which topics would, or should, be developed further.

14 Outline which parts of your thesis might be published.

15 Outline future areas of research.

Post-examination options

After your oral examination the examiners will normally confer. They will seek to take a number of considerations into account, such as whether you have provided an adequate defence of your thesis, as well as showing sufficient knowledge of the field of study and the relevant literature. They will consider the range of evidence you have used and the interpretations you have based on that evidence. The examiners will also wish to confirm that your thesis has a coherent structure and that the presentation of the text and the use and citation of references are satisfactory. They will expect to see evidence of the application of knowledge and understanding, and the ability to find, organise and evaluate material. The examiners will expect you to be able to communicate your ideas effectively and show the relationship between your conclusions and established knowledge in the same field of study. If you have used a particular research method in your project, then you may have to show evidence that you have described this clearly. Your thesis will be expected to critically analyse evidence and not simply present factual data. It will also have to show some evidence that you have made a significant contribution to knowledge and have been able to demonstrate your ability to relate a particular historical topic to other research studies in the same area. If you believe that your work shows evidence of all these qualities then you should feel confident about the outcome of the oral examination.

After the oral examination the examiners may inform you in person of their recommendation, which would be subject to formal approval by your university. No grade is awarded for the submission and examination of a dissertation or thesis: the candidate will either pass or fail. If the examiners recommend that your thesis should be passed, or passed subject to very minor modifications, your university will usually concur with this recommendation. The final decision about whether a thesis passes or fails is determined by the external examiner. In general, most history theses pass outright or require only very minor corrections. The examiners would normally provide candidates and supervisors with a list of items to be amended. Some theses do require major corrections, but only a few fail or are recommended for the award of a lesser degree, such as an MPhil or MLitt or an MSc or diploma. If major corrections are needed and a thesis has to be re-submitted, it is very unlikely that a second oral examination would be held. Most universities provide candidates with guidelines on the procedures involved in the examination of dissertations or theses for research degrees. You should be aware of these guidelines, including the various options open to the examiners and the procedures which must be adopted. If you are successful and the degree is awarded, the next stage involves consideration of how to broaden the potential readership of the results of your research. This is accomplished by getting some or all of your work published. The transition from the award of a degree to the publication of articles and books is the subject of the next section, which concludes Part II of this book.

13

Publication of articles and books

Historical research may commence with the primary objective of publishing work so that it can be brought to the attention of a wider audience, or it may have been originally completed for a research degree. Even in the latter case, most historical researchers usually wish to see their work published, thereby gaining a measure of credibility and academic recognition. The outcome of your research may culminate in a series of journal articles, chapters in edited books or a scholarly monograph. Many research students begin by selecting an appropriate chapter of their dissertation or thesis which might be suitable for publication in a learned journal. Historical research is often perceived as more valuable if it is widely distributed, which it will be if it is published in a reputable academic journal or as a book by a major publisher or well-known university press. Whatever the approach, as a potential author you need to take a number of factors into account when selecting or preparing work for publication.

Journal articles

In general, book publishers are normally less interested than journal editors in work which was originally produced for a dissertation or thesis. This is understandable to the extent that theses are written in a style which is often found to be too cumbersome for most readers to negotiate. Theses are too meticulously documented and may be too detailed in content to be acceptable to many book publishers. Indeed, any thesis worth publishing will almost certainly require extensive revision before it is acceptable to a book publisher. But an individual chapter of a dissertation or thesis, which deals with a specific topic or theme, may be of a suitable length to be of interest to the editor of a scholarly journal, yet not require substantial revision. This is also a useful means of bringing your research much more quickly before a larger readership, particularly as the circulation figures of scholarly journals are usually larger than those of most monographs.

You should begin by preparing a list of history journals which are likely to be interested in publishing material in your specialist subject. In some instances additional research will be necessary in order to write an original and competent article. Your research topic may be of interest to a journal which has broader interests than the specialist field of interest covered in your thesis. The type of original material which might form the basis of a suitable article may range from a case study or survey, through to the provision of new biographical material or the discovery of exciting manuscripts. The inside or back cover of journals should be carefully examined for guidelines on the preparation and submission of material. Guidance will usually cover matters such as format, style and spellings. If you discover that only brief information is given, it may be a good idea to write to the journal asking for a copy of their in-house guidelines. You can supplement this advice by looking at the house style of each journal. The latter will indicate the preferred length of article, the format for citing source material and whether citations are to appear as footnotes or as endnotes typed in a single list at the end of the article.

Target historical journals carefully by examining their contents, style and length of articles requested, particularly as each journal tends to have a slightly different interest and readership. Try also to find out how long it will take for any article to be published. Your primary task is to convince the editor (whose name will usually appear on the inside cover of the journal) that there is some merit in publishing your work. If necessary, send a summary of your article to the editor. It is perfectly permissible to approach the editorial board of different journals prior to submitting a dissertation or thesis to your university. Your academic supervisor may suggest that some of your work is submitted to a journal, and may also be willing to read some material to ascertain whether it merits publication. Ideally, a 200-word summary of your article should be prepared and sent to the editor of an appropriate journal to enquire whether the topic is of interest. If the response is positive, this will be followed by a request to submit an article.

A typical article may be about 25 to 30 pages in length. It should be typed on A4 paper, double spaced and with wide margins. The footnotes or endnotes should also be double spaced. You will have to prepare a brief covering letter and send this to the journal, together with the top copy of the article. Your covering letter should indicate why the article is suitable for the chosen journal and also why it is worth publishing. Journal editors look at the quality of the research and the content of articles, as well as the extent to which the presentation of the material conforms to the stylistic and other requirements of their journal. Material should normally only be sent to one journal at a time, because editors will send your material to referees to obtain their advice on the merits of your work. It may be justifiable to send a synopsis of a book to several publishers simultaneously because of potential delays in receiving replies, but this procedure is not so acceptable with journal articles. It would, however, be acceptable to send the synopsis of an article to several journals simultaneously.

A good article on a historical subject is one which is both readable and relates the subject to current themes and debates. Individual chapters of a dissertation or thesis, or perhaps part of a chapter which deals with a single identifiable topic or theme, would provide suitable material for publication in a journal. Look for interesting ideas or themes which you think might be suitable for an article. The article should be concise, original and avoid jargon or the inclusion of any irrelevant material. Your aim should always be to provide information which readers are unlikely to be aware of, but which they might wish to know. Any personal debts you owe to others in researching material for your article should be acknowledged in a first footnote. You may also wish to obtain an estimate of the probable elapse time between acceptance of an article and its publication. Finally, remember to enclose a stamped addressed envelope for the journal editor's reply.

The aim of any article which is submitted to a journal should be clear, the structure should be sound and the item must be appropriate to the journal to which it is submitted. The editor of a journal normally decides which articles to send to referees for their opinion on the quality of the material submitted. You should be prepared to accept constructive criticism about your article and make appropriate adjustments to the content where necessary. The editor can, however, overrule the comments offered by referees. The task of referees is to look at the quality and originality of an article and assess its suitability for publication, based on their specialist knowledge of the subject covered in the article. If you find that an article is returned by a journal without any comments, it might be useful to write a letter to the editor asking whether it is possible to gain some insight into the reasons why the referees were critical of it, or why the editor thought it was not suitable for publication in that particular journal. You may not agree with everything they say, but it will at least give you some clues as to what aspects might be improved. If your work is rejected by more than one journal then this could indicate that the work is seriously flawed.

The refereeing procedures of journals are intended to guarantee the scholarly value of the work which they publish. So the publication of work can be taken as some evidence of the author's scholarly accomplishments. This is somewhat similar to the situation with those books which win awards or receive favourable reviews, since they also reflect positively on the author of the work. The option of getting your work published as a series of articles will not adversely affect the possibility of getting a book published. Moreover, it could be argued that a published article may attract the attention of a book editor and bring about an invitation to submit material for publication. Book editors are aware that articles which have been submitted to refereed journals have been reviewed by specialists who are competent in the field of study of the article and are also familiar with current research in the subject area. They will also be aware that the work is original, properly researched and documented, and has something interesting and important to say to its intended readership. If your article is accepted for publication, then copyright clearance must be sought if you include quotations or statistical data. Authors are not normally expected to surrender the copyright of their articles because this would prevent the work from being subsequently incorporated in a book.

Books

The publication of a book may arise after you have had a number of articles published. Alternatively, it could be based on a thesis or a substantial piece of independent research. The publication of a scholarly monograph is intended to disseminate new research findings, whereas a textbook summarises existing knowledge. The publication of a book often arises as a result of a commission or a form of early encouragement by a publisher. You can, of course, also approach a publisher directly, but your topic may not fit in with the publisher's programme and therefore could be rejected on that basis alone. If you do decide to approach a publisher on a speculative basis, a letter should be sent to the commissioning editor indicating that you are preparing material on a particular historical subject. This letter should, if possible, be typed on headed notepaper, such as from an academic institution, because this may carry more authority with some publishers. Your covering letter should be accompanied by a synopsis of your proposed book, outlining its scope and content. The synopsis should include a draft title, a table of contents and at least five lines summarising the content of each chapter. It should also include an estimate of the total length of your proposed book, its intended readership, and how it relates to other books in the same subject area. Some publishers prefer to examine a sample chapter, or at least a very detailed outline of each chapter. This enables the publisher to offer a considered view of the content of each chapter. It can also be helpful if you include some brief biographical details which highlight your qualifications for writing the book (i.e. a record of research, publications and academic or professional qualifications). If you are able to obtain an endorsement from an eminent historian or senior academic working in the same field, then so much the better. You may decide that your proposed book should include tables or illustrations, and so this information should also be incorporated in the submission to the publisher. Try to ensure that your work does not exceed 100,000 words; the average preferred length for most books is 80,000 to 90,000 words. It is, of course, not essential to have written the whole book before approaching a publisher, but it will certainly be useful to have prepared a minimum of one or two sample chapters.

You may find it helpful to look at recent books published in your field of interest, as well as consult the current edition of the *Writers' and Artists' Yearbook* to note who has published them. It is acceptable to solicit interest from several publishers simultaneously about your proposed history book, but only submit a complete or partial manuscript to one publisher at a time. The reason for doing so is because at this stage a publisher will probably be investing time and money in the production of a reader's report. A large publisher is more likely to be able to afford to take a chance on a newcomer, and they may have a number of editors specialising in different subjects. Some smaller publishers also deal with specialist subjects and should be approached if they publish books in your chosen field of study. Trade publishers, unlike university presses, publish books that will appeal to a much broader readership than do most monographs. Publishers who acquire and promote works that make current research accessible to a general popular audience may have to offer more competitive terms to authors. Those publishers who decide to take new authors on to their list naturally hope that they will produce more than one book, perhaps building up a reputation as a specialist in a particular area of study. This may also help any later books to sell in larger quantities. The main types of approach which are made to publishers usually arise under the following circumstances: 1 an unsolicited approach by letter, which might be followed up by a meeting with the editor; 2 contact with publishers who visit academic departments or attend conferences; 3 literary agents who will review material and contact suitable publishers on behalf of the author; 4 contacts with senior academics who might read a manuscript and encourage their research students to submit their work to suitable publishers; and 5 visits to a book fair. You will have to decide for yourself which approach is likely to generate the most promising results.

Historians who have completed, or who are nearing completion, of a book, are expected to demonstrate clear evidence of originality and to have identified the potential readership for their book. Publishers do not normally take more than three months to decide whether to accept work for publication. The possession of an advance contract for a book which is still to be fully written may be of value to you in relation to gaining work, promotion, research grants or editorial advice. A contract relieves authors of the worry of finding a publisher, as well as showing a measure of commitment by the publisher to the book. You may have some general preference about when you would like your work to be published, and if this is important it could be written into the publishing contract. However, keep in mind that the process from submission of a manuscript to publication may take anything from four to twelve months, the average being about nine months. September and October are often believed to be the best months to get a book published because of the potential sales likely to be generated in the pre-Christmas period. However, the volume of sales may also depend on the subject matter and whether your book is intended for a general or specialised readership.

In general, authors should not sign a contract until they know when their manuscript will be completed and a typescript delivered to the publisher. If you write on a variety of subjects it may be preferable to be published by more than one publisher. Moreover, even if your books are on a similar subject, the appearance of too many books by one author on the same publisher's list may reduce their sales. Some historians prefer to get a chapter of their book or an article included in an anthology or reader because it can sometimes be a useful means of increasing interest in their book by bringing its existence before a wider readership. An alternative approach is to write articles for a commissioned volume of historical readings, although multi-author books can pose problems for publishers. The principal reasons for the emergence of problems with such books are: there may be an unevenness in the quality of the articles; the contributors may be writing for different audiences; there may be gaps in information which cannot be compensated for; and there may also be some degree of overlap in the coverage of subjects. You will have to make your own assessment of the benefits and disadvantages of getting your research published under different modes of publication.

The quality of scholarship exhibited in any historical monograph is expected to be sound, sources cited should be adequately documented and arguments should be easy to follow. Try to identify why your book is likely to hold the attention of your readers, and assess which readers will want to purchase, not merely consult, your book. A crucial factor involves being able to identify why your book is important, particularly if there are few other similar books published on the same subject. Your work may be distinctive simply because no book has been published on a similar topic. Alternatively, perhaps any work which is available is either out of date or simply out of print. It may be that competing books are weak on historical analysis, or have not taken account of the availability of new published or unpublished source material. Publishers will be attracted to any work which is intrinsically important, well-documented, of an appropriate length and displays originality in content or in the treatment of its subject. This is precisely the type of historical work which will have a larger potential market. No publisher is under any obligation to accept anything offered by an author. However, if your work is exceptionally good then it certainly deserves to be published and made available to a wider public, whether general or scholarly.

Books need to have well-defined markets and the potential sale of a given number of copies over a pre-determined period. If your work is primarily academic in nature then an approach may be made to a specialised publisher, such as a university press. However, specialised books will have a more limited potential audience. An alternative approach might be to get your book adopted on to university courses, particularly if you intend to persuade a publisher to make the material available in paperback. A book will only be published in paperback if there is a good prospect of significant sales being achieved which will justify the larger print run needed. Some books on a publisher's list may be reprinted, whereas others might be issued in a new edition if major changes are incorporated in the material, such as an additional chapter or an updating of the text and bibliography. In new editions, some information needs to be re-checked, such as cross-references to chapters, statistical data in tables, or time-related references in the text. The bibliography may also have to be updated to take account of new publications, new editions of other books and books which have gone out of print. As a general rule, books which have been adopted on courses need to be revised more frequently to ensure that their contents are kept up to date: this may involve extending the chronology and revising the preliminary matter, text and index.

Publishers have their own specific criteria which they use in deciding whether to publish a book. Most publishers will wish to consider the academic merit of the material, its suitability for their list and also estimate the marketability of the proposed book. The last is commonly referred to as getting the right book appearing by the right author at the right price and time. But publishers do use the profits of some books to subsidise the cost of producing others which, although regarded as important, are nevertheless thought unlikely to generate significant sales. Publishers' lists and policies do change and potential authors need not be discouraged too much by negative responses from the first few publishers that are approached; after all, many thousands of books are published each year. However, it is worth stating that there are a number of cost factors which publishers do take into account when deciding whether or not to publish a book: the number of pages; the extent of illustrations and tables; size of print and number of lines per page; the amount of discounts given to bookshops who agree to stock a particular book; the percentage rate of royalties paid to the author; whether the author is well known; and the amount of subsidy received by the publisher to publish the book. You may wish to keep some of these factors in mind when preparing work for publication.

It was mentioned at the beginning of this chapter that some historians choose to approach a publisher with the intention of getting material published which is based on an academic thesis. There are a few general points worth noting if you envisage adopting this type of approach. Firstly, a thesis has a rather rigid structure and uses a scholarly prose, whereas the narrative in a book needs to flow more smoothly, as well as appeal to a wider audience. The purpose in writing a book is to communicate new ideas effectively, whereas in a thesis the writer is invariably more concerned to demonstrate his or her knowledge of the subject and show evidence that it has been adequately researched. In a thesis the content therefore becomes too defensive in style and tone. A thesis or dissertation may tend to adopt a cautious formal style with extensive footnotes which document all significant points, whereas a book needs to have a more readable and confident style with far fewer footnotes. Books have a wider target audience than theses and generally assume less depth of knowledge on the part of readers. It is therefore sensible to indicate to a publisher that your thesis can and will be altered to make it more suitable for publication. If you find it difficult to revise your work without significantly reducing the 100,000 word limit of a thesis, then consider the possibility of submitting several articles to journals by rewriting individual chapters of your thesis or dissertation.

A thesis can be revised to make it more suitable for publication as a book. You may find that you have to reduce the number of headings or subdivisions within each chapter so that the table of contents is not over-elaborate. Less emphasis will also have to be placed on a review of existing historical literature. Other desirable changes might include the following: 1 the introduction of shorter sentences; 2 simplification of specialist language and jargon; 3 elimination of obvious points or transitional devices which signal advances in the argument; and 4 a reduction in the number and length of quoted extracts. You may also discover that unnecessary footnotes need to be excluded, such as those which support reasonable assumptions and therefore do not add anything of substance to the work. The bibliography in a book might also be shorter and more selective than that included in a thesis, unless there are valid reasons for citing a large number of publications. Books do share some common aims with theses because both aim to make a contribution to knowledge, show an adequate knowledge of the field of study and present a unified body of work which is satisfactory in its literary presentation.

You may wish to consider various other methods for publicising the results of your research, such as via research seminars, contacting the press and broadcast media or by using the Internet. The language you use to disseminate your research will have to be tailored to the audience you are hoping to address. For example, a feature in a local, regional or national newspaper should preferably be written in concise non-technical language, with major points highlighted so that the material can be appreciated by non-specialists. Media awareness skills is perhaps an area which relatively few historians have sought to develop, yet it may be helpful if the results of your research are to be publicised outwith the academic community. By bringing your research to a wider audience you may help to stimulate an interesting debate on a historical issue which perhaps may also assist you to obtain funding for future projects. It may also help you make contacts and so obtain assistance from other people interested in your project. The ability to get material published in the press depends to a significant extent upon developing an interesting and newsworthy aspect of your research and bringing this to the attention of appropriate journalists. You will probably have to supply a concise catchy headline, identify a few key points which summarise your research findings, list these points using clear understandable non-technical language and supply a short summary of your work so that the context can be appreciated. If your project contains several interesting themes, you may be able to sustain public interest in it over a period of time by supplying information on different or related topics in stages. If you take part in a radio or television broadcast you will also have to provide short replies to the major points and present these in an interesting and entertaining manner.

The type of media which you contact will depend upon your target audience (i.e. those who will be interested in hearing about or using your research findings). Consider whether your historical research project covers topics which are of local or national significance. Have you completed a historical study of a particular profession which may be of interest to a regular specialist publication or newsletter? If the latter applies, use a reference publication, such as *Willings Press Guide*, to identify suitable outlets for your news story. You may have to monitor several newspapers and broadcast programmes in order to identify which topics or themes they appear to be particularly interested in covering. If you can complete this task successfully you will be able to target your efforts more effectively. It is perhaps useful to generate interest in your project in its early stages. Obviously this may be more difficult to achieve with historical topics because they are often less topical than scientific topics or those within the social sciences. However, it may be worthwhile focusing on aspects of your project which could be of interest to non-specialists, by drawing attention to new, unusual or unexpected results which emerged from your research.

Your subject may link in with other topics currently covered in the press, radio or television and, if so, so much the better. Your aim should be to provide interesting information which will contribute to an understanding of a particular subject or theme which appears to be of topical interest. Put yourself in the place of the journalist or member of the public and ask yourself whether your topic sounds interesting, informative and newsworthy. Think of the type of questions which they are likely to ask and want answered. The amount of information you supply on your project will depend upon which media outlet you choose to approach: a feature article in a magazine weekend supplement or specialist publication can be based on a fuller summary than an article intended for a daily newspaper. If you wish the information to be published or broadcast on a particular day, then find out the closing dates and times for the submission of material. Send your material to your chosen media outlets at the same time because information which appears in a newspaper on one day is less likely to be covered by a rival newspaper the following day. The only exception would occur where you believe there are significant advantages in allowing one source an exclusive story, such as where an important media outlet offers to give detailed coverage of your research findings. Finally, do remember to prepare some answers to any obvious questions you are likely to be asked about the content of your research.

Although established authors find it much easier to get work published, the type of topic and the quality of the work will remain the principal selling points for new authors. Few academic books earn their authors a handsome profit, so most writers of academic books do not require the services of a literary agent. A literary agent is more useful for established authors of popular books who generate a reasonable income from the sale of their books. In these circumstances the literary agent may help an author secure a contract on more favourable terms with a commercial publisher. Moreover, the public lending right (PLR) is probably of little material benefit to authors of academic books because, unlike the authors of popular history books, their publications are not borrowed on such a frequent basis that would result in any payment under the PLR system. The publisher of specialised books is also unlikely to derive any significant financial benefit from publishing such books. Many specialised small publishers and university presses receive a subsidy from a research council or arts body to assist with the financial costs of publishing books which, although of academic merit, might not have been published according to commercial criteria. You should not be deterred from approaching publishers, both large and small, if you have a good proposal for a history book and know how to highlight its advantages. The successful completion and publication of historical research can be a rewarding experience and provide the necessary stimulus for further research on other subjects of historical interest.

PART III   STYLISTIC CONVENTIONS

14

Abbreviations, numbers and punctuation

There are a number of stylistic conventions to which you may be expected to adhere when preparing a dissertation or thesis or published articles and books. This section focuses on three main categories of style: the presentation of abbreviations, numbers and punctuation. Later sections will cover the following aspects: the format of different parts of a typescript; the citation of footnote and bibliographical references; proofreading; and the preparation of an index.

Abbreviations

There are a number of abbreviations which are used in the research and publication of historical work. Some of the most useful ones which you should be aware of are included in the list which follows. Ideally, all abbreviations should be used sparingly. Essential abbreviations which are incorporated in any history project, other than the specific abbreviations mentioned in the list which follows, should be written in full when they are first used. If many different abbreviations have to be used it is best to prepare a separate list of them for inclusion in the preliminary matter of your dissertation, thesis or book. Lower-case letters are used for most abbreviations; those which contain both upper and lower-case letters should be followed by a full stop. Note that no full stop is needed if the final letter of a word also appears in its abbreviation. For example, the word *number* is abbreviated to 'no.' whereas *numbers* is abbreviated to 'nos'. A list of abbreviations should not contain any closing punctuation marks.

app.	appendix
arch.	archaeological
art.	article
b.	born
B.	Bulletin
bk	book
c.	century; chapter (of legal documents)
c. or *ca*	about, approximately, *circa*
caps	capital letters
cat.	catalogue
cf.	compare
ch.	chapter
CIP	Cataloguing-in-Publication
col.	column
comp.	compiler, compiled by
cont.	continued
div.	division
do.	ditto, the same
ed.	edited by, editor
edn	edition
e.g.	for example
et al.	and others
et seq.	and the following, as in p. 36 *et seq.*
etc.	and so forth, and so on, et cetera
f.	following page, as in p. 36f.
ff.	following pages, as in p. 36ff.
fig.	figure
fl.	*floruit*
fol.	folio
hist.	historian, historical, history
ibid.	in the same place, as in the citation of a publication in the immediately preceding footnote, thus ibid., p. 132
i.e.	that is
Inst.	Institute
ISBN	International Standard Book Number

ital.	italic
J.	Journal
l.	line
l.c.	lower case
ll.	lines
loc. cit.	in the place cited
max.	maximum
mic.	microfilm/s
min.	minimum
monog.	monograph
MS	manuscript
MSS	manuscripts
n.	note
n/a	not applicable
NB	nota bene, note well
n.d.	no date (of publication)
nn.	notes
no.	number
nos	numbers
n.p.	no place (of publication)
NS.	new series
o.p.	out of print
op. cit.	in the work cited, such as a publication referred to earlier, but not in the immediately preceding footnote, thus op. cit., p. 172
p.	page
P.	Proceedings or Press
para.	paragraph
passim	in many places, as in ch. 5 *passim*
pbk	paperback book
per.	periodical
per cent	percentage
pl.	plate
pp.	pages
prehist.	prehistorical, prehistory

PS	postscript
pt	part
PTO	please turn over
pub.	publication, publish, publisher
Q.	Quarterly
q.v.	which see, as in q.v., p. 58
r.	recto
R.	Review
rev.	revised
rom.	roman (type)
s.a.e.	stamped addressed envelope, self addressed envelope
sec.	section
ser.	series
sic	so, thus (use this to indicate a spelling error in a quotation)
Soc.	Society
ss.	sections
stet	let it stand, do not erase
T.	Transactions
tr./trans.	translated by, translator
u.c.	upper case
Univ.	University
UP	University Press
v.	verso, versus
viz	that is to say, namely
vol.	volume
vols	volumes
vs.	versus
w.e.f.	with effect from

Numbers

It is normal practice to elide all numbers, except for the teens. Some variations in practice do occur, but the following examples may be recommended:

27–8, 45–6, 49–54, 60–2, 63–72, 198–9, 203–4, 363–73, 470–5, 508–9, 680–4, 1841–5, 1960–1, 1970–5

but note the following
11–19, 16–18, 116–18, 210–11, 211–15, 314–15, 512–16, 1914–18, 1789–1914

In displayed matter, such as in the title of a book, all numbers or dates are normally printed in full, thus 1920–1929. Do not elide the numbers on the titles of published works if they have not been elided by the publisher. Numbers less than one hundred are usually written out (e.g. twenty-four), except where they appear in statistical tables. However, if two numbers are included in a sentence, only one of which is below 100, then use numerals to refer to *both* of them. Do not begin a sentence with a numeral: instead, spell these numbers. Note also that it is preferable to write '22-year-old craftsman' than 'twenty-two-year-old craftsman' because this avoids the use of an additional hyphen.

For other instances involving numerals, proceed as follows.

Fractions

Write '$2^2/_3$' *not* 'two and two-thirds'.

Percentages

Write '8 per cent' in the text, but '8%' in tables or in notes. There is no full stop after 'per cent', unless this abbreviation appears at the end of a sentence.

Span of numbers

Write '280 to 300' or '280–300', *not* 'from 280–300'.

Numerals in a book

Roman numerals are used for the preliminary pages; use figures, not words, when referring to volume, part, chapter and page numbers.

Measurements

It is always best to use numbers, thus '5kW' rather than 'five kW'. Two numbers should not be written together, either as numerals or as words: 'two 50kW transmitters', *not* '2 50kW transmitters' or 'two fifty kW transmitters'. If there are two quantities, use a word to describe one series and a numeral to describe the other (e.g. the two transmitters held 9 masts).

Money

References to decimal currency are written as follows: 45p, £6, £6.50, £6.5m. References to pre-decimal currency are written as follows: 8s, 8s 6d, £8 9s 6d.

Time

Information should appear as follows: 6.30p.m., six o'clock, twelve months.

Dates

References should appear as follows: 1 May 1851, 1922, 1930s, the seventies, 155–135 BC, AD 135–50. Note that whereas 1871/2, or 1871/72 refers to one year, such as a financial year, 1871–2 or 1871–72 refers to two years.

To refer to a period of time, write 'from 1971 to 1972', *not* 'from 1971–1972'; or 'between 1963 and 1964', *not* 'between 1963–4'. A reference to a century should take the form 'the twentieth century', *not* 'the 20th century'.

Roman numerals

These are still sometimes used to identify the volume numbers of old manuscripts, books or journals. They are also printed in lower case in the preliminary pages of a book. A summary of roman numerals is given as follows:

I = 1	VII = 7	L = 50	DC = 600
II = 2	VIII = 8	LX = 60	CM = 900
III = 3	IX = 9	XC = 90	M = 1,000
IV = 4	X = 10	C = 100	
V = 5	XX = 20	CD = 400	
VI = 6	XL = 40	D = 500	

Punctuation

A few comments are offered here on some of the more important aspects relating to the use of punctuation. Choosing and using the correct punctuation can play a significant role in assisting, or hindering, our understanding and enjoyment of a piece of historical writing.

Full stop

A full stop represents a definite pause. It should not be placed after each item in a list or at the end of chapter or section headings. It should be used after abbreviations, except where the final letter of a word also appears in its abbreviation (e.g. edition is abbreviated to edn).

Comma

A comma represents a short pause within a sentence. A comma does not have to be placed before a conjunction such as 'and' in a short sentence; a comma though is often used before 'but'. A single comma provides a longer pause than commas used in pairs. Commas should be placed between a parenthetical phrase or to separate items in a list. In the latter it may be necessary to place a comma before the final 'and' in a list to avoid ambiguity: Scotland, Wales and the English regions, *but* Scotland, Wales, south and west, and the English regions. A comma is normally placed after the words 'however', 'moreover' and 'for example'. The presence, or absence, of a comma can turn a defining relative clause (a) into a commenting relative clause (b), as follows:

(a) the political leader who arrived that morning told the crowd about his historical mission
(b) the political leader, who arrived that morning, told the crowd about his historical mission

Semicolon

This signifies a pause which is longer than a comma, but shorter than a colon or full stop. It should be placed outside inverted commas and parentheses. Semicolons, rather than commas, are normally used to separate numerous lengthy clauses, as in a list. You should use semicolons with coordinate clauses, but not before subordinate clauses, because the latter are too closely linked with the main clause.

Colon

A colon represents a longer pause than a semicolon, but less than that of a full stop. A colon should be used to introduce a list, a quotation or a summary; it can also be placed between two statements of equal weight, or where a second statement elaborates the first. A colon should not be followed by a dash when it introduces a list. Normally a colon is used to link equally balanced clauses which are either closely connected in sense, or which contrast with each other. Colons should always be placed outside inverted commas.

Dash

A dash provides a pause similar to that achieved by the use of parentheses. It may be used at the end of a sentence to separate material which may be classed as an afterthought. Alternatively, a pair of dashes may be used within a sentence to achieve the same effect; used this way, a pair of dashes will provide greater emphasis than a pair of commas. A dash is also used between dates or page numbers. Do not add a dash to a colon which is being used to introduce a list.

Parentheses

Curved or round brackets provide a pause within a sentence similar to that achieved by a dash or a pair of dashes. Parentheses and dashes provide more emphasis than commas. No comma should be placed after a parenthesis, unless a comma was present in the original sentence before the parenthesis was added. If round brackets are placed at the end of a sentence, the full stop should be placed outside the concluding parenthesis, unless the expression represents a separate complete sentence.

Brackets

Square brackets are normally used for an editorial insertion in a quotation. They can also be used in instances where parentheses need to be placed within existing parentheses, so that one set can be distinguished from the other.

Question mark

Question marks should only be used for direct, not indirect, questions. A question mark may also be placed *before* a word or phrase if its accuracy is in doubt. Question marks are placed inside inverted commas if the person who is being quoted is asking a question; otherwise, place question marks outside any inverted commas.

Hyphen

Try not to split a hyphenated word at the end of a line or separate a pair of hyphenated words (e.g. full or part-time). Note that in some instances the omission of a hyphen may lead to some confusion (e.g. 'long standing official', instead of 'long-standing official').

Exclamation mark

Avoid the use of exclamation marks whenever possible. If you do have to use them in a sentence which contains inverted commas, the exclamation mark should be placed inside the latter if the exclamation belongs to the quotation.

Apostrophe

The apostrophe precedes the letter 's' of the possessive case in singular words (e.g. diplomat's) and in plurals that *do not* end in 's'. The apostrophe follows the 's' in plurals that *do* end in 's' (e.g. the diplomats' conference). If you have to refer to a decade, omit the apostrophe (e.g. the 1970s).

Ellipsis points

Three full points are used to omit material at the beginning, middle or end of a sentence. Words can be omitted at the beginning or end of a passage to adjust a quotation to the grammar of the sentence, or to omit less relevant material. However, if the quotation represents only part of a larger sentence, and if the meaning is clear, then it is not essential to use ellipsis points to indicate the omission of material. If ellipsis points are required at the end of a complete sentence, then add a further full stop, so that there are *four* full points. Ellipsis points may precede or follow any punctuation mark within a sentence.

Quotation marks

Use single quotation marks to identify any quoted extract; double quotation marks are normally used to indicate a quotation which appears within a quotation. Quotation marks are also used for a number of other purposes, as follows: to enclose the titles of articles in books, journals or newspapers; to indicate chapters of books or the title of unpublished papers; or to identify slang or technical language. The placing of quotation marks in relation to other punctuation marks is normally guided by the following general principles. A full stop or comma should be placed *outside* quotation marks if the words which are quoted either do not represent a complete sentence, or if they do, they form only part of the main sentence. But if a quotation is a complete sentence and ends with a full stop, then place the full stop *before* the closing quotation mark. Other punctuation marks (e.g. commas, question marks, exclamation marks, a dash or a parenthesis) should also be placed *before* the closing quotation mark if they belong to the extract which is quoted, rather than belong to the main sentence. If they do belong to the latter then they should be placed *outside* the closing quotation mark. Colons and semicolons should be placed outside any quotation marks. Ellipsis points should be placed within the quotation marks if it is clear that the omitted words, which are signified by the ellipsis points, form part of the quotation.

It is important to follow the original spelling and punctuation of quotations exactly. For example, if you have to decide whether a comma should be placed before or after a quotation mark, this will depend upon whether there was a pause in the original quoted extract: if there was a pause, the comma should precede the quotation mark. In most instances you will extract and reproduce a quotation from a much longer sentence and so the full stop is placed *outside* the closing quotation mark. However, if you quote a complete sentence it is normally introduced by a short phrase which is separated from the quotation by either a comma or a colon; in this instance the full stop will be placed *before* the closing quotation mark. In general, all punctuation marks should be placed according to sense, so that if a pause or a question belongs to the quoted extract, then the appropriate punctuation mark should be placed before any closing quotation mark.

15

Typescript format

The publication of historical work in book format requires some familiarity with the structure and functions of each part of a book. Similarly, the submission of work for a higher degree requires research students to be familiar with the various parts of a dissertation or thesis. The purpose of this section is to outline for potential authors the purpose of each part of a book and give advice on the preparation of a typescript intended for publication. The appearance of a dissertation or thesis is not substantially different from that of a book, except that the former will not include a half-title, frontispiece, imprint, dedication or foreword. A history thesis is also unlikely to require the inclusion of an index. But a dissertation or thesis will, unlike a book, include an abstract and a declaration, both of which are normally incorporated in the preliminary matter. Much of the information in this section will therefore be of practical use for the preparation of a typescript for a published book as well as for a dissertation or thesis. The special, and more detailed, requirements involved in the citation of footnote and bibliographical references, in proofreading and in the preparation of an index, are all covered in the remaining three chapters of Part III.

Parts of a book

The sequence in which preliminary matter, text and end-matter appears in a book will normally be similar to the items in the following list. Not all items, of course, will appear in every book. The various parts of a book are listed as follows:

- blank page
- half-title
- frontispiece
- title page
- imprint, copyright notice, ISBN, CIP information
- dedication
- contents list
- list of illustrations (plates, figures, maps, tables)
- foreword
- preface
- acknowledgements
- list of abbreviations
- introduction
- text, subdivided into parts, chapters or sections
- appendices
- glossary
- notes
- bibliography
- index

The preliminary pages are numbered using lower case roman numerals; page numbering begins with the introduction, or the first page of chapter 1 if there is no separate introduction.

Half-title

This page should only contain the title of the book, or a shortened version of a long title. If your book contains a subtitle, it will not be included on this page. The verso of this page is normally left blank, but sometimes it is used to list previous books written by the same author. Numeration begins at the half-title (i.e. this page is counted in the prelims but is not numbered).

Frontispiece

If a book contains a frontispiece it will be included on the verso of the half-title and therefore face the title page. The caption should be placed below the illustration; the source may be referred to in an acknowledgements page. The page on which the frontispiece appears is not numbered.

Title page

This page gives details of the title (and subtitle if there is one), the edition (if other than the first), the name of the author (including, if desired, degrees, distinctions and position held) and the name of the publisher. This page is counted in the prelims but is not numbered.

Imprint, copyright notice, ISBN, CIP information

These details appear on the verso of the title page. This page will contain the name and address of the publisher, year of publication, the copyright notice, the ISBN and Cataloguing-in-Publication data. Details of the printer and the typeface used will also be provided. This page is not numbered.

Dedication

The inclusion of this page is optional; it is used to convey a private message chosen by the author. The dedication is printed on the recto; the verso of this page is left blank.

Contents list

The contents should list all the preliminary pages (except the half-title, title and imprint), parts, chapters or sections, appendices, glossary, notes, bibliography and index. Give the exact title of all chapters, appendices, and so on as they appear in the text. Appendices should be numbered using arabic numerals in one sequence, not individually numbered chapter by chapter. Even if a book is divided into parts, the chapters should normally be numbered in a single sequence. Roman numerals should be used for the preliminary pages. Turnover lines for titles of chapters should be indented. It is not essential to add a full stop between the chapter numbers and the chapter titles. The word 'part' appears in the contents if your book is subdivided into parts, but each chapter should not normally be preceded by the word 'chapter'. The first page of the contents appears as a recto.

List of illustrations

If you include several illustrations, a list of captions should be prepared. Plates, figures, maps and tables should each be listed on separate pages. The words 'list of . . .' should be included in the contents, but omitted from the heading on the page or pages which list the illustrations.

Foreword

Not all books contain a foreword. Where one is included it will be written by someone other than the author who is distinguished in the same field of study. The foreword should refer to the work in general terms, as well as relating the book to other publications in the same subject area. The name of the person who has written the foreword may appear in the contents. The foreword normally appears as a recto.

Preface

The preface is written by the author to indicate the scope and purpose of the book, how it came to be written and to whom the author is obliged for assistance during the course of researching material for the book. If your book is published in a second or subsequent edition, a separate preface will be written and either included after the original preface or replace it entirely. The new preface should indicate how the edition differs from earlier ones. At the end of the preface the author's name (or initials) and a date is sometimes included.

Acknowledgements

The acknowledgements are impersonal and therefore normally list the sources from whom permission has been given to reproduce copyright material, such as text, illustrations and tables. This list may be arranged in alphabetical order according to the name of the copyright owner. It is normally the responsibility of the author to obtain copyright permission in circumstances where a significant amount of material has been quoted or when extensive use has been made of particular source material. Copyright permissions letters should be gathered together and may be submitted to your publisher at a later date, rather than submitted with the typescript. However, these letters must be sent to the publisher prior to publication of your book. It is normally permissible to quote up to 200 words for the purpose of criticism or review without having to seek copyright clearance; some publishers set a higher word limit. In general, there is no need to seek permission to quote brief passages in a scholarly book if the source is acknowledged in a footnote. Otherwise, you should write to the copyright owners giving an exact reference to material which is quoted, and also enclose details of your proposed book, the publisher and the expected date of publication. You will normally be expected to pay for any copyright permissions. Always acknowledge the source of any textual or illustrative material, regardless of whether there is any formal requirement to seek permission to reproduce such material.

List of abbreviations

If you wish to include a list of abbreviations, all items in this list must be in alphabetical order; no full stop is required after each item in the list. The heading for this list should merely be entitled 'Abbreviations'. A list will not be needed if you do not use many abbreviations, or alternatively if those which you do use are commonly known.

Introduction

The introduction to a book should appear prior to chapter 1 if it provides introductory comments on the entire text; otherwise, comments can be incorporated at the beginning of the first chapter. The first page of a book should begin with the introduction, or the start of chapter 1, if there is no separate introduction. The first page number of each chapter or other major division within a book will either be centred and placed at the foot of the page or otherwise omitted; all other page numbers are normally placed in the top right-hand corner of your typescript and aligned with the text. Pages should be numbered continuously throughout your typescript, not chapter by chapter. You may notice that in a book the left-hand pages (verso) are always even numbers, whereas right-hand pages (recto) are always odd numbers. In general your introduction can serve several purposes: outline the problem to be discussed, the themes to be covered, the aims and objectives of your work, and the range of sources consulted. You are unlikely to be in a position to prepare a proper introduction (or conclusion) until you have written all the chapters or sections and know what topics or themes you will be discussing.

Text

Your text may be subdivided into parts, chapters or sections. If several chapters are grouped together into different themes, a book may be divided into perhaps three or four parts. The part-title page will contain the part number and title, but no page number; the verso of each part-title page will be blank, so that the first chapter of each part will always begin on the next recto after the part title. The headings of any part titles, chapters or appendices will normally be centred or ranged left. Headings are not underlined and are best kept as short as possible. Upper case letters are normally used for the first word, main words and proper names within the headings. Publishers tend not to divide words within chapter titles, leave a short word on the last line of a title, or place full stops after any headings. A chapter may be divided into numbered sections, in which case section 2.3 would, for example, represent the third section of chapter 2. Note that the first line of each paragraph is indented, except for the first line in the first paragraph of each chapter or section. Your book may include a conclusion which will either be incorporated in a final chapter or in a separate conclusion. The conclusion is used to review your evidence and present a considered judgement on this evidence. It may draw attention to the importance of your findings, but must not be used as an opportunity to discuss new issues, themes or topics. The conclusion should not simply repeat points which were made in the introduction or examine views which do not agree with those expressed in your preceding chapters. The conclusion can, however, be used to answer any questions which were originally posed in the introduction and, if appropriate, also provide some suggestions for further research.

Appendices

Appendices can be useful if you wish to include material which would otherwise interrupt the flow of the narrative within each chapter. Material which may included in the appendices are tables, charts, graphs, diagrams, maps or reproductions of historical documents. In a book the appendices are normally set in a smaller type, with each appendix separately numbered and starting on a new page. If a book is divided into separate parts, each preceded by a part-title page, then a similar page will be used to precede all the appendices.

Glossary

A glossary may be included if you wish specialist terms used throughout the text to be explained more fully. All entries within your glossary must be in alphabetical order. If the headwords are arranged in a separate column, the turnover lines for any entry will not be indented; if the headwords are not arranged in a separate column, the turnover lines need to be indented so that the headwords can be easily identified. In the latter case the headwords may be printed in bold.

Notes

If you choose not to include notes at the foot of each page of text (i.e. footnotes) or at the end of each chapter (i.e. chapter endnotes), they must be placed at the end of the book just before the bibliography. Your list of notes should be subdivided by chapter. It is helpful to include the chapter numbers and titles in this list because readers will often recall the title of the chapter they are reading, yet seldom recall the chapter number. Full bibliographical details need not be given for each item if you choose to provide a comprehensive bibliography which includes all items referred to in the footnotes or endnotes. Your references should all be carefully checked to ensure that they are accurate and consistent in format.

Bibliography

This will serve as a guide to sources and to further reading. A systematic method has to be adopted for making a record of sources consulted. You may wish to subdivide your bibliography according to type of source material, but note that too many subdivisions will make it difficult for readers to locate any specific item. Turnover lines for any entry in the bibliography need to be indented so that each item can be clearly identified. The bibliography should normally include all items cited in the footnotes or endnotes, unless you want it to serve only as a guide to further reading; in the latter case your readers will be referred to the separate lists of footnotes or endnotes. Your bibliography may also include other source material which, although not cited in the notes, were found to be useful. These are the type of sources to which you believe readers may also wish to refer. The bibliography, in common with the appendices, will normally be set in a smaller type than the rest of the text.

Index

All scholarly history books, although comparatively few dissertations or theses, contain an index. All entries in an index are arranged in alphabetical order. Refer to the detailed notes in chapter 18 on the format of an index and how to prepare an index for a book.

Typescript format

There are a number of general points which you may wish to keep in mind when preparing a typescript. These points are equally applicable whether work is prepared on a computer or typewriter. All material which you prepare should be double spaced and typed on only one side of A4 paper, leaving adequate margins on all sides. Try to allow about sixty to seventy characters per line, including word spaces. If possible, you should aim for some consistency in the length of line and in the number of lines per page. The type should be clear, using only one type size throughout your work. Publishers normally advise against the use of proportional spacing, so right-hand margins should not be justified. Allow for double spacing between paragraphs, not double-double spacing. A page or column should not commence with the last line of a paragraph, but a paragraph may start as the last line of a page. It is best to leave adequate margins of at least one inch at the top, right and foot of the page; a larger left-hand margin of perhaps 1½ to 2 inches may be required, especially for dissertations and theses because these have to be bound. If you need to add or delete material at a later stage then the page numbers can be altered relatively easy if your work has been prepared using a word processor. However, if the work was originally prepared on a typewriter the following procedure should be adopted: if, for example, page 40 is deleted, the preceding page should be numbered 39–40, or page 39 should indicate that page 41 follows; if two pages are added after page 30, then number them 30a and 30b, state at the foot of page 30 that pages 30a–b follow, and state on page 30b that page 31 follows. Cross-references within your typescript should normally be to chapters or appendices rather than to page numbers, because exact page numbers cannot be known until the work is typeset and page proofs are produced. However, if you wish a cross-reference to refer to a page(s), then type 'see p. 000', so that the actual page number(s) can be entered at page proof stage when the precise reference(s) will be known.

Running heads

At page-proof stage each page will incorporate a running head, which is printed at the top of each page of text. If your book is subdivided into parts, the part title may be printed on the verso (left-hand page) and the chapter title on the recto (right-hand page). There are no running heads above part-title pages. Your running heads may need to be abbreviated in length so that they can appear across the top of the page. If a book is divided into chapters and sections, rather than parts, the chapter title may appear on the verso and the section title on the recto. In the preliminary pages, glossary, bibliography and index, the running heads for verso and recto are identical. In the appendices the number of the appendix will normally appear on the verso (e.g. Appendix 2) and the title of the appendix will appear on the recto. No running heads will appear above the first page of each chapter if the chapters begin on a new page. It may be helpful to suggest suitable short titles for running heads if asked to do so by your publisher.

Underlining

In a typescript, underlining is used to indicate changes to the appearance of the text. For example, a single line will indicate that italic type is required, wavy underlining indicates bold type and double underlining indicates small capitals. Italic is used more frequently than bold or small capitals because it has a number of uses. It can be used to indicate the following: titles of books, journals, newspapers, art works, and films and broadcast programmes; foreign words and phrases; words to be emphasised; running heads; and directions, such as *see also* and *continued*. Titles of articles, chapters or unpublished papers are normally enclosed in single quotation marks and not italicised. If a name which is normally italicised does appear in capitalised or italic headings, a publisher will usually place these names within single quotation marks.

Capitalisation

The use of capitals makes a word more specific and limited in its reference. Capitals should be used for places, persons, titles, months, days, laws, organisations and proprietary names. Do not use capitals for seasons of the year. Capitals are normally used when you wish to refer to something in the particular sense, such as 'the Labour Government', rather than in the general sense, such as 'the policy of a government'. The best advice is to use capitals sparingly.

Hyphens

Avoid using hyphens to divide a word at the end of a line unless the word is usually hyphenated, because the hyphen in your typescript copy may be retained in error in the typeset copy which is prepared by the printer. If a word must be split, hyphenate at the correct division within the word by referring to *The Oxford Spelling Dictionary*. Try to leave at least two letters at the end of a line and carry over at least three letters to the following line. Any word which must be divided should not be included at the end of a recto (or a verso if there is a full-page illustration on the recto). Be careful also to distinguish between the attributive and predicative forms of hyphenated words:

> a tenth-century manuscript (attributive form, with one main stress) in the tenth century (predicative form, with two main stresses)

Quotations

You will undoubtedly incorporate some quoted extracts in your work. Quotations should be used selectively and in circumstances where they will be used to best effect, such as to reinforce a particular argument or emphasise the sense and style of the person whose words are quoted. There are a few general points which are therefore worth summarising about the presentation of quotations in typescript copy:

1 Copy the exact text, spelling and punctuation which appear in the original source.
2 Place superscript numerals *after* punctuation marks. These numerals should appear at the end of a sentence or at a major break within a sentence, such as that indicated by a semicolon or parenthesis.
3 Use single quotation marks, except for quotations within a quotation which take double quotation marks.
4 Short quotations can be run on from the main sentence and so no ellipsis points need be placed before the quotation. However, if material is omitted within an extract then ellipsis points (i.e. 3 dots) should be used.

5 For a short quotation it is permissible to alter the initial letter of the first word from capitals to lower case if the extract is run on from the sentence which precedes the quotation. If an extract is not run on (i.e. if the preceding sentence ended with a full stop) then change the full stop to a colon.

6 If a quotation exceeds 50–60 words in length, use a block (or displayed) quotation. Block quotations are normally introduced with a colon, they are indented, and they do not take quotation marks (except for a quotation within a block quotation which will be placed within single inverted commas). No ellipsis points need be used at the beginning or end of block quotations, and the initial letter of the first word can be lower case if the quoted material is extracted from a longer sentence. Remember not to indent either the first line of a block quotation or the first line of the sentence which immediately follows the block quotation, unless, of course, the latter begins a new paragraph.

7 Ellipsis points may need to be included at the beginning or end of a quotation if you think that the extract quoted gives a distorted view of the contents of the original source by being lifted out of context. If an ellipsis is placed at the end of a complete sentence then use four, not three, full points. Similarly, if an ellipsis is placed at the beginning of a sentence, and the preceding sentence ended with a full stop, then four full points will be needed.

8 Any editorial insertion you make within a quotation should be placed in square brackets, not parentheses.

Footnotes and endnotes

Footnotes appear at the foot of each page, whereas endnotes appear at the end of each chapter or at the end of a book. A full discussion of footnotes and endnotes is covered elsewhere in this book, but you may find it helpful if you glance at the following notes relating to the format of footnotes and endnotes in typescript copy.

1 Your notes should be listed on separate sheets, regardless of whether they are to appear as footnotes or endnotes. The footnote numbers will appear as superscript numerals in the text.

2 All notes should be typed double spaced if they are to be published in an article or book.

3 Footnotes are used primarily for documenting historical sources cited in the text. Content footnotes may be used to elaborate upon specific points in the text, but it is often better to incorporate this material in your text, place it in an appendix, or omit it.

4 Number your notes consecutively and separately for each chapter, and avoid placing footnote numbers within headings or subheadings. Footnote numbers should only be placed within a closing parenthesis if they refer to material within the parenthesis. As a general rule, footnote numbers usually follow any punctuation mark, except a dash.

5 Tables and lists which are not immediately relevant to the discussion in the text should be placed in an appendix, not in a footnote. Notes to tables must be separated from notes to your text.

Illustrations

A few general points are noted here for the benefit of historians who intend to include illustrations in their work; notes on the incorporation of tables, charts and graphs in any history project can be found in chapter 11.

1 Illustrations which need to be significantly reduced do not reproduce well.

2 Obtain a black-and-white glossy print rather than reproduce material directly from other publications.

3 Do not use paper clips or write in ballpoint pen on the back of photographs you intend to use; use a soft pencil or affix a self-adhesive label to identify the number and title of any illustration.

4 A publisher may ask you to submit a list of captions. These captions should be numbered and typed on a separate sheet. The source of illustrations will normally be placed within brackets after the captions or listed in an acknowledgements page. Plates are usually numbered in a separate sequence from text illustrations.

5 If only part of an illustration (i.e. a detail) is to be included, the relevant area should be indicated to your publisher using a photocopy of the illustration. The caption will then include the word 'detail' to indicate that only a detail is shown.

6 The choice of appropriate illustrations may be governed by aesthetic qualities, such as composition, as well as technical qualities, such as contrast and clarity.

7 If an illustration has to be positioned sideways on either verso or recto pages, ensure that the top of the illustration is on the left-hand margin of the page. References to illustrations in the text should state, for example, 'see figure 20'. Indicate in the margin of your typescript the approximate position where you would like illustrations to appear.

Final checking procedure

After your typescript has been prepared, the following checking procedure should be implemented before material is submitted to a publisher or university. Note that not all of the items which follow will be relevant to every history project.

1 Check that pages are in the correct order and that no pages are missing.

2 Check that all major divisions in your typescript are properly numbered and are in the correct order.

3 Compare the contents list with the prelims, chapters, appendices, bibliography and index to ensure that wording, capitalisation and punctuation are consistent.

4 Compare any list of illustrations and tables with their captions. Illustrations should be numbered by chapter, with captions provided on a separate sheet.

5 Ensure that no full stop appears at the end of each item in any list.

6 Check that all entries in a list of abbreviations are in the correct order and agree with the format used in the text.

7 Ensure that there is consistency in the format chosen for chapter headings, sections and subsections.

8 Check spelling, punctuation, capitalisation and use of italics in the text.

9 Check the length of paragraphs, noting the occurrence of very long or very short paragraphs.

10 Check the format and accuracy of all quotations.

11 Check that all dates are accurate and presented in a consistent format.

12 Check for consistency in the elision of pairs of numbers.

13 Check the accuracy of all statistical data in the text and appendices.

14 Ensure that all cross-references in the text are both accurate and refer to chapters or appendices, not to page numbers.

15 Ensure that a footnote or endnote exists for each note indicator, and that all note indicators are in superscript and placed in numerical order after punctuation marks.

16 Ensure that all footnotes or endnotes adopt a consistent referencing style and that they also appear in the bibliography.

17 Check that all the appendices are properly numbered and in the correct order.

18 Ensure that all entries in a glossary appear in correct alphabetical order.

19 Check that accurate chapter titles are provided for subheadings in endnotes, if your book or thesis does not use footnotes.

20 Ensure that all entries within the bibliography adopt a consistent format and are arranged in the correct order.

A separate series of checks will have to be made on the index for a book and, less commonly, for a dissertation or thesis. For details on the preparation and checking of an index, refer to chapter 18. The chapter that follows offers representative examples of how source material is cited in footnotes and bibliographies, a task referred to in items 16 to 20 above.

16

Footnote and bibliographical references

Historians have traditionally been expected to provide sufficient details of the sources on which their research has been based. What they have been less successful at is in achieving a level of consistency in the citation of these sources, whether in footnotes, endnotes or in bibliographies. The aim of this section is to provide you with several model examples on the citation of various types of source material which are used in historical research. These examples indicate the preferred formats which should be used for citing the different categories of source material which were identified in chapter 7.

The formats which follow are for guidance only because there is no single standard method for citing all types of source material. Small variations of format in the examples given would be equally acceptable. The notes which follow the examples do draw attention to some of these variations. However, the examples reflect the accepted practice for citing source material within the humanities. Some publishers, universities and university departments do, of course, produce their own style sheets. Some of them are willing to allow authors or research students to devise their own referencing style, providing that such a system is both sensible and consistent. But there are certain conventions to which publishers and academic institutions try to adhere. The problem for many historians and researchers is to know which variations in referencing style are permissible and which are not. The examples which follow will point you in the right direction. The intention of this section is therefore not to impose any standard referencing style, but rather to draw attention to the most sensible and preferred formats and encourage you to use them if you do not already do so. A certain degree of standardisation is beneficial because it makes it easier for historians and readers to understand, and less likely to misinterpret, footnote and bibliographical references.

In the humanities the normal method for citing publications is by use of the short-title system. With this system a full reference is provided the first time a publication is cited, but a shortened version is given in subsequent references. Footnotes and endnotes are numbered in a single consecutive sequence for each individual chapter, with superscript numerals used to identify each note within the text. A full reference is always provided in a bibliography or guide to further reading to enable readers to locate the relevant source material. In a bibliographical listing, items need to be arranged in alphabetical order by author (or title if there is no author). Some types of source material, such as manuscript collections or official publications, may need to be listed separately within a bibliography and perhaps arranged in numerical or chronological order. The order in which you list material should be dictated by the nature of the source material and the ability of your readers to locate it within the bibliography. You may also wish to note that in footnotes the use of the abbreviation 'ibid.' should only be used where a source which is cited is identical to that which occurs in the immediately preceding footnote.

The principal alternative to the short-title system is the author-date system, often referred to as the Harvard system. A few comments are offered here on that system because you may encounter it if you have to refer to social scientific publications. In the Harvard system references are inserted in the text by enclosing the author's surname, the date of publication and a page reference in parentheses. Full references are then provided at the end of the text, in a bibliography, in which publications are listed in alphabetical order. Two or more publications by the same author are listed chronologically by date of publication. The following example indicates how 1 a book and 2 an article would appear as a reference in the text and in a bibliographical list:

Reference in the text

1. (Taylor, 1965, pp. 120–5)
2. (Butterfield, 1955, p. 15)

Reference in a bibliography

1. Taylor, A.J.P. (1965), *English History 1914–1945*, Oxford: Oxford University Press.
2. Butterfield, H. (1955), 'The role of the individual in history', *History* 40, 1–17.

If more than one publication by the same author occurs then these are normally distinguished by placing letters after the date: (Bullock, 1979b). If the author's name is referred to in the text then only the date and page reference need be given in the reference: (1965, pp. 120–5). Where the abbreviation for pages is omitted, a colon will normally precede the page reference: (Taylor, 1965: 120–5). If two publications are referred to in the same reference, the note would appear as follows: (Bullock, 1979a, 1994) or (Taylor, 1965: 120–5; Butterfield, 1955: 15). Where a page reference is provided in the text, only the authors and dates of publication are normally given: (Taylor, 1965; Butterfield, 1955). The Harvard system is not widely used in the humanities, particularly because of the limitations which it imposes in citing some types of source material, notably unpublished material. You will therefore find it much more useful in your own historical research to adhere to the short-title system when citing different types of source material.

1 Manuscripts and archive material

General manuscript reference

Canning to Huskisson, 8 March 1821, Huskisson papers, British Library, Additional MS 38742, fols 187–97.

can be abbreviated to:
Canning to Huskisson, 8 March 1821, Huskisson papers, BL, Add. MS 38742, fols 187–97.

subsequent references:
British Library, Additional MS 38742, fol. 192.
BL, Add. MS 38742, fol. 192.

Letters

Melville Dinwiddie to W.J. Haley, 7 September 1946, BBC WAC, R6/187.

Minutes

Board of Governors: Minutes, 29 September 1955, BBC WAC, R1/1/23, no. 195.

Papers

Board of Governors: paper G.84/51, 27 June 1951, BBC WAC, R1/3/92, fols 2–3.

Memoranda

Neil McLean (Aberdeen Station Director) to J.C.W. Reith (Managing Director, Head Office), memo on staff, 4 September 1926, BBC WAC, R34/731/1.

Scottish Office, 'Broadcasting arrangements in Scotland', memorandum by the Secretary of State for Scotland, 11 January 1952, SRO, ED. 29/1, fol. 2.

Scottish Arts Council, 'Broadcasting and the arts in Scotland', 21 January 1975, SRO, COM.1/620, para. 5(b).

Reports

B.E. Nicolls, 'Post-war Home Programme set-up', 23 April 1945, BBC WAC, R34/574, fols 4, 9.

'Sound broadcasting future', statement by Director of Sound Broadcasting, 9 April 1957, BBC WAC, R34/422/3, fol. 7.

Notes

1 The sequence of items in a reference to unpublished material is as follows: author; title or description of document; date of document; repository; title of archive collection; reference number of collection; and folio, minute or paragraph numbers.

2 Place the titles of individual documents within single quotation marks. Descriptive titles, such as minutes, should be capitalised and not placed within quotation marks.

3 The location of a manuscript collection should be given in full in the first citation; thereafter, an abbreviated form should be used for subsequent references (e.g. Public Record Office, hereafter cited as PRO). If several sources of archive material are frequently cited, they should be included in a list of abbreviations, to be incorporated in the prelims.

4 For citations which are identical to that which occurs in the immediately preceding footnote, use the following format:

1. BL Add. MS 38742, fol. 192.
2. Ibid., fol. 194.
3. Ibid.

5 The titles of manuscript collections are neither italicised, nor placed within quotation marks.

6 With manuscripts, specific references are normally to folios than to page numbers (e.g. fols 17–19), but it is best to avoid placing the superscripts v and r (to denote verso and recto) after folio numbers.

7 In a bibliography, manuscripts should be listed by repository. Individual documents are not listed in a bibliography, but archive files may be listed in numerical or chronological order for each archive collection.

2 Official publications

Parliamentary debates (pre-1909)

212 Parl. Deb. ser. 3, cols 157–61 (25 June 1872).
37 Parl. Deb. ser. 4, col. 445 (17 Feb. 1896).

Parliamentary debates (1909–)

480 HC Deb. ser. 5, cols 594–5 (6 Nov. 1950).

other possible variations include:
480 HC Deb. 1950–51, cols 594–5.
HC Deb. vol. 480, 6 Nov. 1950, cols 594–5.
480 HC Deb. 5s 6 Nov. 1950, cols 594–5.

House of Lords debates:
176 HL Deb. ser. 5, cols 1289–94 (22 May 1952).

written answers to Commons and Lords debates:
500 HC Deb. ser. 5, *col. 42* (7 May 1952).
180 HL Deb. ser. 5, *col. 664* (23 Feb. 1953).

Parliamentary papers (Commons and Lords papers)

Independent Television Authority: Annual Report and Accounts 1955–56 (1956; HC 362), p. 18.
Persons in receipt of Poor Relief (England and Wales) (1937; HC 157), paras 4, 5.

Command papers

Report of the Broadcasting Committee, 1925 (1926; Cmd 2599), para. 9(a).
British Broadcasting Corporation: Annual Report and Accounts for the year 1962–63 (1963; Cmnd 2160), p. 23.

Journals (Commons and Lords)

83 HC J. 184 (20 Mar. 1828).
106 HL J. 75 (21 Apr. 1874).

Bills

Imperial Telegraphs Bill 1928.
Imperial Telegraphs Bill 1928, cl. 2(a).
Carriage by Railway Bill 1972, cl. 7(2)(a), Schedule art. 7.

short citation, omitting the title:
HC Bill 1928–29 [11].
HL Bill 1971–72 (97).

Acts

Public General Acts (pre-1963):
Wireless Telegraphy Act, 1904 (4 Edw. 7, c. 24).
Post Office (Parcels) Act, 1922 (12 & 13 Geo. 5, c. 49), s. 1(c).
Television Act, 1954 (2 & 3 Eliz. 2, c. 55), s. 2(5)(b), Sch. 2, para. 3(a).

Public General Acts (1963–):
Television Act 1964 (c. 21), s. 4(1)(a)(ii), Sch. 1, para. 4(2).
Independent Broadcasting Authority Act 1974 (c. 16).
Independent Broadcasting Authority (No. 2) Act 1974 (c. 42).
Broadcasting Act 1980 (c. 64), Pt. 3, Schs 1, 2 and 3.

Local and Personal Acts (pre-1963):
The Great Northern Railway (Additional Powers) Act, 1873 (36 & 37 Vict. c. xc), s. 14.

Local and Personal Acts (1963–):
British Railways Act 1964 (c. xvi), ss. 6(1)(a), 6(2), Sch. 1 Pt. 2, Sch. 3.

Statutory Instruments

Wool Textile Industry (Scientific Research Levy) (Amendment) Order 1971 (SI 1971 No. 881), r. 3(a).

Ministry of Posts and Telecommunications (Dissolution) Order 1974 (SI 1974 No. 691), rr. 1(5), 2.

short citation, omitting the title:
SI 1974 No. 691.

Notes

1 Prior to 1909, parliamentary debates in the Commons and Lords were printed in the same series of volumes. However, since the start of the fifth series in 1909 the Commons and Lords debates have been printed in separate volumes, each with its own sessional index. So for debates since 1909 it is necessary to state whether these are HC or HL debates. Note that written answers are grouped together at the end of each volume (i.e. after the oral answers) and they also have a different sequence of column numbers. In any footnote, column numbers which refer to written answers should therefore be underlined or printed in italic to distinguish them from oral answers. Note also that if the year or date of a debate is provided, mention of the series can be omitted. There are also verbatim reports of the debates of the various Standing Committees which consider Bills after their second reading; any note which refers to these debates must indicate the relevant committee.

2 The serial numbers of HC and HL papers are printed at the bottom left-hand corner of the title page; only the serial numbers of HL papers appear in round brackets. A new sequence of numbers begins each session, so if you refer to parliamentary papers it is important to quote the year or session as well as the serial number. Unlike HC papers, HL papers and HL Bills are numbered in the same series.

3 Unlike HC and HL papers and Bills, Command papers are not numbered by session. They are numbered in a continuous series extending across several parliamentary sessions. For example, the fourth series extended from 1919 to 1956. Note that in the following list the abbreviation for 'Command' differs for each series and must therefore not be standardised in a footnote or bibliographical reference. The different series are noted as follows:

    1st series: 1–4222 (1833–1869)
    2nd series: C. 1–9550 (1870–1899)

3rd series: Cd 1–9239 (1900–1918)

4th series: Cmd 1–9889 (1919–1956)

5th series: Cmnd 1–9927 (1956–1986)

6th series: Cm 1– (1986–)

It is now common practice to omit the full stop after the abbreviation for 'Command'. Note that the reports of some committees are referred to unofficially by the name of their chairman. For example, the *Report of the Committee on the Future of Broadcasting* (1977; Cmnd 6753) is often referred to as the Annan Report, after its chairman Lord Annan.

4 References to Commons or Lords Journals are normally arranged in the following sequence: volume number; HC or HL Journal; page number; and date.

5 Unlike Acts of Parliament, Bills have no chapter number or authorised short title. Public Bills may become Public General Acts, whereas Private Bills may become Local and Personal Acts. There can be several versions of Bills because their content could be modified during passage through the Commons and Lords. Each new version of a Bill has its own serial number which is printed at the bottom left-hand corner of the title page: this number is enclosed in square brackets for Commons Bills, and in round brackets for Bills which originate in the Lords. A new numerical sequence begins each session, hence any abbreviated reference to a Bill must cite the session and serial number. Note that the main divisions within Bills are referred to as clauses, not sections.

6 Acts are arranged by chapter number within each calendar year. Acts can be located by using the subject index, or the numerical list of chapter numbers if you know the number of the Act you wish to locate. The inclusion of the chapter number is helpful because it assists readers to locate a specific Act within the bound volumes. Acts can be referred to by their short title, but those which have no short title should be cited by regnal year, chapter number and, unless previously indicated in the text, the calendar year: 14 & 15 Vict. c. 64 (1851). Acts prior to 1963 are cited by regnal year, whereas those from 1963 onwards are cited by calendar year. A comma was normally placed between the short title and the year in Acts prior to 1963, but it is not essential to retain this convention. Use the ampersand when referring to regnal years (e.g. 2 & 3 Eliz. 2). A parliamentary session may

extend over more than one regnal year, so both years will need to be given (11 & 12 Geo. 6; 12, 13 & 14 Geo. 6). A session may also cover the reign of two sovereigns (15 & 16 Geo. 6 & 1 Eliz. 2). The abbreviation for 'chapter' is preceded by a comma only when the Sovereign's designation ends in a numeral (5 Geo. 1, c. 11) or is a complete word (13 Anne, c. 13); otherwise, omit the comma (49 & 50 Vict. c. 31).

7 Note that the chapter number of Local Acts is printed in small roman numerals, and for Personal Acts an arabic number is used, printed in italics. All Acts, Public or Local, can be subdivided into parts, sections and schedules. A very specific reference within an Act would give the section number, subsection number, paragraph and subparagraph: s. 4(1)(c)(ii). A very broad reference would merely refer to a part: Television Act 1954, Pt. 3. Schedules are numbered consecutively and are located towards the end of an Act. You will find that some schedules are divided into paragraphs and subparagraphs, so a specific reference would appear as follows: Television Act 1954, Sch. 3, para. 1(2). Other schedules may be divided into parts: Sch. 3, Pt. 2. Reference to more than one section within an Act may be indicated as follows: ss. 1, 2.

8 Statutory Instruments have no uniform divisions, although they are subdivided by rules, regulations and articles, which correspond to the section of an Act. Note that the SI year may differ from the year given in the short title. If you refer to the title in the text, the footnote can be abbreviated as follows: SI 1974 No. 691.

9 Some types of official publications, such as reference to specific parliamentary debates, are not listed in a bibliography. However, parliamentary papers and Acts of Parliament can be listed in a bibliography; their format should be identical to that used in footnotes, except for the omission of specific references to pages, paragraphs or sections. If you do need to include official publications in a bibliography, they should be listed in chronological order. A separate list may be required if you also refer to several non-parliamentary publications. Note that in the HMSO sessional indexes, parliamentary publications are cited according to the following sequence: title; session; paper or Command number; volume number; and page number of volume. This is illustrated in the following examples:

> *First special report from the Select Committee on Nationalised Industries: the Electricity Supply Industry*; 1963–64 (67) vii, 525.
>
> *Report of the National Assistance Board Report for 1963*; 1963–64 Cmnd 2386, viii, 1553.

However, this type of reference is helpful only for your own use in identifying which bound volumes within a session to consult when locating specific parliamentary papers.

3 Theses and dissertations

Stan H. Nicholas, 'The BBC, British morale, and the Home Front war effort, 1939–45' (DPhil thesis, University of Oxford, 1992).

Rosemary E. Horrox, 'The extent and use of Crown patronage under Richard III' (PhD thesis, University of Cambridge, 1977).

A. Birch, 'The development and organisation of the British iron industry, 1815–67' (MA dissertation, University of Manchester, 1951).

Monica C. Hodgson, 'The working day and the working week in Victorian Britain, 1840–1900' (MPhil dissertation, University of London, 1974).

A.K. Aldgate, 'The use of film as a historical source: British newsreels and the Spanish Civil War' (PhD thesis, University of Edinburgh, 1976).

comparison of 1 footnote and 2 bibliographical references:

1 M.C. Reed, 'Investment in Railways in Britain, 1820–44' (DPhil thesis, University of Oxford, 1971), pp. 25–7.

2 Reed, M.C., 'Investment in Railways in Britain, 1820–44', DPhil thesis, University of Oxford, 1971.

Notes

1 The sequence of items in a reference to a thesis or dissertation is as follows: author; title of thesis or dissertation; degree; university; year; and page number(s).

2 Note that the titles of dissertations and theses, in common with all unpublished documentary material, are printed in roman with single quotation marks.

3 Dissertations and theses represent unpublished work, the copyright of which belongs to the author. The author's written permission may be required if substantial parts of a dissertation or thesis are to be quoted or incorporated as paraphrased extracts, although the bibliography can normally be copied without permission.

4 Broadcasts and filmed material

references to broadcasts:

The Richard Dimbleby Lecture, BBC1, 15 July 1987.

Europe since Hitler, BBC Radio 4, 6 April 1971.

The Search for the Nile, Episode 2, BBC2, 29 September 1971.

America, a personal history by Alistair Cooke, BBC2, 26 November 1972.

The Ascent of Man, Part 7, The Majestic Clockwork, BBC2, 16 June 1973.

The Triumph of the West, Part 6, An Exploring Civilisation, BBC2, 14 October 1985.

Europe since Hitler, presented by Dr Alan Bullock, Part 2, The Recovery of Western Europe, BBC Radio 4, 13 April 1971.

comparison of 1 footnote and 2 bibliographical references:

1 *Civilisation*, Part 8, The Light of Experience, BBC2, 12 April 1969.

2 *Civilisation*, Part 8, The Light of Experience. BBC2. 12 April 1969.

references to filmed material:

All Quiet on the Western Front, film, directed by Lewis Milestone. USA: Universal, 1930.

The Thirty-Nine Steps, film, directed by Alfred Hitchcock. GB: Gaumont British, 1935.

Triumph of the Will, film, directed by Leni Riefenstahl. Germany: Nazi Party, 1936.

Gone with the Wind, film, produced by David O. Selznick. USA: MGM, 1939.

Great Expectations, film, directed by David Lean. GB: Rank/Cineguild, 1946.

comparison of 1 footnote and 2 bibliographical references:

1 *The Grapes of Wrath*, film, directed by John Ford. USA: TCF, 1940.

2 *The Grapes of Wrath*. Film. Directed by John Ford. USA: TCF, 1940.

Notes

1 The type of information required to identify broadcast material is as follows: title (of individual programme or series); number of episode and title of programme within a series; broadcasting channel; and date of broadcast. The type of information required to identify filmed material is as follows: title of film; name of director or producer; country of origin; film production company; and year of release.

2 Films and programmes are collaborative ventures with no single 'author', hence the title is given first. The title of films may be followed by the name of the director (or producer). Note that the titles of broadcast and filmed material are always underlined to indicate that

they should appear in italics. If you refer to a single episode in a radio or television series, this should be distinguished typographically from the title of the series by being printed in roman, not italics.

3 Refer to British Standards 1629 and 5605 for guidelines on the citation of other non-book media.

5 Interviews

(the following fictional examples indicate variations in the format used)

Interview with A. MacDonald, Cambridge, 29 May 1972.

Interview with J. Grant, military historian, Edinburgh, 21 September 1990.

Interview with Robert Whitehouse, Company Archivist, Tweedbank Textile Company, Leeds, 29 April 1988.

Recorded interview with George Bolton, Local Secretary of the Transport and General Workers' Union, Oxford, 1 May 1986.

Notes

1 The sequence of items in a reference to an interview is as follows: name of interviewee; occupation of interviewee; and place and date of interview.

2 Information derived from interviews is more likely to be used extensively in oral history projects. It is helpful if you can indicate whether or not the interview was recorded. The occupational details of the interviewee may be given in the reference if they are not referred to in the text.

3 A list of interviewees may be incorporated in a bibliography if extensive use has been made of interviews, such as for an oral history project. The suggested format for bibliographical references is as follows:

Stewart, Martin. BBC Arts Producer. Recorded interview, London, 9 November 1992.

The list of interviewees would normally be arranged in alphabetical order within a bibliography.

6 Books

The examples which follow relate to 1 footnote and 2 bibliographical references:

One author

1 G.R. Elton, *The Practice of History* (London, 1987), p. 68.

2 Elton, G.R., *The Practice of History*, London: Fontana Press, 1987.

1 E.P. Thompson, *The Making of the English Working Class* (Harmonds-worth, 1968), pp. 259–62.

2 Thompson, E.P., *The Making of the English Working Class*, Harmonds-worth: Penguin, 1968.

Two authors

1 H.G. Koenigsberger and George L. Mosse, *Europe in the Sixteenth Century* (London, 1968), pp. 54–8.

2 Koenigsberger, H.G. and George L. Mosse, *Europe in the Sixteenth Century*, London: Longman, 1968.

Editor(s) as author(s)

1 John Cannon (ed.), *The Historian at Work* (London, 1980), pp. 2–9.

2 Cannon, John (ed.), *The Historian at Work*, London: George Allen & Unwin, 1980.

1 Colin Chant and John Fauvel (eds), *Darwin to Einstein: Historical Studies on Science and Belief* (Harlow, 1980), pp. 45–6.

2 Chant, Colin and John Fauvel (eds), *Darwin to Einstein: Historical Studies on Science and Belief*, Harlow: Longman, 1980.

Editor not as author

1 *Blackwell Dictionary of Historians*, ed. John Cannon *et al.* (Oxford, 1988), p. 50.

2 *Blackwell Dictionary of Historians*, edited by John Cannon *et al.*, Oxford: Basil Blackwell, 1988.

1 R.G. Collingwood, *The Idea of History*, ed. Jan Van Der Dussen (Oxford, 1993), p. 366.

2 Collingwood, R.G., *The Idea of History*, edited by Jan Van Der Dussen, Oxford: Clarendon Press, 1993.

Later edition

1 John Tosh, *The Pursuit of History*, 2nd edn (London, 1991), p. 136.

2 Tosh, John, *The Pursuit of History*, 2nd edn, London: Longman, 1991.

Revised edition

1 A.G. Dickens, *The English Reformation*, rev. edn (London, 1967), pp. 386–92.

2 Dickens, A.G., *The English Reformation*, revised edn, London: Fontana, 1967.

Compiled work

1 *History Theses 1971–80*, comp. Joyce M. Horn (London, 1984), p. 122.

2 *History Theses 1971–80*, compiled by Joyce M. Horn, London: Institute of Historical Research, 1984.

Revised work

1 H.W. Fowler, *A Dictionary of Modern English Usage*, 2nd edn, rev. Sir Ernest Gowers (Oxford, 1965), pp. v–xii.

2 Fowler, H.W., *A Dictionary of Modern English Usage*, 2nd edn, revised by Sir Ernest Gowers, Oxford: Oxford University Press, 1965.

Translated work

1 Maurice Crouzet, *The European Renaissance since 1945*, trans. Stanley Baron (London, 1970), pp. 11–15.

2 Crouzet, Maurice, *The European Renaissance since 1945*, translated by Stanley Baron, London: Thames & Hudson, 1970.

Named author of introduction

1 Walter Bagehot, *The English Constitution*, with an introduction by R.H.S. Crossman (London, 1963), pp. 214–21.

2 Bagehot, Walter, *The English Constitution*, introduction by R.H.S. Crossman, London: Fontana, 1963.

Title and subtitle

1 Carl N. Degler, *Out of Our Past: The Forces that shaped Modern America*, 3rd edn (New York, 1984), ch. 2.

2 Degler, Carl N., *Out of Our Past: The Forces that shaped Modern America*, 3rd edn, New York: Harper & Row, 1984.

Series

1 Arthur Marwick, *British Society since 1945*, The Pelican Social History of Britain (Harmondsworth, 1982), pp. 118–23.

2 Marwick, Arthur, *British Society since 1945*, The Pelican Social History of Britain, Harmondsworth: Penguin, 1982.

1 E.J. Hobsbawm, *Industry and Empire*, The Pelican Economic History of Britain, 3 (Harmondsworth, 1969), pp. 60–2.

2 Hobsbawm, E.J., *Industry and Empire*, The Pelican Economic History of Britain, 3, Harmondsworth: Penguin, 1969.

1 Thomas S. Kuhn, *The Structure of Scientific Revolutions*, 2nd edn, International Encyclopaedia of Unified Science, 2:2 (Chicago, 1970), pp. 4, 7.

2 Kuhn, Thomas S., *The Structure of Scientific Revolutions*, 2nd edn, International Encyclopaedia of Unified Science, 2:2, Chicago: University of Chicago Press, 1970.

1 Sydney and Olive Checkland, *Industry and Ethos: Scotland 1832–1914*, The New History of Scotland, no. 7 (London, 1984), pp. 47–50.

2 Checkland, Sydney and Olive, *Industry and Ethos: Scotland 1832–1914*, The New History of Scotland, no. 7, London: Edward Arnold, 1984.

Reprint

1 W.H. Walsh, *An Introduction to Philosophy of History* (Bristol, reprint 1992), pp. 98–101.

2 Walsh, W.H., *An Introduction to Philosophy of History*, Bristol: Thoemmes Press, reprint 1992.

Multivolume work with a general title

1 *New Cambridge Modern History*, vol. 11, pp. 49–52 *or* xi, 49–52.

2 *New Cambridge Modern History*, vol. 11.

1 *New Cambridge Modern History*, vol. 11: *Material Progress and World-Wide Problems 1870–1898* (Cambridge, 1962), pp. 49–52.

2 *New Cambridge Modern History*, vol. 11: *Material Progress and World-Wide Problems 1870–1898*, Cambridge: Cambridge University Press, 1962.

1 *Cambridge Economic History of Europe*, vol. ii: *Trade and Industry in the Middle Ages*, 2nd edn (Cambridge, 1987), p. 614.

2 *Cambridge Economic History of Europe*, vol. II: *Trade and Industry in the Middle Ages*, 2nd edn, Cambridge: Cambridge University Press, 1987.

1 *Fontana Economic History of Europe*, 3: *The Industrial Revolution* (London, 1973), pp. 15–20.

2 *Fontana Economic History of Europe*, 3: *The Industrial Revolution*, London: Fontana, 1973.

Multivolume work with one author

1 Asa Briggs, *The History of Broadcasting in the United Kingdom*, vol. 2 (London, 1965), pp. 23–6.

2 Briggs, Asa, *The History of Broadcasting in the United Kingdom*, vol. 2, London: Oxford University Press, 1965.

1 Asa Briggs, *The History of Broadcasting in the United Kingdom* (5 vols, Oxford, 1961–95), II (1965), 23 or 2 (1965), 23.

2 Briggs, Asa, *The History of Broadcasting in the United Kingdom*, 5 vols, Oxford: Oxford University Press, 1961–95.

Multivolume work with one author and separately titled volumes

1 Asa Briggs, *The History of Broadcasting in the United Kingdom*, vol. 2: *The Golden Age of Wireless* (London, 1965), p. 23.

2 Briggs, Asa, *The History of Broadcasting in the United Kingdom*, vol. 2: *The Golden Age of Wireless*, London: Oxford University Press, 1965.

Notes

1 The sequence of items in a book reference is as follows: author(s); title; edition; editor(s); compiler, reviser or translator; named author of introduction, if applicable; title and number of series; number of volumes in multivolume works; volume number and title if volume is separately titled; place of publication; publisher; date of publication, including details of any reprint edition; and page number(s), which should be elided. Not all items will, of course, apply to every reference to a published book.

2 Capitalise the first word and all significant words in book titles, including those which have a subtitle. The title of any named series is not underlined.

3 The first time you refer to any book within a chapter you should provide sufficient details for it to be identified. In subsequent references, a short title can be provided as follows:

Degler, *Out of Our Past*, p. 52

Fontana Economic History of Europe, vol. 3, p. 20

Briggs, *The Golden Age of Wireless*, p. 23

If you find that a number of pages separate references to the same book, and if there are no intermediate references to other publications on these pages, it is better to repeat the title in shortened form rather than use the abbreviation 'ibid'. The latter should be used if you refer to the same publication in the immediately preceding footnote or endnote.

4 In multivolume works, if the publication date given refers only to the volume cited, the volume number should precede the publication details. But if the publication dates refer to the span of years over which a series of volumes were published, the volume number will follow the publication details. There is no need to give the total number of volumes when citing a separately titled volume. Volume numbers can be printed in roman or arabic, with references appearing as follows: II, 23 *or* vol. 2, p. 23. As noted in the examples given, the abbreviations 'vol.' and 'p' may be omitted if there is no confusion about whether a number refers to a volume or to a page. In all page references try to elide page numbers as far as possible, except those in the teens (e.g. 11–15, *not* 11–5).

5 In a bibliography, books should be listed in alphabetical order by author (or title if there is no author). In comparison with footnotes, fuller details of each publication must be provided in a bibliography, but, as noted in the examples, punctuation can be simplified. The second and subsequent lines in each bibliographical entry are normally indented so that each entry is easier to identify. If a number of books by the same author appear in a bibliography, the author's name can be replaced in the second and subsequent references by a short title. Two or more publications by the same author are normally listed in chronological order by date of publication; for works published in the same year by the same author, you should arrange the titles in alphabetical order. Books by the same author can be arranged according to the following sequence:

(a) books written by the author; (b) books edited by the author; and (c) books where the author is a co-author.

7 Book articles

The example relates to 1 footnote and 2 bibliographical references:

1 S.B. Saul, 'The American impact on British industry, 1895–1914', in Clive Emsley (ed.), *Essays in Comparative History: Economy, Politics and Society in Britain and America, 1850–1920* (Milton Keynes, 1984), p. 182.
2 Saul, S.B., 'The American impact on British industry, 1895–1914', in Clive Emsley (ed.), *Essays in Comparative History: Economy, Politics and Society, 1850–1920*, Milton Keynes: Open University Press, 1984, pp. 179–95.

Notes

1 The basic sequence of items in a reference to a book article is as follows: author(s); title of article; editor(s); title of book; edition; place of publication; publisher; date of publication; and page number(s).
2 Capitalise the first word and proper names in the titles of book articles. The titles should be enclosed within single quotation marks; any quotation marks which appear within a title should therefore be double, not single, so that they can be easily identified.
3 A shortened reference can be given in the footnotes after the first full citation of a book article. If a book is listed in your bibliography under the author of the article, the shortened footnote reference should appear as follows:

> Saul, 'American impact on British industry', p. 182

But if a book is listed in your bibliography under its editor, the shortened footnote reference would appear as follows:

> Saul, 'American impact on British industry' in Emsley, *Essays in Comparative History*, p. 182

Note that in a bibliographical entry the span of pages over which a book article extends should be given.

8 Pamphlets

The examples relate to 1 footnote and 2 bibliographical references:

Individual pamphlet

1 Hugh Carleton Greene, *The BBC as a Public Service* (London, 1960), p. 7.

2 Greene, Hugh Carleton, *The BBC as a Public Service*, London: BBC, 1960.

General series

1 Donald Read, *Edwardian England*, General Series G.79 (London, 1972), p. 45.

2 Read, Donald, *Edwardian England*, General Series G.79, London: The Historical Association, 1972.

1 William K. Ritchie, *Edinburgh in its Golden Age*, Then and There Series (London, 1967), pp. 58–62.

2 Ritchie, William K., *Edinburgh in its Golden Age*, Then and There Series, London: Longmans, 1967.

Lectures

1 F.M.L. Thompson, *Victorian England: The Horse-Drawn Society*, Inaugural Lecture 1970 (London, 1970), pp. 8–9.

2 Thompson, F.M.L., *Victorian England: The Horse-Drawn Society*, Inaugural Lecture 1970, London: University of London, 1970.

1 A.J.P. Taylor, *Lloyd George: Rise and Fall*, The Leslie Stephen Lecture, 21 April 1961 (Cambridge, 1961), pp. 22–3.

2 Taylor, A.J.P., *Lloyd George: Rise and Fall*, The Leslie Stephen Lecture, 21 April 1961, Cambridge: Cambridge University Press, 1961.

1 David Douglas, *The Norman Conquest and British Historians*, The David Murray Lectures, 13 (Glasgow, 1971), p. 31.

2 Douglas, David, *The Norman Conquest and British Historians*, The David Murray Lectures, 13, Glasgow: University of Glasgow, 1971.

Named papers

1 M.A. Hicks, *Richard III as Duke of Gloucester: A Study in Character*, Borthwick Paper no. 70 (York, 1986), p. 27.

2 Hicks, M.A., *Richard III as Duke of Gloucester: A Study in Character*, Borthwick Paper no. 70, York: University of York, 1986.

1 Cyril Hart, *The Early Charters of Essex: The Saxon Period*, Occasional Paper no. 10 (Leicester, 1957), pp. 10–11.

2 Hart, Cyril, *The Early Charters of Essex: The Saxon Period,* Occasional Paper no. 10, Leicester: University of Leicester Press, 1957.

Edited pamphlet

1 Gordon Donaldson (ed.), *Common Errors in Scottish History,* General Series G.32 (London, 1956), p. 5.
2 Donaldson, Gordon (ed.), *Common Errors in Scottish History,* General Series G.32, London: The Historical Association, 1956.

Notes

1 The basic sequence of items in a reference to a pamphlet is as follows: author or editor; title; title and number of series; place of publication; publisher; date of publication; and page number(s).
2 Capitalise the first word and all significant words in the titles of pamphlets. The title and number of any series should be provided, but do not underline the title of the series. Shortened references to pamphlets should follow the same format as that indicated for books.
3 In a bibliography, all entries should be arranged in alphabetical order by author or editor (or title if there is no author). If you make use of several pamphlets in any historical project, these may be listed separately from books in your bibliography.

9 Journal articles

The examples relate to 1 footnote and 2 bibliographical references:

Volume number (journal paginated continuously)

1 R.H.C. Davis, 'The content of history', *History,* 66 (1981), 371.
2 Davis, R.H.C., 'The content of history', *History,* 66 (1981), 361–74.

Issue number (journal not paginated continuously)

1 E.J. Hobsbawm, 'The social function of the past: some questions', *Past and Present,* no. 55 (May 1972), 10–12.
2 Hobsbawm, E.J., 'The social function of the past: some questions', *Past and Present,* no. 55 (May 1972), 3–17.

Volume and issue numbers (journal not paginated continuously)

1 David Thomson, 'The writing of contemporary history', *Journal of Contemporary History*, 2:1 (January 1967), 28.

2 Thomson, David, 'The writing of contemporary history', *Journal of Contemporary History*, 2:1 (January 1967), 25–34.

New series (journal paginated continuously)

1 R.W. Fogel, 'The new economic history: 1. Its findings and methods', *Economic History Review*, 2nd series, 19 (1966), 654.

2 Fogel, R.W., 'The new economic history: 1. Its findings and methods', *Economic History Review*, 2nd series, 19 (1966), 642–56.

No author, volume number (journal not paginated continuously)

1 'The state of history today: 75 years of the Historical Association', *History Today*, 31 (April 1981), 5.

2 'The state of history today: 75 years of the Historical Association', *History Today*, 31 (April 1981), 5.

Notes

1 The sequence of items in a reference to a journal article is as follows: author; title of article; title of journal; series, if applicable; volume and/or issue number; year (or month and year) of publication; and page number(s).

2 Journal articles are placed within single quotation marks. If quotation marks are required within the title of any article, these should appear as double quotation marks. Capitalise the first word and proper names in the titles of articles. Journals which are frequently referred to can be abbreviated (e.g. *SHR* for *Scottish Historical Review*) and also included in a separate list, to be incorporated in the prelims.

3 Arabic numerals are normally used to indicate volume numbers, even if journal volumes print these as roman numerals. If a journal is paginated continuously, you only need to provide the volume number and year of publication. However, if a journal is not paginated continuously, give the issue number as well (if there is one), together with the month and year of publication. If a journal is identified only by an

issue number, this number should be preceded by the abbreviation 'no.' so that it will not be mistaken for a volume number.

4 A shortened reference can be given in the footnotes after the first full citation of a journal article as follows:

> Hobsbawm, 'The social function of the past', p. 10
> *or*
> Hobsbawm, *Past and Present*, no. 55 (May 1972), 10

5 In a bibliography, journal articles are arranged alphabetically by author (or title if there is no author). The span of pages over which an article extends should be given in a bibliographical reference, but in a footnote only the page number(s) of material referred to within an article is normally given.

10 Newspaper articles

The Times, 14 July 1789.

'The opening of the Great Exhibition', *The Times*, 2 May 1851, pp. 4–6.

'Stock markets: General depression', *The Scotsman*, 30 October 1929, p. 4.

'At war with Germany', *The Times*, 4 September 1939, p. 8.

'Local history', *Times Educational Supplement*, 25 January 1963, p. 131.

'Mr. Wilson forms his Government', *Glasgow Herald*, 17 October 1964, p. 1.

'Apollo's spacecraft at rest in Moon crater', *The Scotsman*, 21 July 1969.

THES, 5 November 1971, p. 2.

Philippa Ingram, 'Carr announces major retraining plans', *TES*, 4 February 1972, p. 3.

John Warden, 'Missionary role for British MPs in European Parliament', *Glasgow Herald*, 2 January 1973, p. 2.

Sunday Times, 9 April 1978, p. 3.

TLS, 24 May 1985, pp. 567–8.

Financial Times, 20 October 1987, p. 1.

Adam Clymer, 'Democrats promise quick action on a Clinton plan', *New York Times*, 5 November 1992, p. B6.

Notes

1 The sequence of items in a reference to a newspaper article in a footnote is as follows: author; title of article; title of newspaper; date of publication; and page number(s).

2 Newspaper articles are placed within single quotation marks. Capitalise the first word and proper names in the titles of articles. A title may be omitted if you provide sufficient descriptive material in the text. The full date (e.g. day, month and year) is required to identify articles in daily and weekly newspapers. Inclusion of the page number will help readers locate any specific article, news item or editorial comment.

3 A shortened reference can be given in the footnotes after the first citation of a newspaper article, as follows:

Warden, 'Missionary role for British MPs', p. 2
or
Warden, *Glasgow Herald*, 2 January 1973, p. 2

4 Individual newspaper articles are not normally listed in a bibliography, but a list of newspapers consulted could be included if you make extensive use of them as source material.

17

Proofreading

The preparation of any historical work which is intended for publication has to be very carefully checked for accuracy prior to being submitted to a publisher. The purpose of this section is to outline, from the point of view of the author, what tasks and procedures are involved in proofreading this work. But before you can begin the task of checking the proofs, you will have to examine the copy-edited typescript which will, in due course, be sent to the typesetter so that the proofs can be produced.

After your typescript has been checked and delivered to a publisher it will be forwarded to a freelance or in-house copy-editor. The task of the copy-editor is to read carefully through the author's typescript and look at the sense, style and general presentation of the material. This involves looking at a number of matters, as follows: spelling; grammar; punctuation; the use of capitals and italics; the elision of numbers; consistency in the format adopted for references and type style; the layout of the text; and the clarity of the arguments used in the material. Although the copy-editor will not have an in-depth knowledge of the subject matter covered in your typescript, he or she may be able to identify parts of the material which may be unclear to your intended readers. So the copy-editor performs a vital dual role by looking at typographical matters, such as style and punctuation, as well as clarity, sense and understanding. These two principal functions are interrelated because the presence, or absence, of certain punctuation marks can alter significantly the meaning of any piece of historical writing.

The copy-editor will mark up the text for the printer and then return the copy-edited typescript to you for checking. The typescript may also be accompanied by a list of questions which you will be expected to answer. The primary purpose of this work is to enable the copy-editor to provide clear and unambiguous instructions to the typesetter so that the appearance and content of the text will be in accordance with what you intended to occur. The copy-edited typescript will therefore have to be checked very carefully. This will involve looking, not only at obvious matters such as spelling and punctuation, but also at the content of the material with the following purposes in mind: to ensure that your meaning is clear; that statistical data are accurate; that page numbers are in the proper sequence; and that there is consistency in the use of references and displayed quotations. Indeed, the arrival of the copy-edited typescript provides authors with the last opportunity to make any important corrections to the text before page proofs are produced, since only corrections of typesetting errors are normally permitted at page-proof stage. If changes have to be made to the copy-edited typescript you will normally be expected to list these changes so that the copy-editor can incorporate them in the typescript prior to sending the material direct to the typesetter or publisher.

During the next stage the typesetter will use the copy-edited typescript to produce page proofs. These proofs, together with the copy-edited typescript, will be returned to the publisher prior to being forwarded to the author. The publisher will normally forward two sets of page proofs to you: one set will have to be checked and returned to the publisher, and the second set will be used to prepare the index (if you have already informed your publisher that you agree to prepare the index). Proofreading involves checking for both sense and for typographical errors. However, given that only limited corrections are possible at page-proof stage because of the prohibitive cost involved in making extensive alterations, changes should normally be confined to the identification and correction of typographical errors. These errors can be identified by comparing the copy-edited typescript carefully against one set of the page proofs.

There are a number of useful preliminary steps which you can take prior to commencing a detailed examination of the page proofs, and these are noted as follows:

1 Check that all the pages in both sets of page proofs are in numerical order. Note that page numbers will be counted but *not* printed on some pages, such as blank pages, the title page or part-title pages.

2 Read any guidance notes and instructions relating to proofreading which are provided by your publisher.

3 Check whether the amendments which you included in the typescript have been incorporated by the copy-editor in the copy-edited typescript. Those which have not been entered in the copy-edited typescript will not be incorporated by the typesetter in the page proofs.

4 Check the accuracy of the running heads in the page proofs. Note that no running heads will appear above some pages, such as those which begin a chapter or part, or where an illustration has been turned on the page. Take this opportunity to examine the position of all illustrative material, such as tables, charts or graphs.

After these preliminary checks have been completed, the checking of the page proofs can begin. The purpose of checking the page proofs is to ensure that they incorporate accurately all the material which appears in the copy-edited typescript.

The process of checking the page proofs is best tackled in stages. The first stage is to check the copy-edited typescript against the first set of page proofs. Place a ruler or blank card on the copy-edited typescript and carefully check line by line against the page proofs. Look for letters or words in the wrong type or size, punctuation errors, spelling errors (which are more difficult to spot in familiar words), or missing words or letters. Only essential changes should be made: this task should not be used as an opportunity to make major revisions to your text. If an error is detected, re-read the entire line carefully to check for any further errors. Also, remember to correct any errors that were originally overlooked during the copy-editing stage. You may be able to identify errors on the page proofs that were originally overlooked on the typescript. However, try to keep changes to an absolute minimum, especially if these changes are likely to alter the page layout, and consequently also the pagination. If you have to include new material, try to delete an equivalent amount of less essential text. Similarly, if you discover that some material has to be deleted, try to incorporate an equivalent amount of new material. By making these subtle adjustments you may prevent the need for a paragraph, a page or several pages of text to be re-set. Do remember that any changes in the pagination will affect the page references in the index. If there are any cross-references to pages, it may be advisable to enter the relevant page numbers in red ink in the text; page numbers would also be entered in red ink on the list of contents.

Typographical errors should be marked on the first set of page proofs using the British Standard recommended symbols for proofreading. These symbols can be found in BS 5261:part 2:1976; your publisher may also supply you with a set of proof-correcting symbols. All corrections to the proofs are colour-coded according to the following accepted criteria: typesetters mark their own corrections in green ink; red ink should be used to identify errors made by the typesetter; and blue ink should be used for all other minor corrections, such as those which you wish to incorporate in the proofs. Sometimes publishers or copy-editors use black ink to identify their own corrections. The corrections are colour-coded so that the cost of making alterations can be fairly allocated between typesetter, publisher and author. Typesetters charge for all corrections other than their own. Authors may have to pay for corrections, other than those made by the publisher and typesetter, which exceed 10 per cent of the cost of setting the work. You should indicate corrections by entering a proof correction mark in the margin (to indicate the nature of the correction required) as well as marking the text (to indicate exactly where the correction is required). If you identify several corrections which need to be made in a line of text, the marginal proof-correcting marks should appear from left to right in the same order in which the errors occur in the line. An oblique line should be used to separate each marginal mark which occurs in the same line.

If you wish to include additional instructions for the typesetter you should encircle them so that they can be distinguished from material which is intended to be printed. These additional notes would normally be written in the margin in pencil, and perhaps preceded by the word 'printer' or 'editor'. The typesetter may have listed queries for your attention or that of your publisher: answer these queries or, if they do not require corrections, strike through them. If any words must be deleted at page proof stage, or if the typesetter has printed additional material in error, try to be helpful and substitute other words which contain the same number of characters. There may exist doubt over whether certain material should be altered and, if so, it is best in these circumstances to list the points and deal with them separately, rather than make alterations to the proofs. Alterations made by the typesetter to the proofs can, after all, be time-consuming and expensive.

After the page proofs have been checked it is important to re-check all the errors identified to ensure that the correct proof correction marks have been used and that they have been properly colour-coded. By doing so you will ensure that the correction of errors has not inadvertently introduced new errors. You will also be able to decide whether corrections were really necessary, and whether they are clear and can be readily understood. The next stage is to copy the typographical errors, together with the appropriate mark-up symbols, from the first set of page proofs to the second set. The marked set of proofs can now be returned to your publisher for onward transmission to the typesetter. You will now be able to prepare the index using the first set of proofs which you have retained. The proofing procedure should operate smoothly if you accept that the purpose of checking the proofs is to search for errors made by the typesetter, rather than provide an opportunity for you to introduce new and significant alterations to the text. The procedure will also work smoothly if the correct proof correction marks are used, so that clear and precise instructions are given to the typesetter on how the material is to be typeset. Similar considerations apply if you are asked to check the proofs of the index. Some publishers do, however, check the index proofs in-house rather than forward them to authors for checking. But the detailed knowledge which authors have of their books may be advantageous by assisting them to identify typographical errors in the index. These errors may include misprints of index entries, mistakes in the indentation of subheadings and turnover lines, punctuation errors, lines omitted or printed twice, and misprints in the lists of page references. Details on how to prepare an index are included in the following chapter.

A few errors may be discovered *after* your work has been printed but prior to publication. These errors can be noted by using an erratum/ errata slip, particularly if you consider that it is essential for your readers to be informed of them. However, if any errors are discovered after your work has been published, you may wish to prepare a list of them, together with the page and line numbers where they occur. But note that any significant alterations to the text may affect the index, which would then certainly need to be revised. Your list of errors can be forwarded to your publisher at an early stage so that the changes can be incorporated in any subsequent reprinting of the book, whether issued as a reprint or as a new edition.

18

Indexing

Most books, and certainly all scholarly history books, will be provided with an index. This contrasts with dissertations or theses that are normally not expected to contain an index. A carefully prepared, accurate and well-designed index can be a great asset to a book. The index should obviously indicate to readers the scope of the book, as well as highlighting the connection between various subjects, themes or topics. It will also provide readers with information about which subjects the author has covered in detail, and which ones have been given a more superficial treatment. The nature of the subject matter will probably determine how detailed an index needs to be. A good index, in which careful thought has been given to layout, punctuation and cross-references, will assist your readers to identify and retrieve information quickly and easily. A poorly designed index can be offputting to readers and will almost certainly detract from the value of the research.

The author is perhaps the best person to compile the index because of a special understanding of the contents of the book and choice of keywords and cross-references that readers will find most helpful. The author will know what information is important (and which should therefore be included in the index), and what information is peripheral (and so can safely be excluded). Also, authors generally have a much better understanding of the level of detail which is required under each subheading, and this will invariably depend upon the intended readership of the book. The notes which follow are designed to give sufficient information for historians who wish to compile their own index, whether manually or on computer. A computer will certainly reduce the time taken to prepare an index, but the best indexes are those compiled manually. The production of a good index is much more than a mechanical process: it requires thought based upon a sufficient understanding of the content of the material. A computer is not a substitute for human thought. It will provide an average index but not an excellent one. If you initially decide to use a computer to generate an index, you will still need to refer to much of the advice given in this section. The compilation of an index may appear a tedious task but it is a worthwhile investment of your time and effort, particularly as index pages are often the first pages to which readers will turn when seeking specific information or reviewing the scope of a publication.

Selecting index entries

The index proper cannot be prepared until page proofs are produced, because it is only at this stage that all the page numbers will be known. However, it is sensible to prepare a list of index entries well before the page proofs arrive, particularly as publishers normally allow very little time for the preparation of the index after the page proofs have been produced. So the period between the submission of your typescript to the publisher, and the arrival of the page proofs from the publisher, should be used to prepare index entries based on that typescript. There is no need to await the arrival of the page proofs before beginning the task of preparing your index: compile the entries from the typescript, review them and then enter the page references when the page proofs arrive. Although all the chapters and appendices in your material have to be indexed, the notes and bibliography do not need to be indexed. The exception to this rule occurs where content footnotes are used, since these contain information which does not appear elsewhere in the text.

The first task in preparing an index is to read carefully through your typescript and highlight names, subjects, themes and titles which should appear in the index. The best method for identifying these index entries is to use coloured highlighter pens. For example, you may choose to high-light names using a red pen, subjects and themes using a yellow pen, and titles of publications using a green pen. Try to aim for an even coverage of items which you index, by avoiding the temptation to index some pages or chapters more heavily than others. You will probably find that more items will be highlighted than will be eventually included in your index because the primary purpose of highlighting items is to identify all key names, subjects, themes and titles as they occur. However, the final index should exclude items for which there is only a passing mention. You should not be surprised that many items which you decide initially to highlight will not be included in the index. On a first reading it may be difficult to decide which items receive only a passing mention, and should not be indexed, and those which will be commented on in more detail, and will have to be included. Sometimes a further review of your typescript will reveal that new items need to be indexed, some deleted and a few subsumed under other headings. Overall, there is perhaps a greater danger in under-indexing than in over-indexing, because lost entries cannot be recovered without re-reading the entire typescript.

Preparation of index cards

After suitable index entries have been highlighted in your typescript, the next stage is to prepare an index card for each item. A computer can be used to generate index entries but for a complex and detailed index there is no substitute for preparing the index manually. A computer is less useful than the human mind in distinguishing between similar words whose meanings differ depending on the context in which they are used. To pre-pare a manual index you should use a record card (8 × 5 inches) for each main heading and subheading. Your record cards can then be arranged in alphabetical order and filed within a set of A–Z guide cards. The index entries chosen to be included on these cards will need to be those which you believe readers are most likely to look up, and these will tend to be nouns rather than adjectives. You should also decide whether the titles of chapters and appendices might also merit inclusion in your index. For example, an entire chapter which is devoted to a specific subject should certainly be included in the index. Do not, however, index the following: the title page; table of contents; preface; foreword; a synopsis of a chapter; passing mention of individuals; source footnotes; and the bibliography.

In general, there is no need to index references to a subject or person which provides no factual information about them. For items which do require to be included in the index, try to choose index entries from the terminology used in your text. A thesaurus may be useful in identifying synonyms which can be included in the index to provide suitable cross-references to main headings or subheadings. The layout of the text in your typescript will not be identical to that which appears in the page proofs of your book, hence page numbers cannot be entered on the record cards until the page proofs are ready.

Types of indexing

Index entries may consist of a number of different types of information as follows:

- names (personal, corporate, geographical)
- technical terms
- subjects and themes (including titles of chapters if they are devoted to a single subject)
- titles of publications (which should be underlined in your index to indicate that they must be printed in italic)
- abbreviations
- numbers and dates

To highlight an important reference within any of these categories, consider the use of bold type. Bold type can be indicated by placing a wavy line below any page reference which you consider offers the fullest information on that topic. Page references which refer to text illustrations are easier to identify in an index if they are printed in italic. Roman capitals can be used where references are to plate numbers (i.e. illustrations printed separately from the text). If too many page numbers follow a reference, it may be useful to devise a number of subheadings. However, you should try to avoid the inclusion of several levels of indentation because this can lead to very short lines in a two-column index.

There are two basic types of indexing available: analytic indexing and synthetic indexing. The type which you use will depend upon the subject matter and the level of detail required in your index. Examples of both types of indexing are noted as follows:

Analytic indexing

audience research, broadcasting and
cable, broadcasting on
historical development, of broadcasting
licences, broadcasting
radio, broadcasting on
television, broadcasting on
transmitter coverage, broadcasting and

Synthetic indexing

broadcasting: audience research; on cable; historical development; licences; on radio; on television; transmitter coverage

You will see that the first example analyses individual aspects of broadcasting, whereas in the second example all the entries are gathered under the single term 'broadcasting'. These two examples illustrate how analytic indexing provides a more detailed index in comparison with the use of synthetic indexing.

Length and layout of an index

Index entries are normally set in a smaller type than the rest of the text, similar to that used for footnotes and endnotes. Your index should be typed in one column, but will be typeset by a printer using two columns per page. As a general guide, a typical index may represent about 8 per cent of the length of the text, but more detailed indexes representing a higher percentage of the text may be needed if your subject matter requires it. A publisher may either indicate the number of pages over which your index will extend, or alternatively leave you to decide the length of the index. In the latter case the length will probably be governed by the nature and complexity of the subject. It may be helpful to calculate the number of entries required by noting the following general guidelines: if a book is 300 pages long with 40 lines per page, then the total length of the book will be approximately 12,000 lines; a 12-page index of 50 lines per page is equivalent to 600 lines, which represents

5 per cent of 12,000 lines; and if there are two columns on each index page, 600 lines per single column will allow for about 1,200 entries. Normally this figure will be much less than 1,200 because some entries will be longer than the width of the column and therefore occupy more than one line of text. Also, entries which are followed by several page references will obviously take up more space than those with only a few page references. Nevertheless, this method of calculation does provide at least some indication of the approximate number of entries an index might be expected to contain.

The layout of your index also has to be carefully considered. There are two methods which can be used for arranging the entries: the entries can either be run on or set out, as follows:

Run-on entries

broadcasting, 1–15; audience, 30, 35, 41; coverage, 61–4; governmental control, 45, 50; local radio, 70–82; network radio, 65–70; social influence, 107, 112; standards, 115–16; television, 90–105

Set-out entries

broadcasting, 1–15
   audience, 30, 35, 41
   coverage, 61–4
   governmental control, 45, 50
   local radio, 70–82
   network radio, 65–70
   social influence, 107, 112
   standards, 115–16
   television, 90–105

You will see that run-on entries take up less space, but cannot easily accommodate sub-subheadings. Run-on entries also make it more difficult for readers to identify specific entries. If there is only one subheading then it is better to opt for run-on entries, otherwise consider placing the entries in the set-out format. Set-out entries do take up more space, yet make it much easier for readers to identify specific entries. This particular format should be chosen if you decide to include sub-subheadings. In the latter case the normal practice is to set out the subheadings and run on the sub-subheadings, as the following format illustrates:

Set-out subheadings with run-on sub-subheadings

> broadcasting, 1–15
>   audience, 30, 35, 41
>   local radio, 70–82
>   network radio, 65–70
>   television, 90–105; cable television, 94–6; colour television, 92
>   transmitter coverage, 122–7

Note that in this example the sub-subheadings are run on *and* placed in alphabetical order. Subheadings and any turnover lines are normally indented two spaces. The inclusion of a comma between any heading or subheading and its corresponding page reference is optional, but commas must be used to separate individual page references. Entries are usually printed in lower case, unless a word is normally capitalised, and no punctuation marks are placed at the end of any entry. Note that the right-hand margins of an index are not justified. Finally, be careful not to split words arbitrarily to provide a main heading and a subheading because this can sometimes cause confusion: an entry for 'programme allowance' would not be split to make 'programme' a main heading and 'allowance' a subheading.

Alphabetisation and capitalisation

Entries in your index can be arranged in word-by-word or letter-by-letter alphabetical order. In historical publications word-by-word alphabetisation is normally used, whereas in scientific publications letter-by-letter alphabetisation is preferred. In word-by-word alphabetisation shorter words precede longer ones, and a space always precedes a letter. For example, 'broadcast history' would precede the word 'broadcasters'. Abbreviations are treated as one word, unless each letter is separated by a space, hyphen, dash, oblique line or ampersand. For example, 'BBC' would be placed after 'Baird Television Company'. Initials which are not separated by spaces are treated as one word, whether or not they contain full stops. An exception would be if the full stop was used to separate a forename from a surname (e.g. A.A. Milne), but in this case the entry would be filed under the surname, not the forename. Some publishers take a different view and file, for example, the abbreviation 'B.B.C.' under 'B' rather than as 'BBC', so that each letter is treated as a separate word. A hyphenated word should be treated as one word if either the prefix or suffix cannot stand alone (e.g. pre-television age). Otherwise, a hyphenated word should be regarded as two words, so that 'broadcast-receiving licence' would be filed under the word 'broadcast'. Alphabetise only significant words, so that 'on television' is filed under 'television'. The following prepositions are normally ignored when indexing entries: 'and', 'of', 'in', 'at', 'a', 'the'. Mac/Mc/M should be filed as given (e.g. Mac before Mc), or otherwise treated as if they were all 'Mac'. If a word is abbreviated then it may have to follow the full word which it represents, so 'doctor' would therefore precede 'Dr'.

If you find that several numeric entries need to be included in your index, then place them before the main alphabetical sequence in numerical order, so that '1914–18' will come before '1939–1945'. But if there are few numeric entries then these can be placed within the main alphabetical sequence. Numeric entries which are added to this sequence should be entered at the place which corresponds with how the number is spelt out (e.g. '200' is indexed under 'two hundred'). Entries which are distinguished numerically should be placed in numerical order, thus 'Radio 1', 'Radio 2', 'Radio 3', and so on. If two persons with the same name occur, try to distinguish them by adding qualifying information, such as a date of birth or occupation. Titles are normally ignored in alphabetising, unless two or more people have the same name, as follows:

Scott
Scott, Dr
Scott, Sir Andrew
Scott, Lady Antonia
Scott, Dr Bruce
Scott, Charles
Scott, Charles (1850–1925)
Scott, Charles, historian
Scott, Thomas
Scott, Dr Thomas
Scott, Sir Thomas

If you have headings which relate to the same words but these have different meanings, they can be placed in the following order: people;

places; subjects; titles of publications. Indexers normally alphabetise to the first comma or punctuation mark, then renew the alphabetical sequence beyond this point, as follows:

television advertising
television broadcasting
television broadcasting, colour systems
television broadcasting: monochrome systems
television broadcasting history
Television Broadcasting Report
television drama
televisions, sale of

The format in which your entries should appear in the index will correspond to the following hierarchy: main entry; entry with subheading; entry with qualifier; and entry as the first element in a longer entry. This will appear, as in the following example:

broadcasting
broadcasting
    radio
    television
broadcasting, radio drama
broadcasting stations

Apart from alphabetisation, the capitalisation of entries also has to be considered. As a general rule you should capitalise any entry that is capitalised in the text, otherwise use lower case. Subheadings are always lower case, unless they refer to proper names. Be careful to use the same spelling and hyphenation as that used in the text. The following example illustrates the use of capitals and lower case in a sequence of index entries:

ABC Television, 205
Aberdeen Station (2BD), 24–6
advertising, on television, 71–8
Annan Committee (1974), 352–5
Assistant Controller, Scotland, 23–4
ATV, 18
audience research, 103–9
Baird, John Logie, 11–14
BBC Charter, 16–18

British Broadcasting Corporation, 40–55
broadcasting stations, 55–72
commercial broadcasting, 125–54

Page numbers

All page references should be separated by commas. You will see in the above example that there are no leaders (i.e. full points) between an index entry and its corresponding page reference; separate the two with a comma or simply leave a space. Also, try to elide page numbers as far as possible, except for the teens. You will discover that one of your main tasks is to distinguish between scattered references to a topic and the continuous discussion of such a topic. In manually prepared indexes it will be possible to distinguish continuous from scattered mentions of a subject by referring to the record cards on which the index entries are listed. Using these cards, commas can be inserted to separate page numbers where there are only scattered mentions of a subject, whereas hyphens could be placed between page numbers to indicate the continuous discussion of a subject. The following example illustrates how these page references would appear, both on your index card and in the typed index:

scattered references

(a) index card 50, 52, 53, 54, 58, 71, 72
(b) typed index 50, 52, 53, 54, 58, 71, 72

continuous discussion

(a) index card 50, 52–53–54, 58, 71–72
(b) typed index 50, 52–4, 58, 71–2

For very scattered mentions of a subject in the text, then indicate as follows:

history of broadcasting, 50–62 *passim*

However, you should try to avoid including *passim* references if possible: it is much better to provide exact page references because readers will find these more helpful. You may also wish to help your readers by not placing six or seven page references after a heading or subheading. If there are too many page references you can always subdivide the entry. If the index entries at the foot of a recto (i.e. right-hand page) continue at the top of the next page, then remember to repeat the main heading at the top of the left-hand column on this page, followed by the abbreviation *cont.* within parentheses. As mentioned earlier, footnotes or endnotes should only be indexed if they provide substantive information about a subject which is not covered in the text. If you do wish to indicate to readers that a reference is to a note, use the following formats:

radio programmes, 121n [this refers to the footnote on page 121]
radio programmes, 161n5 [this refers to the fifth footnote on page 161]

It is also permissible to place a full stop after the letter 'n' in the previous examples (e.g. 121n. and 161n.5). Page numbers which refer to illustrations are normally printed in italics so that they can be distinguished from page references to the text or to footnotes.

Cross-references

You will find that almost all indexes contain cross-references so that readers can be directed to preferred entries, or to entries which they might not have looked up, yet which are linked together by subject, theme or concept. If you discover that only a few pages of text contain information relating to two subject headings, then prepare two entries. This double entry would appear as in the following example:

radio, music programmes, 11–15
music programmes, on radio, 11–15

Be careful to ensure that both entries contain the *same* page references. But if it appears that there will be too many page references to a subject under two headings, it is probably better to include all the entries under one heading and provide a cross-reference to this heading from the other entry. This split entry would appear as follows:

broadcasting, licences *see* licences, for broadcasting
licences, for broadcasting, 9–16, 27–30, 36, 41–50, 64–8

Avoid splitting page references between two synonyms: include them under one entry and provide a cross-reference from the other entry. Try, where possible, to use specific and familiar terms to which your readers will wish to refer, rather than vague or broad ones. For example, the entry 'radio programmes, influence of' is much better than 'influence of radio programmes'. Anticipate which entries you believe readers will wish to look up in the index. If an entry has an obvious synonym, prepare a cross-reference. You may also find it helpful to include those entries which readers might not think about looking up, but to which they ought to refer (e.g. classical music *see also* Radio 3). If two words are closely related, but not synonyms, put the references under each and add a cross-reference. If the same subject appears as part of another entry, you should check to ensure that both refer to the same page numbers. You may also encounter words which have more than one meaning, but these can be distinguished by providing a separate entry for each meaning as follows:

historical records (1), accounts
historical records (2), archives
historical records (3), discs

One of the most important tasks in indexing is to ensure that entries do exist for all of your cross-references because their absence may leave an unfavourable impression on readers. Cross-references may consist of 'see' or 'see also' entries. The use of 'see' occurs where an author includes entries which were not indexed, but which cross-refer to entries which were chosen to be included in the index. This can be useful in directing readers to preferred entries (e.g. wireless *see* radio broadcasting). However, if the cross-reference forms part of an existing index entry then this must be indicated by a 'see also' entry, as follows:

broadcasting, 1–35
  local radio, 49–54
  network radio, 42–8
  network television, 60–9
  see also regional services

A cross-reference may also appear as part of a sub-entry to direct readers to related headings which do not refer to the same page references. If several cross-references follow a subheading, then they should be placed in alphabetical order. The example which follows illustrates the inclusion of cross-references which follow subheadings:

Typing and checking the index

The arrival of page proofs from your publisher will enable you to add in the exact page references. It will also enable you to check how well you have differentiated between scattered mentions of a subject and continuous discussion of a subject. If your index is being prepared manually then before typing the index do check to ensure that all the index cards are in alphabetical order and that all 'see' and 'see also' cross-references are correct. After these tasks have been completed, the index will be ready to be typed directly from the information contained on your index cards. A number of important points can now be summarised about the typing of the index and these are noted in the numbered list which follows:

1 Use A4 paper, allow double spacing for headings and subheadings, and type the entries in a *single* column with a specified number of characters per line, probably up to forty-five. The typesetter will set your index in a double-column format using a smaller type size than that used for the text.

2 Leave the following margins: 1 inch at the top and foot of the page; 1½-inch left-hand margin; and 3-inch right-hand margin.

3 Number each page of your index separately from the rest of the text (i.e. the first page of the index will begin on page 1). After the index has been typed, these pages must be checked to ensure that they are in numerical order.

4 Use word-by-word alphabetisation for all headings and subheadings. Alphabetise to the first punctuation mark in each entry and continue using alphabetical order after it.

5 Leave one extra line space between groups of entries included under each successive letter of the alphabet. This will assist readers to locate index entries and improve the overall layout of the index.

6 For set-out entries, indent subheadings two spaces; turnover/continuation lines for subheadings should be indented four spaces so that the subheadings can be easily identified. Any 'see also' cross-references which appear at the end of an entry should be aligned with the subheadings and so should be indented two spaces. If any entry has to be continued at the top of a left-hand page, then repeat the heading followed by the abbreviation *cont.* in parentheses at the top of the first column on this page.

7 A comma is normally placed between headings and page references, although some publishers omit the comma. No comma follows a heading if it is not followed by a page reference. Sub-subheadings and run-on subheadings should be separated by semicolons. If several cross-references appear at the end of an entry, they should be listed in alphabetical order and separated by semicolons. No punctuation is needed at the end of a row of page references which are not followed by a further entry.

8 Important page references can be highlighted for readers by being printed in bold type. Ensure that your page references distinguish continuous discussion of a subject from scattered mentions.

9 Try to avoid many levels of indentations for sub-entries because this tends to produce very short lines which look awkward on the printed page. Entries can be either run on or set out. If subheadings are set out, sub-subheadings are usually run on.

10 Check the following items in your index:

- alphabetical order of headings and subheadings
- cross-references
- spelling
- numerical sequence of page references for each entry
- capitalisation
- punctuation
- use of bold and italic
- elision of page numbers
- double entries, which must refer to the same page numbers
- surnames, which should ideally be accompanied by initials, a forename or a title
- subheadings, which must be followed by page references

A manually prepared index which has been typed should be checked for accuracy against your record/index cards. Publishers normally request two copies of the index, and they will arrange for the index to be typeset. Some publishers forward the proofs of the index to authors for checking, whereas others carry out this task in-house. If you are given the opportunity to check the proofs of your index do remember that this will be your last opportunity to check the accuracy of the printed index prior to publication. If you have been able to make full use of the advice in this section you should be able to produce a very helpful index for your readers.

Glossary

The following list contains many of the terms which you are likely to come across when preparing material for a dissertation or thesis, or for publication as an article or book. You may also wish to refer to the separate list of abbreviations which are included in chapter 14.

abstract a summary of the contents of a dissertation or thesis.

acknowledgements a list of copyright owners whom the author acknowledges for the use of quoted extracts; the list may also include the names of individuals or organisations to whom the author is obliged for assistance received, if this information is not to be included in a preface.

alphanumeric data consisting of a series of letters and numerals.

archive the archives of an institution; a building containing archival material; to prepare a safe copy of computer-generated data.

author-date system a system whereby an item in a bibliography is referred to in the text by the author's surname and date of publication; it is also known as the Harvard system and is normally used in the social sciences, but not in the humanities.

back-up the creation of copies of computer programs and data on floppy or hard disks as security against loss of the original information.

block quotation a long quotation which is displayed (i.e. indented) and set on separate lines, sometimes in smaller type.

blurb a description of a book which is incorporated on the jacket or cover of the book, or used in a publisher's catalogue to promote the book.

camera copy copy, such as typescript or artwork, which is ready for photographic reproduction by the printer; also known as camera-ready copy.

caption the descriptive title for an illustration, printed below the illustration; the heading of any chapter, section or table.

CD-ROM compact disk read-only memory; a computer disk which permanently holds large quantities of information more securely than a computer hard disk.

cliometrics the application of quantitative and model-building methods to economic history; also known as econometrics or new economic history.

corrigenda a list of corrections included in a book and not printed separately, as in an erratum/errata slip.

cursor a flashing symbol on a computer monitor to indicate the location of the next task.

database a collection of information stored in computer files which can be displayed or retrieved.

DBMS database management system; a computer program which provides access to a database.

directory a group of computer files, normally assigned a name by the user.

disk a computer magnetic disk which stores information (e.g. a floppy or hard disk).

edition printings of a book which contain the same text and are issued in the same binding; a book published with only small alterations would be classified as a reprint, whereas major corrections or the re-set of type would be regarded as a new edition.

electronic mail the sending of messages between computers, known as e-mail.

elision a pair of numbers which are run together (e.g. 25–26 becomes 25–6).

ellipsis the use of three points or dots to signify the omission of text.

endmatter material which follows the main text, such as the appendices, bibliography and index.

endnotes bibliographical notes included at the end of a chapter or book, rather than printed at the foot of each relevant page as footnotes.

errata a list of corrections on a slip of paper attached to, or placed in, a book.

figure an illustration incorporated within the text; an arabic numeral.

floppy disk a portable magnetic disk used in computers to store programs and text.

folio a page number assigned to the leaf of a manuscript or book; a sheet of typescript or manuscript.

font typeface which incorporates a similar size and design of characters, such as letters, numerals, punctuation marks and symbols.

foreword comments on the content of a book and its author which are written by someone else.

frontispiece an illustration which faces, and precedes, the title page.

gigabyte computer storage capacity, equivalent to one thousand million bytes.

graphical user interface a system in computing whereby the user can control a computer through the use of images (icons) on a screen, rather than through textual commands.

guide cards cards with a projecting tab, labelled alphabetically or numerically, and placed within a set of record cards to assist the location of entries.

half-title the first printed page of a book which incorporates only the title of the book and precedes the title page.

halftone images produced by an array of numerous black dots of various sizes.

hard copy copy produced on paper in contrast to output in electronic form, such as on a computer monitor, a computer disk, or a microform.

hard disk a permanent magnetic disk in a computer which stores programs and text.

house style typographical style associated with different publishers.

icon graphical symbol on a computer monitor which indicates the task to be performed by the computer.

impression copies of a book printed at the same time and containing the same text; a new impression will contain minor alterations to the original text.

imprint publisher's name, including date and place of publication; the imprint is included on the verso of the title page.

inkjet printer a printer which prints characters by squirting small amounts of ink on to the paper.

justified setting alteration of the space between words to provide lines of text of equal length, thus ensuring alignment of the text in the right-hand margin.

keyword a significant word which is selected from the text for use as an index entry; a subject word used to search a computer database.

kilobyte computer storage capacity, equivalent to 1,024 bytes.

landscape indicates that the width of an illustration or table is greater than its height; the foot of such an illustration or table should appear at the right-hand side of the page.

laptop a small portable computer.

laser printer a high-quality printer producing rapid output and operating similarly to a photocopier.

leaders a line of dots which appear in contents lists or tables to assist the reader in identifying information.

letter-by-letter indexing an alphabetical list where the entries are arranged according to the letters of the words of each entry so that punctuation and spaces between words are ignored; this type of indexing is normally used in scientific publications.

mark-up the inclusion of typographical instructions on a typescript for use by a typesetter.

megabyte computer storage capacity, equivalent to 1,024 kilobytes.

menu a list of options provided for users of a computer.

microfiche a transparent film containing microimages which are arranged in rows and columns.

microfilm photographic film containing microcopies.

microform generic term covering microfiche and microfilm.

modem a modulator/demodulator device for transmitting and decoding information on a computer network, sent via a telephone line.

monograph a major academic work published on a single subject.

page proof final typeset proof which is divided into pages.

pagination page numbering; the total number of pages in a publication.

parenthesis round brackets, in contrast to square brackets, angle brackets or braces.

plate an illustration which is printed separately from the text on paper of a different quality; plates are not included in the pagination of a book.

portrait indicates that the height of an illustration or table is greater than its width.

preface comments by an author on the origin, purpose and content of a book; the preface may also acknowledge assistance received during the research and writing of the book.

prelims the preliminary pages of a book (e.g. the half-title, title page, contents list, foreword and preface); the prelims are paginated in roman numerals.

print run the number of copies of a book printed at the same time.

printout printed copy of work completed on a computer and obtained as output from a printer.

proportional spacing a printing facility whereby the width of characters and the space between them is used to justify text and so produce a straight right-hand margin.

RAM the random access memory of a computer, which holds the program and data being used.

recto a right-hand page.

run on text which continues on the same line, rather than starts a new line or paragraph.

running head the heading printed at the top of each page of text; the book title is printed on the verso, the chapter or section title on the recto.

scanner a device used to convert paper images into electronic format.

short-title system a system whereby a shortened version of the title of a publication is included in footnotes or endnotes after the first citation of the full title; this system of citation is normally used in the humanities.

spreadsheet computer software which holds numerical data in cells (i.e. rows and columns).

stub the left-hand column of a table which identifies the contents of each row.

superscript a small number or letter printed slightly above the line of text, as in footnote numbers.

turnover lines the second and subsequent lines of an index entry which are indented.

unjustified setting the space between words is equal and so the right-hand margin appears ragged rather than even.

verso a left-hand page.

word-by-word indexing an alphabetical list where the entries are arranged according to the individual words of each entry, so that spaces between words will file before the first character of the next word; this type of indexing is normally used in arts and social science publications.

wysiwyg what you see is what you get; a term used in word processing whereby the image which the user sees on the screen corresponds with how the printed version of the text will appear.

Guide to further reading

The following selective guide to reading material has been subdivided into three sections so that published material relating to different aspects of historical research can be easily identified. The three sections cover 1 historiography and historical research, 2 reference sources and 3 research, publishing and style guides.

Some of the books and articles which are listed in section 1 contain excellent bibliographies which offer many suggestions for further reading on the nature and study of history. Some additional sources may also be found in the notes to Part I of this hook. The books by Bloch, Carr, Elton, Evans, Marwick, Thompson, Tosh and Walsh are good introductions to the study and writing of history; those by Greenstein, Mawdsley and Munck, and Harvey and Press, offer sensible advice on the role of the computer in historical research. It may also be worthwhile looking at some of the following history journals which have published interesting articles on the writing of history and on the work of historians: *American Historical Review* (1895/96–); *Historical Journal* (1923–); *History* (1966–); *History and Computing* (1989–); *History and Theory* (1960–); *History Today* (1951–); *Journal of Contemporary History* (1966–); *Past and Present* (1952–); and *Royal Historical Society Transactions* (1873–).

Section 2 lists the most useful general reference works which you are likely to find helpful at some stage in your own historical research. In particular, the *Annual Bibliography of British and Irish History*, the three volumes of *History Theses* and *Historical Research for Higher Degrees* (which is published annually in two parts, covering theses in progress and theses completed), all provide detailed information on both published material and unpublished dissertations and theses covering a vast range of historical subjects. All of these publications are produced by the Institute of Historical Research in London. There are many other reference works which will be of use in the investigation of specific historical research topics, and these should be examined after a suitable topic has been chosen. Many of the publications listed in section 2 should be available for consultation in the reference room of any university or public library.

Section 3 provides a selection of publications on general research methods, as well as on the preparation of work for publication. In particular, the publications by Barzun and Graff, Hoffmann, and Phillips and Pugh give useful advice on research techniques; Legat and the current edition of the *Writers' and Artists' Yearbook* offer information on various aspects of publishing; and Anderson, Butcher (1992) and Hart provide sensible and helpful guidance on stylistic matters. Section 3 also provides an up-to-date listing of the most relevant British Standards which may need to be consulted when preparing an academic thesis or dissertation, or articles and books. In particular, the following British Standards are the most useful ones to refer to: BS 5261 parts 1 and 2 offer recommendations on stylistic matters relating to the preparation of typescripts, and on proofing procedure and proof correction marks; BS 7581 will be found to be particularly informative where illustrative material, such as tables and graphs, are to be incorporated in a research project; and BS 1749 and BS ISO 999 should be referred to for further constructive advice on the various aspects involved in preparing an index for a book.

1 Historiography and historical research

Abrams, Philip, 'The sense of the past and the origins of Sociology', *Past and Present*, no. 55 (May 1972), 18–32

Abrams, Philip, *Historical Sociology*, Shepton Mallet: Open Books, 1982

Barker, Ernest, 'History and Philosophy', *History*, no. 7 (1922), 81–91

Becker, Carl, 'Everyman his own historian', *American Historical Review*, no. 37 (1932), 221–36

Beeching, Cyril Leslie, *A Dictionary of Dates*, 2nd edn, Oxford: Oxford University Press, 1997

Berlin, Isaiah, 'History and theory: the concept of scientific history', *History and Theory*, no. 1 (1960), 1–31

Bloch, Marc, *The Historian's Craft*, Manchester: Manchester University Press, reprint, 1992

Bullock, Alan, 'Has history ceased to be relevant?', *The Historian*, no. 43 (Autumn 1994), 16–20

Bunzl, Martin, *Real History: Reflections on Historical Practice*, London: Routledge, 1997

Burke, Peter, *Sociology and History*, London: Allen & Unwin, 1992

Burston, W.H. and D. Thompson (eds), *Studies in the Nature and Teaching of History*, London: Routledge & Kegan Paul, 1967

Butterfield, Herbert, *The Whig Interpretation of History*, London: G. Bell & Sons, 1931

Butterfield, Herbert, *Man on his Past*, Cambridge: Cambridge University Press, 1955

Cannadine, David, 'British history: past, present – and future?', *Past and Present*, no. 116 (August 1987), 169–91

Cannadine, David, 'On reviewing and being reviewed', *History Today*, 49:3 (March 1999), 30–3

Cannon, John (ed.), *The Historian at Work*, London: Allen & Unwin, 1980

Cannon, John (ed.), *The Oxford Companion to British History*, Oxford: Oxford University Press, 1997

Carr, E.H., *What is History?*, 2nd edn, London: Penguin, 1987

Catterall, Peter and Harriet Jones (eds), *Understanding Documents and Sources*, Oxford: Heinemann, 1994

Caunce, Stephen, *Oral History and the Local Historian*, London: Longman, 1994

Clark, G. Kitson, *The Critical Historian*, London: Heinemann, 1967

Clark, G. Kitson, *Guide for Research Students working on Historical Subjects*, 2nd edn, Cambridge: Cambridge University Press, 1968

Collingwood, R.G., *The Idea of History*, rev. edn, Oxford: Clarendon Press, 1993

Collingwood, R.G., *The Principles of History*, Oxford: Oxford University Press, 1999

Cook, Chris and John Stevenson, *The Longman Handbook of Modern European History 1763–1985*, Harlow: Longman, 1987

Cook, Chris and John Stevenson, *The Longman Handbook of Modern British History 1714–1995*, 3rd edn, Harlow: Longman, 1996

Elton, G.R., 'The historian's social function', *Transactions of the Royal Historical Society*, 5th series, 27 (1977), 197–211

Elton, G.R., *The Practice of History*, London: Fontana Press, 1987

Evans, Richard J., *In Defence of History*, London: Granta, 1997

Floud, Roderick, *An Introduction to Quantitative Methods for Historians*, 2nd edn, London: Routledge, 1979

Fogel, R.W., 'The New Economic History: 1. Its findings and methods', *Economic History Review*, 2nd series, 19 (1966), 642–56

Fogel, Robert William, 'The limits of quantitative methods in history', *American Historical Review*, 80 (1975), 329–50

Gardiner, Patrick, *The Nature of Historical Explanation*, London: Oxford University Press, 1952

Gottschalk, Louis, Clyde Kluckhohn and Robert Angell, *The Use of personal documents in History, Anthropology and Sociology*, New York: Social Science Research Council, 1945

Graham, Gordon, *The Shape of the Past*, Oxford: Oxford University Press, 1997

Greenstein, Daniel I., *A Historian's Guide to Computing*, Oxford: Oxford University Press, 1994

Harvey, Charles and Jon Press, *Databases in Historical Research*, Basingstoke: Macmillan Press, 1996

Hey, David (ed.), *The Oxford Companion to Local and Family History*, Oxford: Oxford University Press, 1996

Hobsbawm, E.J., 'The social function of the past: some questions', *Past and Present*, no. 55 (May 1972), 3–17

Howarth, Ken, *Oral History: A Handbook*, Stroud: Sutton, 1998

Hughes, H. Stuart, 'The historian and the social scientist', *American Historical Review*, 66 (1960), 20–46

Igartua, José E., 'The computer and the historian's work', *History and Computing*, 3 (1991), 73–83

Jackson, Martin A., 'Film as a source material: some preliminary notes', *Journal of Interdisciplinary History*, 4 (1973), 73–80

Jenkins, Keith, *On 'What is History?': from Carr and Elton to Rorty and White*, London: Routledge, 1995

Kemnitz, Thomas Milton, 'The cartoon as a historical source', *Journal of Interdisciplinary History*, 4 (1973), 81–93

Kenyon, J.P., *The History Men*, 2nd edn, London: Weidenfeld & Nicolson, 1993

Krieger, Leonard, 'The horizons of history', *American Historical Review*, 63 (1957), 62–74

Lowenthal, David, *The Past is a Foreign Country*, Cambridge: Cambridge University Press, reprint, 1995

McCord, Norman, 'Photographs as historical evidence', *Local Historian*, 13:1 (February 1978), 23–36

McCullagh, C. Behan, *The Truth of History*, London: Routledge, 1998

Marczewski, Jean, 'Quantitative history', *Journal of Contemporary History*, 3:2 (April 1968), 179–91

Marwick, Arthur, *The Nature of History*, 3rd edn, Basingstoke: Macmillan, 1989

Mawdsley, Evan and Thomas Munck, *Computing for Historians: An Introductory Guide*, Manchester: Manchester University Press, 1993

Meyerhoff, Hans (ed.), *The Philosophy of History in our Time*, New York: Doubleday Anchor Books, 1959

Middleton, Roger and Peter Wardley, 'Information technology in economic and social history: the computer as philosopher's stone or pandora's box?', *Economic History Review*, 2nd series, 43 (1990), 667–96

Miller, Stuart T., 'The value of photographs as historical evidence', *Local Historian*, 15:8 (November 1983), 468–73

Munslow, Alan, *Deconstructing History*, London: Routledge, 1997

Munslow, Alan, *The Routledge Companion to Historical Studies*, London: Routledge, 2000

Nicholson, Heather Norris, 'In amateur hands: framing time and space in home-movies', *History Workshop Journal*, no. 43 (Spring 1997), 199–212

'Oral history', *History Workshop Journal*, no. 8 (Autumn 1979), i–iii

Passmore, J.A., 'The objectivity of history', *Philosophy*, 33 (1958), 97–111

Perks, Robert and Alistair Thomson, *The Oral History Reader*, London: Routledge, 1998

Pollard, Sidney, 'Economic history – a science of society?', *Past and Present*, no. 30 (April 1965), 3–22

Portelli, Alessandro, 'The peculiarities of oral history', *History Workshop*, no. 12 (Autumn 1981), 96–107

Porter, Roy, 'Seeing the past', *Past and Present*, no. 118 (February 1988), 186–205

Roads, Christopher H., 'Film as historical evidence', *Journal of the Society of Archivists*, 3 (1966), 183–91

Rundle, David, 'Internet history', *History Today*, 48:11 (November 1998), 14–15

Skinner, Quentin, 'Sir Geoffrey Elton and the Practice of History', *Transactions of the Royal Historical Society*, sixth series, 7 (1997), 301–16

Stanford, Michael, *A Companion to the Study of History*, Oxford: Blackwell, 1994

Stern, Fritz (ed.), *The Varieties of History*, London: Macmillan, 1970

Stone, Lawrence, 'The revival of narrative: reflections on a new old history', *Past and Present*, no. 85 (November 1979), 3–24

Stone, Lawrence, *The Past and the Present Revisited*, London: Routledge & Kegan Paul, 1987

Thane, Patricia M., 'Oral history, memory and written tradition: an introduction', *Transactions of the Royal Historical Society*, sixth series, 9 (1999), 161–8

Thompson, Paul, *The Voice of the Past*, 3rd edn, Oxford: Oxford University Press, 2000

Thomson, Alistair, 'Making the most of memories: the empirical and subjective value of oral history', *Transactions of the Royal Historical Society*, sixth series, 9 (1999), 291–301

Tosh, John, *The Pursuit of History*, 3rd edn, Harlow: Longman, 2000

Trevor-Roper, H.R., 'The past and the present: history and sociology', *Past and Present*, no. 42 (February 1969), 3–17

Vischer, Wilhelm, 'On the limits of historical knowledge', *History and Theory*, 25 (1986), 40–51

Walsh, W.H., *An Introduction to Philosophy of History*, Bristol: Thoemmes Press, reprint, 1992

Williams, Michael A., *Researching Local History: the Human Journey*, London: Addison Wesley Longman, 1996

Wilson, B.R., 'Sociological methods in the study of history', *Transactions of the Royal Historical Society*, 5th series, 21 (1971), 101–18

2 Reference sources

Annual Bibliography of British and Irish History, 1975–
  (formerly, *Writings on British History* 1901–74)
Annual Bulletin of Historical Literature, 1911–
Aslib, *Index to Theses*, 1950/51– (annual)
  (for earlier years refer to *The Retrospective Index to Theses of Great Britain and Ireland 1716–1950* (5 vols); see especially volume 1: *Social Sciences and Humanities* (1975); there is also a CD-ROM index of theses covering the period from 1970 onwards, and current copies of *Index to Theses* now incorporate abstracts)
Aslib, *Directory of Literary and Historical Collections in the United Kingdom*, London: Aslib, 1993
Aslib, *Directory of Information Sources in the United Kingdom*, 10th edn, London: Aslib, 1998
British Humanities Index, 1962– (annual)
  (BHI is also available on CD-ROM covering the period since 1985; BHI was formerly known as the *Subject Index to Periodicals* 1915–16 to 1961; current copies of BHI now incorporate abstracts)
British Library, *British National Bibliography*, 1950– (annual) (weekly and quarterly lists are also published for the current year)
British Library, *General Catalogue of Printed Books*
  (multivolume series covering books catalogued to 1975; it is also available on CD-ROM)
British Library, *Serials in the British Library*, 1981– (annual)
  (also available on microfiche)

British Qualifications (annual)

Chambers Biographical Dictionary, 6th edn, Edinburgh: Chambers, 1997

Chambers Dates, 2nd edn, Edinburgh: W and R Chambers, 1989

Cheney, Christopher Robert (ed.), *Handbook of Dates for Students of English History* (Royal Historical Society Guides and Handbooks 4), Cambridge: Cambridge University Press, 1996

Current Research in Britain, 1985– (annual) (4 vols)
(formerly *Research in British Universities, Polytechnics and Colleges*; refer to the following two volumes: *The Humanities* and *The Social Sciences*)

Dewey Decimal Classification, 20th edn (1989)

Dictionary of National Biography, 1885– (multivolume series)
(a CD-ROM version is also available from Oxford University Press)

Dissertation Abstracts International, 1952– (annual)
(a CD-ROM version is also available from University Microfilms Inc.; formerly *Microfilm Abstracts* 1938–51)

Dod's Parliamentary Companion, 1965– (annual)

Dunsire, Gordon (ed.), *Scottish Library and Information Resources*, 12th edn, Hamilton: Scottish Library Association, 2000

Encyclopaedia Britannica, 15th edn (1991)
(also available online)

Foster, Janet and Julia Sheppard (eds), *British Archives: A Guide to Archive Resources in the United Kingdom*, 3rd edn, Basingstoke: Macmillan, 1995

Grants Register (annual)

Historical Research for Higher Degrees in the United Kingdom (annual)
(issued by the Institute of Historical Research in two parts, *Theses in Progress* and *Theses Completed*)

History Theses 1901–70, compiled by P.M. Jacobs, London: Institute of Historical Research, 1976

History Theses 1971–80, compiled by Joyce M. Horn, London: Institute of Historical Research, 1984

History Theses 1981–90, compiled by Joyce M. Horn, London: Institute of Historical Research, 1994

HMSO Annual Catalogue, 1985–
(previously known as *Government Publications*; there are also monthly catalogues, and a CD-ROM of UK official publications since 1980 is also available)

Index to the Local and Personal Acts 1850–1995, 4 vols, compiled by Rosemary Devine, London: HMSO, 1996

Index to The Times, 1785– (annual)
(indexes are also available for some other newspapers, some on CD-ROM, but they cover a smaller timescale than *The Times*)

Jellinek, Dan, *Official UK: the Essential Guide to Government Websites*, London: Stationery Office, 1998

Keegan, John and Andrew Wheatcroft, *Who's Who in Military History: from 1453 to the Present day*, London: Routledge, 1996

Kirkham, Sandi, *How to Find Information in the Humanities*, London: Library Association, 1989

Lea, Peter W. and Alan Day, *The Reference Sources Handbook*, 4th edn, London: Library Association, 1996

Manual of Legal Citations, Part 1, London: University of London, Institute of Advanced Legal Studies, 1959

Mitchell, B.R., *British Historical Statistics*, Cambridge: Cambridge University Press, 1988

Pemberton, John E., *British Official Publications*, 2nd edn, Oxford: Pergamon Press, 1973

Postgrad (annual)
(a directory of graduate studies)

Researcher's Guide to British Film and Television Collections, 4th edn, London: British Universities Film and Video Council, 1993

Richard, Stephen, *Directory of British Official Publications: A Guide to Sources*, 2nd edn, London: Mansell Publishing, 1984

Scottish Record Office, *Guide to the National Archives of Scotland*, Edinburgh: Stationery Office, 1996

The Statesman's Yearbook, 1864– (annual)

Teachers of History in the Universities of the United Kingdom, compiled by Joyce M. Horn, London: Institute of Historical Research, 1995

Walford's Guide to current British Periodicals in the Humanities and Social Sciences, London: Library Association, 1985

Walford's Guide to Reference Material, vol. 3: *Generalia, Language and Literature, the Arts*, 7th edn, London: Library Association, 1998

Whitaker's Almanack, 1868– (annual)

Whitaker's Books in Print (monthly)
(available on microfiche and CD-ROM)

Who Was Who, 1897– (multivolume series)

Who's Who, 1849– (annual)

Who's Who in Scotland, Irvine: Carrick Media, 2000

Willing's Press Guide, 2 vols (annual)

3 Research, publishing and style guides

Anderson, M.D., *Book Indexing*, Cambridge Authors' and Publishers' Guides, Cambridge: Cambridge University Press, 1985

Barzun, Jacques and Henry F. Graff, *The Modern Researcher*, 5th edn, Orlando, FL: Harcourt Brace Jovanovich, 1992

Berry, Ralph, *How to Write a Research Paper*, 2nd edn, Oxford: Pergamon Press, 1986

Blackwell Guide for Authors, Oxford: Basil Blackwell, 1991

British Standards:

BS 1629:1989	*References to published materials*
BS 1749:1985	*Alphabetical arrangement and the filing order of numbers and symbols*
BS 2846:part 1:1991	*Statistical Interpretation of Data (part 1: Routine analysis of quantitative data)*

BS 4148:1985   *Abbreviation of title words and titles of publications*

BS 5261:part 1:2000   *Copy Preparation and Proof Correction (part 1: Design and Layout of Documents)*

BS 5261:part 2:1976   *Copy Preparation and Proof Correction (part 2: Specification for typographic requirements, marks for copy preparation and proof correction, proofing procedure)*

BS 5408:1976   *Glossary of Documentation terms*

BS 5605:1990   *Citing and Referencing published material*

BS 6371:1983   *Citation of Unpublished Documents*

BS 7581:1992   *Presentation of Tables and Graphs*

BS ISO 832:1994   *Information and Documentation: Bibliographic references*

BS ISO 999:1996   *Information and Documentation: Indexes*

PD 6506:1982   *Guide for Typewriting*

Brown, S., E. McDowell and P. Race, *500 Tips for Research Students*, London: Kogan Page, 1995

Burbidge, P.G., *Prelims and End-Pages*, Cambridge Authors' and Printers' Guides, 2nd edn, Cambridge: Cambridge University Press, 1969

Butcher, Judith, *Typescripts, Proofs and Indexes*, Cambridge Authors' and Publishers' Guides, Cambridge: Cambridge University Press, 1980

Butcher, Judith, *Copy-Editing*, 3rd edn, Cambridge: Cambridge University Press, 1992

Carey, G.V., *Mind the Stop*, London: Penguin, reprint, 1976

Chicago Manual of Style, 14th edn, Chicago: University of Chicago Press, 1993

Concise Oxford Dictionary

Copinger and Skone James on Copyright, 14th edn, London: Sweet & Maxwell, 1998

Copyright, Designs and Patents Act 1988 (c.48)

Fowler, H.W., *A Dictionary of Modern English Usage*, 2nd edn revised by Sir Ernest Gowers, Oxford: Oxford University Press, 1965 (paperback 1983)

Gowers, Sir Ernest, *The Complete Plain Words*, 3rd edn revised by Sidney Greenbaum and Janet Whitcut, London: Penguin, 1987

Hart's Rules for Compositors and Readers at the University Press Oxford, 39th edn, Oxford: Oxford University Press, reprint 1991

Hoffmann, Ann, *Research for Writers*, 5th edn, London: A. & C. Black, 1996

Legat, Michael, *An Author's Guide to Publishing*, rev. edn, London: Robert Hale, 1991

Luey, Beth, *Handbook for Academic Authors*, 3rd edn, Cambridge: Cambridge University Press, 1995

MHRA Style Book, 5th edn, London: Modern Humanities Research Association, 1996

Oxford Dictionary of Abbreviations, Oxford: Oxford University Press, 1993

Oxford Spelling Dictionary, compiled by R.E. Allen, Oxford: Oxford University Press, 1986; paperback 1991

Oxford Writers' Dictionary, compiled by R.E. Allen, Oxford: Oxford University Press, 1990

Phillips, Estelle M. and D.S. Pugh, *How to get a PhD*, 2nd edn, Milton Keynes: Open University Press, 1994

Roget's Thesaurus

Turabian, Kate L., *A Manual for Writers of Term Papers, Theses and Dissertations*, 6th edn, London: University of Chicago Press, 1996

Watson, George, *Writing a Thesis: A Guide to Long Essays and Dissertations*, London: Longman, 1987

Writers' and Artists' Yearbook (annual)

Index